Interactive Approaches to
Second Language Reading

THE CAMBRIDGE APPLIED LINGUISTICS SERIES
Series editors: Michael H. Long and Jack C. Richards

This new series presents the findings of recent work in applied linguistics which are of direct relevance to language teaching and learning and of particular interest to applied linguists, researchers, language teachers, and teacher trainers.

In this series:

Interactive Approaches to Second Language Reading *edited by Patricia Carrell, Joanne Devine, and David Eskey*

Second Language Classrooms – research on teaching and learning *by Craig Chaudron*

Language Learning and Deafness *edited by Michael Strong*

The Learner-Centred Curriculum *by David Nunan*

Interactive Approaches to Second Language Reading

Edited by

Patricia L. Carrell
Southern Illinois University

Joanne Devine
Skidmore College

David E. Eskey
University of Southern California

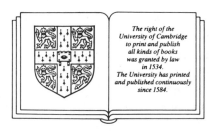

The right of the
University of Cambridge
to print and publish
all kinds of books
was granted by law
in 1534.
The University has printed
and published continuously
since 1584.

Cambridge University Press
Cambridge
New York   New Rochelle
Melbourne   Sydney

To our parents

Published by the Press Syndicate of the University of Cambridge
The Pitt Building, Trumpington Street, Cambridge CB2 1RP
32 East 57th Street, New York, NY 10022, USA
10 Stamford Road, Oakleigh, Melbourne 3166, Australia

First published 1988

Printed in the United States of America

Cover design by Tom Wharton

Library of Congress Cataloging-in-Publication Data
Interactive approaches to second language reading.
(The Cambridge applied linguistics series)
Includes bibliographies and index.
1. Language and languages – Study and teaching.
2. Reading.   3. Second language acquisition.
I. Carrell, Patricia L.   II. Devine, Joanne.
III. Eskey, David E.   IV. Series.
P53.75.I58   1988   418'.007   87–23878

ISBN 0 521 35360 2 hardcover
ISBN 0 521 35874 4 paperback

Contents

Contributors

J. Charles Alderson, University of Lancaster, Lancaster, England
Richard C. Anderson, University of Illinois at Urbana-Champaign
Patricia L. Carrell, Southern Illinois University at Carbondale
Mark A. Clarke, University of Colorado at Denver
Andrew Cohen, Hebrew University, Jerusalem
Joanne Devine, Skidmore College, Saratoga Springs, New York
Joan C. Eisterhold, Northwestern University, Evanston, Illinois
David E. Eskey, University of Southern California, Los Angeles
Jonathan Ferrara, Givat Washington Teachers College, Jerusalem
Jonathan Fine, Bar-Ilan University, Ramat Gan
Hilary Glasman, Hebrew University, Jerusalem
Kenneth Goodman, University of Arizona, Tucson
William Grabe, Northern Arizona University, Flagstaff
Thom Hudson, University of California at Los Angeles
Michael L. Kamil, University of Illinois at Chicago
P. David Pearson, University of Illinois at Urbana-Champaign
Pat Rigg, American Language and Literacy, Tucson, Arizona
Phyllis R. Rosenbaum-Cohen, Hebrew University, Jerusalem
S. Jay Samuels, University of Minnesota, Minneapolis
Margaret S. Steffensen, Illinois State University, Normal
A. H. Urquhart, College of St. Mark and St. John, Plymouth, England

Series editors' preface

Interactive Approaches to Second Language Reading, edited by Patricia Carrell, Joanne Devine, and David Eskey, is a welcome addition to the Cambridge Applied Linguistics series. The series provides a forum for the best new work in applied linguistics by those in the field who are able to relate theory, research, and practice.

Although reading has always had a prominent position in the interests of both second language teachers and researchers in second language teaching and learning, in recent years new views of the nature of the reading process have revitalized both theory and practice in second language reading. Originating in the work of theoreticians and researchers in first language reading, these new perspectives are typically associated with those who reject views of reading as largely a process of decoding and who see it instead as an interaction of both "top-down" and "bottom-up" processes – that is, processes that utilize background knowledge and schemata and are hence concept driven, as well as those that are primarily text or data driven.

This is the position advocated in this timely collection of original and reprinted papers spanning the literature in both first language and second language reading. The interaction between top-down and bottom-up processes in second language reading is examined from the perspectives of theory, research, and instruction. The book considers different models of reading as an interactive process, clarifying the nature and role of background knowledge, topic of discourse, schemata, and inferencing. At the same time the importance of such factors as vocabulary recognition, syntactic recognition, text structure, as well as the contribution of language proficiency itself are examined. Throughout, however, the authors resist the tendency to reduce complex issues to simplistic pedagogical formulas. Rather, they outline an agenda both for further research as well as for experimentation and testing in the design of classroom materials and instructional strategies. Thus the book will be a useful reference for those interested in understanding more about the nature of second language reading, and in developing approaches to the teaching of second language reading that result in effective top-down and bottom-up reading strategies in learners.

Michael H. Long
Jack C. Richards
University of Hawaii at Manoa

Preface

This book had its origins at the 1984 TESOL Convention in Houston, Texas, when the three of us began collaborating on proposing, organizing, and presenting the Colloquium on Research in Reading in a Second Language. Our collaboration has continued since, not only on the continued life of the colloquium, but on other projects as well as this book. The responsibility and the effort in the production of this book have been shared jointly by all three of us.

We wish to thank the authors of the chapters which were specifically commissioned for this volume, as well as the authors of the reprinted chapters, who kindly gave us permission to incorporate their materials. We also wish to thank and acknowledge the support of our respective academic institutions (Southern Illinois University at Carbondale, Skidmore College, University of Southern California) for their support of our individual research as well as for their support in the production of this book.

It goes without saying that a book such as this could not have been produced without the guidance of the series' editors, Jack C. Richards and Michael H. Long, and our editors and others at Cambridge University Press. We thank all of them. Special words of thanks go to Thomas Scovel for his helpful comments and valuable suggestions in reviewing earlier drafts of this book.

Last, but not at all least, we wish to thank our spouses (Craig, Ron, and Elena) and families (Michael and Jennifer; Oliver; Megan, Jennifer, and Katherine) for their understanding and support during the several years it took to produce this book.

Patricia L. Carrell
Joanne Devine
David E. Eskey

Introduction: Interactive approaches to second language reading

Patricia L. Carrell

For many students, reading is by far the most important of the four skills in a second language, particularly in English as a second or foreign language. Certainly, if we consider the study of English as a foreign language around the world – the situation in which most English learners find themselves – reading is the main reason why students learn the language. In addition, at advanced proficiency levels in a second language, the ability to read the written language at a reasonable rate and with good comprehension has long been recognized to be as important as oral skills, if not more important (Eskey 1970). In second language teaching/learning situations for academic purposes, especially in higher education in English-medium universities or other programs that make extensive use of academic materials written in English, reading is paramount. Quite simply, without solid reading proficiency, second language readers cannot perform at levels they must in order to succeed, and they cannot compete with their native English-speaking counterparts. Thus, for at least these three groups of students (those in EFL contexts, those at advanced levels of proficiency, and those with a need for English for academic purposes), effective reading in a second language is critical. Professionals in second language education should be vitally concerned with approaches that can improve the reading skills of learners. Interactive approaches to reading hold much promise for our understanding the complex nature of reading, especially as it occurs in a second or foreign language and culture.

In order to understand the interactive approach to reading in a second language that is promoted in this book, it is helpful to understand a bit about the recent history of theories of reading in a second language.

That reading is not a passive, but rather an active, and in fact an interactive, process has been recognized for some time in first or native language reading (Goodman 1967, 1971; Kolers 1969; Wardhaugh 1969; Smith 1971; Rumelhart 1977; Adams and Collins 1979). However, only recently has second language or foreign language reading been viewed as an active, rather than a passive process. Early work in second language reading, specifically in reading in English as a second language, assumed a rather passive, bottom-up, view of second language reading;

1

that is, it was viewed primarily as a decoding process of reconstructing the author's intended meaning via recognizing the printed letters and words, and building up a meaning for a text from the smallest textual units at the "bottom" (letters and words) to larger and larger units at the "top" (phrases, clauses, intersentential linkages). Problems of second language reading and reading comprehension were viewed as being essentially decoding problems, deriving meaning from print (see, for example, Rivers 1964, 1968; Plaister 1968; Yorio 1971).

Furthermore, before 1970, reading in a second language was viewed primarily as an adjunct to oral language skills (Fries 1945, 1963, 1972). The strong influence of the audiolingual method dictated the primacy of listening over reading and of speaking over writing. The importance assigned to phoneme-grapheme relationships by structuralists such as Fries and Lado (1964) was also responsible for the promulgation and implementation of the decoding perspective on second language reading. Even among those who had a somewhat broader conception of the second language reading process (Rivers 1968), decoding sound-symbol relationships and mastering oral dialogues were considered to be the primary steps in the development of reading proficiency.

At the same time, there was recognition of the importance of background knowledge and in particular of the role of sociocultural meaning in second language reading comprehension. According to Fries (1963), a failure to relate the linguistic meaning of a reading passage to cultural factors would result in something less than total comprehension. Rivers (1968) also recognized that the strong bond between culture and language had to be maintained for a nonnative reader to have a complete understanding of the meaning of a text. However, despite the acknowledged importance of the role of background knowledge, and, in particular, culture-specific knowledge (what today we call "schemata," although the term was not in use at the time), these concepts played no real role in early theories of second language reading, and the methodological and instructional focus remained on decoding, or bottom-up processing.

About a decade ago, the so-called psycholinguistic model of reading, which had earlier exerted a strong influence on views of first or native language reading (Goodman 1967, 1971; Smith 1971), began to have an impact on views of second language reading. Goodman had described reading as a "psycholinguistic guessing game," in which the "reader reconstructs . . . a message which has been encoded by a writer as a graphic display" (Goodman 1971:135). In this model, the reader need not (and the efficient reader *does* not) use all of the textual cues. The better the reader is able to make correct predictions, the less confirming via the text is necessary (Goodman 1973:164). According to this point of view, the reader reconstructs meaning from written language by using the graphophonic, syntactic, and semantic systems of the language, but he or she merely uses cues from these three levels of language to predict meaning, and, most important, confirms those predictions by relating them to his or her past experiences and knowledge of the language.

Although Goodman did not characterize his theory as a top-down model, and continues to resist this characterization himself (Goodman 1981), several other reading experts (Anderson 1978; Cziko 1978) have recently characterized it as basically a concept-driven, top-down pattern in which "higher-level processes interact with, and direct the flow of information through, lower-level processes" (Stanovich 1980:34). In any event, the impact that Goodman's psycholinguistic theory had on both first or native language reading, and later on second or foreign language reading, was to make the reader an active participant in the reading process, making and confirming predictions, primarily from his or her background knowledge of the various linguistic levels (graphophonic, syntactic, and semantic, in the broadest sense of that term).

Goodman did not initially relate his theory to ESL readers, but by the early 1970s the first of what was to become a flood of articles making this connection began to appear in the literature. Among the first of the most widely distributed, and, one assumes, most widely read articles, were those of Eskey (1973) and Saville-Troike (1973). According to Eskey (1973), the decoding model was inadequate as a model of the reading process because it underestimated the contribution of the reader; it failed to recognize that students utilize their expectations about the text based on their knowledge of language and how it works. Other second language reading specialists such as Clarke and Silberstein (1977), Clarke (1979), Mackay and Mountford (1979), and Widdowson (1978, 1983) began to view second language reading as an active process in which the second language reader is an active information processor who predicts while sampling only parts of the actual text.

At this same time, dissatisfaction was growing with the audiolingual method and teachers were becoming aware that aural-oral proficiency did not automatically produce reading competency. Reading researchers began to call for teaching reading in its own right, rather than merely as an adjunct to the teaching of oral skills (Eskey 1973; Saville-Troike 1973).

In 1979 Coady elaborated on this basic psycholinguistic model for ESL reading and suggested a model in which the ESL reader's background knowledge interacts with conceptual abilities and process strategies to produce comprehension (Coady 1979:5–12). Only since 1979 has a truly top-down approach been advanced in second language reading (Steffensen, Joag-dev, and Anderson 1979; Carrell 1981, 1982; Carrell and Eisterhold 1983 – reprinted as Chapter 5 in this volume; Johnson 1981, 1982; Hudson 1982 – reprinted as Chapter 13 in this volume).

In the top-down view of second language reading, not only is the reader an active participant in the reading process, making predictions and processing information, but everything in the reader's prior experience or background knowledge plays a significant role in the process. In this view, not only is the reader's prior linguistic knowledge ("linguistic" schemata) and level of proficiency in the second language important, but the reader's prior background knowledge of the content area of the text ("content" schemata) as well as of the rhetorical structure of the text ("formal" schemata) are also important. Research done by and reviewed by Carrell (1983a, 1983b, 1983c, 1984a, 1984b, 1984c, 1985; Carrell and Eisterhold 1983; Carrell and Wallace 1983) within the general framework of schema theory has shown the significant roles played in ESL reading by both content and formal schemata.

The introduction of a top-down processing perspective into second language reading has had a profound impact on the field. In fact, it has had such a profound impact that there has been a tendency to view the introduction of a strong top-down processing perspective as a *substitute* for the bottom-up, decoding view of reading, rather than its complement. However, as schema theory research has attempted to make clear, efficient and effective reading – be it in a first or second language – requires *both* top-down and bottom-up strategies operating *interactively* (Rumelhart 1977, 1980; Sanford and Garrod 1981; van Dijk and Kintsch 1983). The purpose of this book is to present approaches to second language reading which involve *both* top-down *and* bottom-up processes functioning interactively.

This book presents a timely collection of theoretical, empirical, and pedagogical perspectives on interactive approaches to second language reading, particularly in relation to reading in English as a foreign or second language. The chapters in this volume integrate earlier, traditional, so-called bottom-up approaches to reading with more recent, contemporary approaches (e.g., schema theory), which include top-down processing perspectives. The purpose of the collection is to demonstrate that both top-down and bottom-up processing, functioning interactively, are necessary to an adequate understanding of second language reading and reading comprehension.

The book is organized into four major sections. Part I presents models of reading in general, and interactive models in particular. This section contains four chapters – by Goodman, Samuels and Kamil, Anderson and Pearson, and Grabe.

Part II presents interactive approaches to second language reading from a theoretical perspective. This section contains four theory or position chapters – by Carrell and Eisterhold, Eskey, Carrell, and Clarke.

Part III contains six chapters dealing with empirical investigations of second language reading conducted within an interactive framework –

by Devine, Steffensen, Cohen et al., Alderson and Urquhart, Hudson, and Rigg.

Part IV presents the classroom implications and applications of interactive approaches to second language reading. This section contains three chapters, each addressing pedagogical issues related to the introduction of interactive approaches to second language reading into ESL reading classrooms. These chapters are by Eskey and Grabe, Carrell, and Devine.

References

Adams, M. J., and A. Collins. 1979. A schema-theoretic view of reading. In *New directions in discourse processing*, R. O. Freedle (Ed.), 1–22. Norwood, N.J.: Ablex.

Anderson, R. C. 1978. Schema-directed processes in language comprehension. In *Cognitive psychology and instruction*, A. M. Lesgold, J. W. Pellegrino, S. D. Fokkema, and R. Glaser (Eds.), 67–82. New York: Plenum Press.

Carrell, P. L. 1981. Culture-specific schemata in L2 comprehension. In *Selected papers from the ninth Illinois TESOL/BE annual convention, the first Midwest TESOL conference*, R. Orem and J. Haskell (Eds.), 123–132. Chicago: Illinois TESOL/BE.

1982. Cohesion is not coherence. *TESOL Quarterly* 16(4): 479–488.

1983a. Three components of background knowledge in reading comprehension. *Language Learning* 33(2): 183–207.

1983b. Background knowledge in second language comprehension. *Language Learning and Communication* 2(1): 25–34.

1983c. Some issues in studying the role of schemata, or background knowledge, in second language comprehension. *Reading in a Foreign Language* 1(2): 81–92.

1984a. Evidence of a formal schema in second language comprehension. *Language Learning* 34(2): 87–112.

1984b. The effects of rhetorical organization on ESL readers. *TESOL Quarterly* 18(3): 441–469.

1984c. Schema theory and ESL reading: classroom implications and applications. *Modern Language Journal* 68(4): 332–343.

1985. Facilitating ESL reading comprehension by teaching text structure. *TESOL Quarterly* 19(4): 727–752.

Carrell, P. L., and J. C. Eisterhold. 1983. Schema theory and ESL reading pedagogy. *TESOL Quarterly* 17(4): 553–573. [Reprinted as Chapter 5 in this volume.]

Carrell, P. L., and B. Wallace. 1983. Background knowledge: context and familiarity in reading comprehension. In *On TESOL '82*, M. Clarke and J. Handscombe (Eds.), 295–308. Washington, D.C.: TESOL.

Clarke, M. A. 1979. Reading in Spanish and English: evidence from adult ESL students. *Language Learning* 29(1): 121–150.

Clarke, M. A., and S. Silberstein. 1977. Toward a realization of psycholinguistic principles in the ESL reading class. *Language Learning* 27(1): 135–154.

Coady, J. 1979. A psycholinguistic model of the ESL reader. In *Reading in a second language*, R. Mackay, B. Barkman, and R. R. Jordan (Eds.), 5–12. Rowley, Mass.: Newbury House.

Cziko, G. A. 1978. Differences in first- and second-language reading: the use of syntactic, semantic and discourse constraints. *Canadian Modern Language Review* 34(3): 473–489.

Dijk, T. A. van, and W. Kintsch. 1983. *Strategies of discourse comprehension.* New York: Academic Press.

Eskey, D. E. 1970. A new technique for the teaching of reading to advanced students. *TESOL Quarterly* 4(4): 315–321.

    1973. A model program for teaching advanced reading to students of English as a second language. *Language Learning* 23(2): 169–184.

Fries, C. C. 1945. *Teaching and learning English as a foreign language.* Ann Arbor: University of Michigan Press.

    1963. *Linguistics and reading.* New York: Holt, Rinehart, and Winston.

    1972. Learning to read English as part of the oral approach. In *Readings on English as a second language: for teachers and teacher-trainers*, K. Croft (Ed.), 168–173. Cambridge: Winthrop Publishers.

Goodman, K. S. 1967. Reading: a psycholinguistic guessing game. *Journal of the Reading Specialist* 6(1): 126–135.

    1971. Psycholinguistic universals in the reading process. In *The psychology of second language learning*, P. Pimsleur and T. Quinn (Eds.), 135–142. Cambridge: Cambridge University Press.

    1973. On the psycholinguistic method of teaching reading. In *Psycholinguistics and reading*, F. Smith (Ed.), 158–176. New York: Holt, Rinehart and Winston.

    1981. Letter to the editor. *Reading Research Quarterly* 16(3): 477–478.

Hudson, T. 1982. The effects of induced schemata on the "short circuit" in L2 reading: Non-decoding factors in L2 reading performance. *Language Learning* 32(1): 1–31. [Reprinted as Chapter 13 in this volume.]

Johnson, P. 1981. Effects on reading comprehension of language complexity and cultural background of a text. *TESOL Quarterly* 15(2): 169–181.

    1982. Effects on reading comprehension of building background knowledge. *TESOL Quarterly* 16(4): 503–516.

Kolers, P. A. 1969. Reading is only incidentally visual. In *Psycholinguistics and the teaching of reading*, K. S. Goodman and J. T. Fleming (Eds.), 8–16. Newark, Del.: International Reading Association.

Lado, R. 1964. *Language teaching: a scientific approach.* New York: McGraw-Hill. (See esp. Chapter 13, "Reading," pp. 131–142.)

Mackay, R., and A, Mountford. 1979. Reading for information. In *Reading in a second language*, R. Mackay, B. Barkman, and R. R. Jordan (Eds.), 106–141. Rowley, Mass.: Newbury House.

Plaister, T. 1968. Reading instruction for college level foreign students. *TESOL Quarterly* 2(3): 164–168.

Rivers, W. 1964. *The psychologist and the foreign-language teacher.* Chicago: University of Chicago Press.

    1968. *Teaching foreign language skills.* Chicago: University of Chicago Press.

Rumelhart, D. E. 1977. Toward an interactive model of reading. In *Attention and performance*, Vol. 6, S. Dornic (Ed.), 573–603. New York: Academic Press.

    1980. Schemata: the building blocks of cognition. In *Theoretical issues in reading comprehension*, R. J. Spiro, B. C. Bruce, and W. F. Brewer (Eds.), 33–58. Hillsdale, N.J.: Erlbaum.

Sanford, A. J., and S. C. Garrod. 1981. *Understanding written language*. New York: Wiley.

Saville-Troike, M. 1973. Reading and the audio-lingual method. *TESOL Quarterly* 7(4): 395–405.

Smith, F. 1971. *Understanding reading: a psycholinguistic analysis of reading and learning to read*. New York: Holt, Rinehart and Winston.

Stanovich, K. E. 1980. Toward an interactive-compensatory model of individual differences in the development of reading fluency. *Reading Research Quarterly* 16(1): 32–71.

Steffensen, M. S., C. Joag-dev, and R. C. Anderson. 1979. A cross-cultural perspective on reading comprehension. *Reading Research Quarterly* 15(1): 10–29.

Wardhaugh, R. 1969. *Reading: a linguistic perspective*. New York: Harcourt, Brace and World.

Widdowson, H. G. 1978. *Teaching language as communication*. London: Oxford University Press.

1983. *Learning purpose and language use*. London: Oxford University Press.

Yorio, C. A. 1971. Some sources of reading problems for foreign language learners. *Language Learning* 21(1): 107–115.

PART I:
INTERACTIVE MODELS OF READING

The chapters in this section introduce, develop, and then further explore the notion that reading is not a passive but rather an active process, involving the reader in ongoing interaction with the text. Goodman's chapter introduces the idea that reading, far from being passive, is an active process, with emphasis on both *active* and *process*. In presenting his macro model of the reading process, Goodman situates reading within the broader context of communicative, meaning-seeking, information processing. He further highlights both the psycholinguistic aspects of reading (how language and thought interact), as well as the sociolinguistic aspects of reading (language operating in a social context including writers as well as readers). Whether or not one agrees with Goodman that there is indeed a *single* reading process, or that miscue analysis is the best or even an appropriate way to access this process, Goodman's model sets the stage for approaching reading as an *active process*.

The chapter by Samuels and Kamil presents an overview of several models of reading, all from the perspective of reading as an active process. Depending on the particular foci or interests of the specific model builders, different aspects of reading as an active process are emphasized in these different models. Samuels and Kamil not only touch on various aspects of a number of models, but they go into some detail on two models in particular – Rumelhart's interactive-activation model, and Stanovich's interactive-compensatory model. In discussing these two models, Samuels and Kamil introduce the notions of top-down and bottom-up processing, and *interactive* models, models that have interacting hierarchical stages, rather than discrete stages that are passed through in a strictly linear fashion. In terms of the desired characteristics of any model, Samuels and Kamil show how interactive models of reading, models which allow processing at one level or stage (e.g., word perception) to interact with processing at another level or stage (e.g., semantic knowledge), are superior to linear models in either direction (either strictly bottom-up, decoding or strictly top-down, predicting).

The Anderson and Pearson chapter details another type of interactive model of reading, namely a schema-theoretic model. In a state-of-the-art presentation on schema theory, these authors show how reading comprehension involves the interaction between old and new information. They focus on, as they say, "how the reader's *schemata*, or knowledge already stored in memory, function in the process of interpreting new information and allowing it to enter and become a part of the knowledge store."

Part I concludes with Grabe's chapter relating interactive models of reading, which were developed primarily with native reading in mind, to the domain of second language reading. In making this connection to second language reading, Grabe also highlights the different senses in which a model may be *interactive* – that is, it may focus on the relation of the reader to the text, or it may focus on the processing among the various component skills and stages, or it may even focus on features of the text itself.

In reading the chapters in this section, the reader may find it useful to keep the following questions in mind, and to read the chapters with the purpose of learning the answers to these questions: (1) How have models of the reading process evolved recently, from passive, to active, to interactive? (2) What are the different senses in which the term *interactive* is used to describe and to think about reading? (3) What are some of the different levels, stages, factors, and aspects of reading that "interact"? (4) What is meant by *bottom-up* and *top-down* processing of text? (5) What is the particular role in reading comprehension of prior background knowledge already stored in memory?

1 *The reading process*

Kenneth Goodman

In a very real sense this chapter is a progress report. Some years ago I decided that a major reason for the lack of forward motion in attempts to develop more effective reading instruction was a common failure to examine and articulate a clear view of the reading process itself. Knowledge, I felt, was non-cumulative in improving reading instruction largely because we either ignored the reading process and focussed on the manipulation of teacher and/or pupil behaviors or because we treated reading as an unknowable mystery.

Ironically two opposite views were and still are widely found in the professional literature:

1. Reading is what reading is and everybody knows that; usually this translates to 'reading is matching sounds to letters.'
2. 'Nobody knows how reading works.' This view usually leads to a next premise: therefore, in instruction, whatever 'works' is its own justification.

Both views are non-productive at best and at the worst seriously impede progress.

My effort has been to create a model of the reading process powerful enough to explain and predict reading behavior and sound enough to be a base on which to build and examine the effectiveness of reading instruction. This model has been developed using the concepts, scientific methodology, and terminology of psycholinguistics, the interdisciplinary science that is concerned with how thought and language are interrelated. The model has also continuously drawn on and been tested against linguistic reality. This reality has taken the form of close analysis of miscues, unexpected responses in oral reading, produced by readers of widely varied proficiency as they dealt with real printed text materials they were seeing for the first time.

The model isn't done yet. No one yet claims a 'finished' model of any language process. But the model represents a productive usable view of

Reprinted by permission from Frederick W. Gollasche, ed., *Language and literacy: The selected writings of Kenneth Goodman*, pp. 5–16 (London: Routledge and Kegan Paul, 1975).

what I believe, at this point in time, about the way the reading process works.

A definition of reading

Reading is a receptive language process. It is a psycholinguistic process in that it starts with a linguistic surface representation encoded by a writer and ends with meaning which the reader constructs. There is thus an essential interaction between language and thought in reading. The writer encodes thought as language and the reader decodes language to thought.

Further, proficient readers are both efficient and effective. They are effective in constructing a meaning that they can assimilate or accommodate and which bears some level of agreement with the original meaning of the author. And readers are efficient in using the least amount of effort to achieve effectiveness. To accomplish this efficiency readers maintain constant focus on constructing the meaning throughout the process, always seeking the most direct path to meaning, always using strategies for reducing uncertainty, always being selective about the use of the cues available and drawing deeply on prior conceptual and linguistic competence. Efficient readers minimize dependence on visual detail. Any reader's proficiency is variable depending on the semantic background brought by the reader to any given reading task.

Source for the model

All scientific investigation must start with direct observation of available aspects of what is being studied. What distinguishes scientific from other forms of investigation is a constant striving to get beneath and beyond what is superficially observable. That involves finding new tools for making otherwise unavailable aspects observable. Such a tool is the microscope in all its variations designed to extend observation far beyond the limits of the human eye. Scientists also devise classification systems, taxonomies, paradigms as they constantly seek for essences, structures, interrelationships; they are aware of the distractions the obvious can cause and they are aware of how easy it is to overlook vital characteristics of phenomena they study.

The primary source of data for the view of the reading process presented here is observation of oral reading. But little can be learned from such observation if a naïvely empirical position is maintained. As the chemist must peer into the molecular structure, as the astronomer must ponder the effects of heavenly bodies on each other, as the ecologist must pursue the intricate web of interrelationships in a biological community, so the scientist in dealing with reading must look beyond behavior to process. Understanding reading requires depth analysis and a constant search for the insights which will let us infer the workings of the mind as print is processed and meaning created.

Oral miscue analysis is the tool I've found most useful in the depth analysis of reading behavior as I've sought to understand the reading process (Goodman 1969).

Miscue analysis compares observed with expected responses as subjects read a story or other written text orally. It provides a continuous basis of comparison between what the readers overtly do and what they are expected to do. A key assumption is that whatever the readers do is not random but is the result of the reading process, whether successfully used or not. Just as the observed behavior of electrons must result from a complex but limited set of forces and conditions, so what the readers do results from limited but complex information sources and interactive but limited alternatives for their use.

When readers produce responses which match our expectations we can only infer successful use of the reading process. When miscues are produced, however, comparing the mismatches between expectation and observation can illuminate where the readers have deviated and what factors of input and process may have been involved. A simple illustration: there has long been concern over reversals in reading, changes in the sequences of letters, apparently involved in word substitution miscues. If 'was' is substituted for 'saw' there appears to be some kind of visual or perceptual aberration in the reader. Our miscue analysis data, however, tells us two things: (1) Such reversals are far less common in reading continuous texts than in word lists. (2) When such reversals do occur they are in only one direction: 'saw' is replaced by 'was' but virtually never is 'was' replaced by 'saw.' The reversal miscue must be influenced by factors other than the obvious visual or perceptual ones. Frequently, syntactic predictability and the range of semantic possibility clearly are involved.

In this depth miscue analysis several basic insights have emerged which have become foundational both to the research and to the model of the reading process:

— Language, reading included, must be seen in its social context. Readers will show the influence of the dialect(s) they control both productively and receptively as they read. Further, the common experience, concepts, interests, views, and life styles of readers with common social and cultural backgrounds will also be reflected by how and what people read and what they take from their reading.
— Competence, what readers are capable of doing, must be separated from performance, what we observe them to do. It is competence that results in

the readers' control of and flexibility in using the reading process. Their performance is simply the observable result of the competence.

Change in performance, whether through instruction or development, is important only to the extent that it reflects improved competence. Researchers may use performance or behavioral indicators of underlying competence, but they err seriously in equating what readers do with what they are capable of doing.

- Language must be studied in process. Like a living organism it loses its essence if it is frozen or fragmented. Its parts and systems may be examined apart from their use but only in the living process may they be understood. Failure to recognize this has led many researchers to draw unwarranted and mis-conceived conclusions about both reading and reading instruction from con-trolled research on aspects of reading such as word naming, word identification, skill acquisition, and phonic rule development.

Researchers, particularly, have tended to fall into the unexamined view that reading is recognizing the next words. An example is the study of reading acquisition by Singer, Samuels, and Spiroff (1974).

They concluded that words were more easily 'learned' in isolation than in text or with illustration. They drew this conclusion from a study in which four words were taught to a number of learners in three conditions:
(a) in isolation
(b) in 'context': each word was presented in a three word sentence
(c) with an illustrative picture.

The key misconception in this study is that reading is a matter of identifying (or knowing) a series of words. It is then assumed that learning to read is learning to identify or know words. Further it is assumed that known words are known under all linguistic conditions. Implicit is the assumption that the task of 'learning' four words is representative of the general task of learning to read.

- Language must be studied in its human context. That's not a humanistic assertion. It's a scientific fact. Human language learning and the general function of language in human learning are not usefully described with learn-ing theories derived from the study of rats, pigeons, and other non-language users.

A revised model

Three kinds of information are available and used in language, whether productive or receptive. These come from 'the symbol system' which uses sounds in oral languages and graphic shapes in written languages. For literate language users of alphabetic languages there is also a set of relationships between sounds and shapes: 'the language structure' which is the grammar, or set of syntactic relationships that make it possible to express highly complex messages using a very small set of symbols. The same syntax underlies both oral and written language: 'the semantic system' which is the set of meanings as organized in concepts and con-ceptual structures. Meaning is the end product of receptive language,

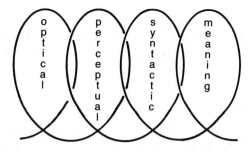

Figure 1

both listening and reading; but meaning is also the context in which reading takes on reality. Listener/readers bring meaning to any communication and conduct themselves as seekers of meaning.

A model of the reading process must account for these information sources. It must also respond to the following realities:

– Written language is displayed over space in contrast to oral language which is displayed in a time continuum.
– Writing systems make arbitrary decisions about direction in using space. The reader must adjust to a left-to-right, right-to-left, top-to-bottom, or other arbitrary characteristic of written language. Reading employs visual input. The eye is the input organ. It has certain characteristics and limitations as an optical instrument. It has a lens which must focus; it requires minimal light; it has a limited field; the area of view includes a small area of sharp detail.
– Reading must employ memory; it must hold an image, briefly store information, retain knowledge and understanding.

Cycles

Though reading is a process in which information is dealt with and meaning constructed continuously, it can be usefully represented as a series of cycles [see Figure 1]. Readers employ the cycles more or less sequentially as they move through a story or other text. But the readers' focus, if they are to be productive, is on meaning, so each cycle melts into the next and the readers leap toward meaning. The cycles are telescoped by the readers if they can get to meaning.

Processes

As the readers move through the cycles of reading they employ five processes. The brain is the organ of information processing. It decides what tasks it must handle, what information is available, what strategies it must employ, which input channels to use, where to seek information. The brain seeks to maximize information it acquires and minimize effort and energy used to acquire it. The five processes it employs in reading are:

1. *Recognition-initiation.* The brain must recognize a graphic display in the visual field as written language and initiate reading. Normally this would occur once in each reading activity, though it's possible for reading to be interrupted by other activities, examining pictures, for example, and then to be reinitiated.
2. *Prediction.* The brain is always anticipating and predicting as it seeks order and significance in sensory inputs.
3. *Confirmation.* If the brain predicts, it must also seek to verify its predictions. So it monitors to confirm or disconfirm with subsequent input what it expected.
4. *Correction.* The brain reprocesses when it finds inconsistencies or its predictions are disconfirmed.
5. *Termination.* The brain terminates the reading when the reading task is completed, but termination may occur for other reasons: the task is non-productive; little meaning is being constructed, or the meaning is already known, or the story is uninteresting or the reader finds it inappropriate for the particular purpose. At any rate, termination in reading is usually an open option at any point.

These processes have an intrinsic sequence. Prediction precedes confirmation which precedes correction. Yet the same information may be used to confirm a prior prediction and to make a new one.

Short circuits

Any reading that does not end with meaning is a short circuit. Readers may short circuit in a variety of ways for a variety of reasons. In general, readers short circuit when they can't get meaning or lose the structure; when they've been taught or otherwise acquired non-productive reading strategies; when they aren't permitted to terminate non-productive reading. Theoretically, a short circuit can occur at any point in the process. Here is a list of short circuits with successively more complex points:

Letter naming: A very old method of reading instruction taught young readers to spell out to themselves any unfamiliar words. This short circuit still occurs but it is not too common.
Recoding: Since print is a graphic code and speech is also a code, it is possible for readers to concentrate on matching print to sound with no meaning resulting. Since the readers go from code to code such short circuits may be considered recoding. Recoding may take place on several levels. 'Letter-sound recoding' is the most superficial. Sounds are matched on a one-to-one basis to the print. This sounding-out requires the readers to blend sounds to syn-

TABLE I. THE REVISED MODEL

Cycles	Inputs	Output
Start Recognize task as reading known language.	Graphic display Memory: recognition-initiation Activate strategies in memory	Optical scan cycle
1. *Optical* a) Scan in direction of print display.	Start: Memory: strategies for scanning appropriate to graphic display. Adjust speed of scan to processing speed.	Optical fixation cycle To memory: predict relation of information to direction of display.
b) Fix-focus eyes at point in the print.	Light reflects from graphic display. Visual field includes sharp and fuzzy input. Memory: prior prediction of meaning, structure, graphic redundancy, expectation of locus of key graphic cues.	Perception cycle To memory: cues for image formation.
2. *Perception* a) Sample-select. Choose cues from available graphic display.	Fix: cues available in sharp and blurred input. Memory: sampling strategies. Prior predictions and decodings to meaning.	To memory: selected cues. To feature analysis
b) Feature analysis. Choose features necessary to choose from alternate letters, words, structures.	Sampled features: From memory: Assign allosystem(s) (type style, cursive, etc.). Prior predictions.	Confirm prior prediction. Correct if necessary by return to scan, fix. If no system available, try best approximation or terminate; otherwise proceed to image formation.
c) Image formation. Form image of what is seen, and expected to be seen. Compare with expectations.	From: feature analysis, cues appropriate to allosystem(s) chosen. From memory: graphic, syntactic, semantic constructs. Prior predictions.	If no image possible, return to feature analysis or prior cycle for more information. Confirm prior predictions. If correction needed

TABLE I. (CONTINUED)

Cycles	Inputs	Output
	Cues from parallel phonological system (optional)	return to prior cycle, scan back for source of inconsistency. If image formed, store in memory and go to syntactic cycle.
3. *Syntactic cycle* a) Assign internal surface structure.	From image formation From memory: rules for relating surface display to internal surface structure. Prior predictions and decodings.	If no structure possible, recycle to perception or optical cycles. If inconsistent with predictions, try alternate or correct by recycling and scanning back to point of mismatch. If structure is possible, go to deep structure.
b) Assign deep structure. Seek clauses and their inter-relationships	From: internal surface structure. From memory: transformational rules for relating surface and deep structures. Prior predictions and decodings.	If no structure possible try alternative. If still no structure, recycle. If inconsistent with prediction, correct by recycling. If deep structure possible, predict graphic, semantic, syntactic features. Go to meaning. If oral reading, assign appropriate intonation contour. Terminate if no success.
4. *Construct meaning* a) Decode	From: deep structure From memory: stored experiences, conceptual constructs, lexicon. Prior predictions.	If meaning not acceptable, recycle to point of inconsistency. If no meaning possible, try alternate deep structure or recycle to seek more information. If still no meaning, hold all information in memory and return to scan. Terminate if no meaning results.

TABLE I. (CONTINUED)

Cycles	Inputs	Output
		If acceptable meaning, go to assimilate/ accommodate.
b) Assimilate/ Accommodate	From: decode	If no assimilation possible and no accommodation possible, recycle to correct or obtain more information.
If possible, assimilate.	From memory: prior predictions, prior meaning.	
If not possible, accommodate prior meaning.	Conceptual attitudinal constructs.	If still not possible, hold and return to scan for possible clarification as reading progresses.
		Accommodations possible; modify meaning of story/text to this point
		modify predictions of meaning
		modify concepts
		modify word definitions
		restructure attitudes
		If task complete, terminate.
		If task incomplete, recycle and scan forward, predict meaning, structure, graphics.

thesize words. 'Pattern-matching recoding' involves the readers fitting spelling patterns to sound patterns. Readers focus on features which contrast patterns such as rat-rate, hat-hate, mat-mate. Recoding is often by analogy: since 'bean' looks like 'mean' it must sound like it too. This recoding produces words or word-like utterances without requiring synthesizing.

'Internal surface-structure recoding' involves using the rules needed to relate print to underlying surface structure. Instead of going beyond to deep structure, however, the reader generates an oral surface representation. This recoding can produce words and phrases with approximate intonation patterns.

Syntactic nonsense. The readers may treat print as syntactic nonsense, generating an approximate deep structure without going beyond to meaning. Even proficient readers resort to this short circuit when conceptual load is too great or when they lack relevant background. With this short circuit the oral reading may be relatively accurate and yet involve little comprehension. Because readers do employ this short circuit we have come to regard the separation of syntactic deep structure from meaning as a useful view.

Partial structures. Readers may resort to one or more of these short circuits with alternating periods of productive reading. Furthermore, because the brain is always actively seeking meaning, some comprehension will often 'leak' through even the most non-productive short circuits. It will most likely result in fragments of meaning, a kind of kaleidoscopic view, rather than an integrated understanding.

I suspect that many of these short circuits result from instruction, but the studies to demonstrate this remain to be done.

Uses and limitations of the Goodman model

The Goodman model built through miscue analysis is a general model of the reading process based on the premise that there is a single reading process. In that sense it is an unlimited macro model of reading.

It is psycholinguistic, since it deals with how language and thought are interactive. But it operates within a sociolinguistic context. Language is social and it is through language that people mean things to each other. Reading, like all language, operates in a social context that includes readers and writers.

Since reading is a unitary process, several key premises follow: The model deals with reading in the context of written language in the context of language. It focusses on the proficient reader, but is applicable to all stages of development. It has been built through the study of English reading, but it must be applicable to reading in all languages and all orthographies.

Reading comprehension, as the model represents it, must be consistent with language comprehension and general comprehension.

All this means the model may not be inconsistent with any model of a larger context except in factors peculiar to the use and physical aspects of written English. Reading is language, so what's true for language must apply to reading. Reading and listening are both receptive language, so they cannot differ except in the linguistic medium and use. What the model predicts for English reading must also work for any other language except in terms of how specific characteristics of the syntax or orthography are accommodated by the reading process.

The reading model may be criticized for being inconsistent with valid theories of more general processes, but is not responsible for dealing explicitly with more than reading. It cannot be attacked for what it need not do.

Similarly, the model must be inclusive of all factors of reading under all conditions, though it need not explicitly or completely stipulate them. It must be applicable to:

1. All characteristics of text, text structure, text length.
2. All characteristics of the reader: linguistic and cognitive background, values and beliefs, motivation, proficiency, physical and mental condition.
3. All characteristics of syntax and grammar.
4. All characteristics of semantic systems: propositional structures, idioms and metaphors, pragmatics, functions, cohesion, inference.
5. All characteristics of memory as they involve language and cognition.
6. All characteristics of perception as it is involved in language and cognition.
7. All characteristics of orthography: symbols, system, features, directionality, relationship to meaning, relationship to phonology.
8. All conditions of reading: purpose, task, setting, third party influences, context.

The model, to be defensible, must be able to include or accommodate detail in any aspect of the reading process or its use without distorting either the model or the detail. It may, of course, offer a reconceptualization of the detail on the basis of the model's internal coherence. Thus, research findings by others that appear inconsistent with the model may be shown to be consistent through reconceptualizing them.

The model cannot be criticized for being incomplete, though it can be criticized for being unable to accommodate detailed micro modeling of any factor or aspect.

There are some things the model isn't. It isn't complete in detail in any aspect. It isn't a theory of comprehension, cognition, or perception. And it isn't a theory of reading instruction. That last must be consistent with a model of the reading process. But it must include a learning theory and theories of curriculum and instruction. A theory of reading instruction building on a theory and model of reading is the ultimate bridge to the classroom. The model presented here is not "something to use on Monday morning." It is the necessary base for the theory that will generate things to do on Monday and explain why they do or do not help people to read more efficiently and effectively.

References

Goodman, K. S. 1969. Analysis of oral reading miscues: applied psycholinguistics. *Reading Research Quarterly* 5: 9–30.

Singer, H., S. S. Samuels, and J. Spiroff. 1974. The effects of pictures and contextual conditions on learning responses to printed words. *Reading Research Quarterly* 9: 555–67.

2 Models of the reading process

S. Jay Samuels *and* Michael L. Kamil

Some context

A brief history of models

Reading research is just a little more than a hundred years old. In fact, it was the year 1879 when Emile Javal published his first paper on eye movements; James McKeen Cattell's still-cited paper on seeing and naming letters versus words was published in 1886. Surprisingly, serious attempts at building explicit models of the reading process – models that describe the entire process from the time the eye meets the page until the reader experiences the "click of comprehension" – have a history of a little more than thirty years.

This is not to say that early reading researchers were not concerned about all aspects of the reading process or that there were no scholarly pieces from which a model could be deduced fairly easily. It is perhaps more accurate to speculate that until the mid-1950s and the 1960s, there simply was not a strong tradition of attempting to conceptualize knowledge and theory about the reading process in the form of explicit reading models.

There are a variety of factors that account for the observed burst in model-building activity from, say, 1965 to the present. Surely the changes that occurred in language research and the psychological study of mental processes played a major role by elevating reading research to a more respectable stature. Just as surely, the advent of what has come to be known as the psycholinguistic perspective (Goodman 1967/1976, 1970; Smith 1971) pushed the field to consider underlying assumptions about basic processes in reading, as did a geometrically accelerating body of empirical evidence about basic processes. . . .

During the 1960s and early 1970s, a number of scholars developed more or less formal models of the reading process. Hockberg (1970), Mackworth (1972), and Levin and Kaplan (1970) all speculated about what a model describing the processes of skilled reading must account for.... Carroll (1964) provided a definition of reading along with a simple one-way flow diagram from visual stimulus to an oral language recoding to meaning responses. Carroll's purpose was to be illustrative not definitive; consequently, his model leaves many stages imprecisely specified.

Ruddell (1969) developed a system of communication model of reading that differed categorically from its predecessors in its excruciating detail of component processes and stages....

Goodman also worked out a model of reading over several years (1965, 1966, 1967/1976) that culminated in a relatively formal statement of the model's components and stages (1970), complete with a flow diagram. During that period and in the subsequent years, Goodman and his colleagues have amassed an extensive array of oral reading data to evaluate and support the model or at least the key features of the model. Often dubbed "reading as a psycholinguistic guessing game," its most distinctive characteristic is its procedural preference for allowing the reader to rely on existing syntactic and semantic knowledge structures, so that reliance on the graphic display and existing knowledge about the sounds associated with graphemes (graphophonemic knowledge) can be minimized. This is not to say that his model does not allow for a reader to go from symbol to sound to meaning – such mediation will not occur in predictable situations (as a function of familiarity and, perhaps, instructional history). It is more accurate to assert that his model always prefers the cognitive economy of reliance on well-developed linguistic (syntactic and semantic) rather than graphic information.

Another interesting distinction between Goodman's model and other models center on his use of the term *decoding*. Whereas others typically reserve this term to describe what happens when a reader translates a graphemic input into a phonemic input, Goodman uses it to describe how either a graphemic input or a phonemic input gets translated into a meaning code. Goodman uses the term *recoding* to describe the process of translating graphemes into phonemes. Thus, *decoding* can be either direct (graphemes to meaning) or mediated (graphemes to phonemes to meaning). Most of the extensive research efforts of Goodman and his colleagues have been directed toward demonstrating the strong procedural preference readers of all ages have for relying upon the meaning (as opposed to the graphic and graphophonemic) cues available in the printed message. A final unique aspect of Goodman's model is that it, among all earlier and later models, has had the greatest impact on conceptions about reading instruction, particularly early instruction. So strong has been this impact that it is not uncommon to hear or read about *the* psycholinguistic approach to reading or *the* whole-language approach to reading.

It is difficult to know what to say about Frank Smith's (1971) seminal work describing reading as a psycholinguistic process. It is not so much a model of reading as it is a description of the linguistic and cognitive processes that any decent model of reading will need to take into account. Like Goodman, he is careful to distinguish between mediated (through recoding to sound) and immediate meaning identification (print to meaning). Also, like Goodman, his account of reading exhibits a procedural preference for reliance on language factors instead of graphic information. But to call it a model of reading would misrepresent Smith's aim. Perhaps the greatest contribution of Smith's work is to explain how the redundancy inherent at all levels of language (letter features, within letters, within words, within sentences, within discourses) provides the reader with enormous flexibility in marshaling resources to create a meaning for the text at hand.

With the publication of Gough's (1972) model of reading, the impact of the information processing approach to studying mental processes is seen within the reading field. Controversial because of Gough's assumption that all letters in the visual field must be accounted for individually by the reader prior to the assignment of meaning to any string of letters, Gough's model has probably generated as much controversy about basic processes as Goodman's has about instrumental practice. The appearance of LaBerge and Samuels's (1974) model emphasizing automaticity of component processes and Rumelhart's interactive model (1977) emphasizing flexible processing and multiple information sources, depending upon contextual circumstances, provided convincing evidence that the information processing perspective was here to stay within the reading field.

Since the publication of Rumelhart's model, there have been other notable efforts deserving mention. Carver (1977–8) has provided us with a model that hearkens back to that of Gough (because of its unidirectional emphasis from letters to sounds to meaning) and to Holmes and Singer (because Carver, more than any other recent model builder, has emphasized the empirical evaluation of all aspects of his model). Stanovich (1980) has developed an interesting twist to the Rumelhart model. Kintsch and van Dijk (1978) have built a model emphasizing comprehension to the exclusion of word identification (most other models, including Rumelhart's, seem to have a bias for explaining word identification). Most recently, Just and Carpenter (1980) have built a model to account for comprehension processes based upon studies of eye movements.

With this brief history, we now turn to describing and explaining some of the models we have mentioned. . . . But first, a few words about some thorny problems all models must address and about the nature of information-processing models.

Some problems in model evaluation

When researchers attempt to describe the reading process, we must be aware of two major problems that lead to misunderstandings among model builders. The first of these problems is that the developer of a model of reading has only a limited knowledge base to draw upon, and this knowledge base is influenced by the scientific philosophies and studies dominant within the historical context in which the model was developed. Thus, if one contrasts the models that were developed during the pre-1960 period of behaviorism with those developed during the post-1965 period of cognitive psychology, one can find conceptualizations and components in the newer models not found in earlier ones. Before the mid-1960s, because of the emphasis on behaviorism, the models attempted to describe how stimuli, such as printed words and word-recognition responses, became associated. During this period, because the emphasis was on directly observable events external to the individual, little attempt was made to explain what went on within the recesses of the mind that allowed the human to make sense of the printed page. After the mid-1960s, with the emergence of cognitive psychology as a major force, the models began to show how processes, such as memory and attention, which went on within the recesses of the human mind, played a role in reading. As more became known about comprehension, an attempt was made to model this process through conceptual networks.

Even during this current period, in which cognitive psychology dominates so much thinking about reading, one can observe how changes in thinking have influenced the models of human information processing. For example, the models of the 1970s tended to be linear information processing models, whereas the later models tended to be interactive with opportunities for feedback loops from components in the later stages to influence components in the earlier stages. Thus, as we attempt to evaluate the models of reading of the last three decades, we must do so in terms of the information available and the conceptualizations current during the period in which they were developed.

The second major problem which we must keep in mind as we study and evaluate these different reading models is that each scholar who describes the process is influenced by information gathered during experiments. Unfortunately, researchers have tended to ignore the fact that information gathered during an experiment is influenced by four interacting factors. These are the age and skill of the experimental subjects, the tasks which the subjects are asked to perform, the materials which are used, and the context (e.g., classroom, laboratory, type of school, etc.) which surrounds the study. A change in any of these variables can alter the results of a study and the researcher's view of the process....

Because of the interactive nature of the variables in a study, we must attempt to evaluate the different reading models in terms of their generalizability.... As we investigate and study... models, we ought to be asking questions, such as, Does this model adequately describe both fluent and beginning reading? Does this model describe reading across a variety of tasks and purposes? Does the model describe the word-recognition process as well as the comprehension process? Does the model describe the reading process for different materials as well as different contexts? At the present time... [no] model[s] can do all of the above. Hence, our need to study models carefully to know what they can and cannot do.

[In the original work, a section follows on building information-processing models.]

Characteristics of models

... A good model has certain important characteristics. The three characteristics of a good model are: (a) it can summarize the past, (b) it can help us to understand the present, and (c) it can predict the future. Some models are developed only after a considerable amount of research has been done and data collected on a topic. When the model is developed, it can synthesize much of the information which was gathered in the past....

The second function of models is that they help us to understand the present. It is unfortunate, but almost everything we are interested in turns out to be complex. Even so-called simple things, upon proper investigation, turn out to be extraordinarily complex. At one time, for example, psychologists thought the stimulus-response bond would turn out to be a simple, basic element in learning; but the more they studied it, the more they found out that it too was complex, involving both stimulus learning and response learning as well as the problems of associating the two. Thus, the development of a model which can help us to understand a complex phenomenon can serve as a most important scientific and social function. It helps us to understand by eliminating the nonessential aspects of the phenomenon, by focusing our attention on the essential, and by showing how these essential parts interrelate and function.

The third characteristic of a good model is that it enables us to formulate hypotheses which are testable, that is, it helps us predict the future.... Model building is a game in which almost anyone can engage. We are all familiar with models that were developed in the past which, on the surface, helped us to understand complex phenomena but, in the face of testing, could not stand up to the facts. For example, at one time the Earth was thought to be flat. Models of the solar system showed the planet Earth as its center. However, Copernicus and, a century later, Galileo were able to destroy the old model that showed the centrality of the Earth in the solar system. Consequently, it is important that we test our models in order to eliminate the invalid ones and to retain the ones which deserve to be saved but may be in need of fine tuning. Thus, an absolutely critical characteristic of a good model is that it be precise enough to lead to testable hypotheses. It is only through the process of testing a model that we are able to determine its validity.

Current models

The Rumelhart model

[The original paper also describes the Gough Model and the LaBerge and Samuels Model.]

Information processing models tend to be linear and to have a series of noninteractive processing stages. Each stage in a noninteractive model does its work independently and passes its production to the next higher stage. According to Rumelhart (1977), linear models which pass information along in one direction only and which do not permit the information contained in a higher stage to influence the processing of a lower stage contain a serious deficiency.

Deficiencies in linear models

The deficiencies in linear models of reading are such that they have difficulty accounting for a number of occurrences known to take place while reading. However, an interactive model, which permits the information contained in higher stages of processing to influence the analysis which occurs at lower stages of processing, can account for those well-known occurrences in reading.

What each of the well-known occurrences and observations share in common is that they can be explained with a model which permits the information found in a higher processing stage to influence the analysis of a lower stage. The first of these observations is that more letters can be apprehended in a given unit of time if they spell a word than if the same letters are used in a nonword (Huey 1908/1968). For example, more letters are apprehended in a word like *alligator* than in a letter string like *rllaagtio*.

Similarly, more letters can be apprehended in a nonsense letter string which conforms to rules of English spelling than in a nonsense letter string which does not conform to English spelling rules (Miller, Bruner, and Postman 1954), for example, *vernalit* as opposed to *nrveiatl*. To account for the fact that apprehension of letters is superior in real words and in nonsense strings which conform to English orthographic rules, one must posit a mechanism whereby the knowledge of lexical items and orthography contained in higher-order stages can influence the perception of letters which occurs earlier at lower stages in the information processing system.

The second category of observations pertinent to reading relates to syntactic effects on word perception. It is commonly observed that when an error in word recognition is made, there is a strong tendency for the word substitution to maintain the same part of speech as the word for which it was substituted (Kolers 1970; Weber 1970). In a now classic study, Miller and Isard (1963) found that auditory perception of words in a noisy environment was superior when normal syntax was used than when there was a violation of normal syntax.

The third type of observation about reading relates to the fact that semantic knowledge influences word perception. For example, using an experimental procedure in which the subject must decide as quickly as possible if a letter string spells a word, it was found that the decision can be made faster when a pair of words are semantically related, as in *bread-butter* or *doctor-nurse*, than if they are semantically unrelated, as in *bread* and *doctor* or *nurse* and *butter* (Meyer and Schvaneveldt 1971; Meyer, Schvaneveldt, and Ruddy 1975). Using a different procedure, Tulving and Gold (1963) were able to demonstrate that speed of word recognition was progressively faster as increased amounts of a sentence were exposed prior to presenting the target word than if the target word was presented by itself.

The fourth observation is that perception of syntax for a given word depends upon the context in which the word is embedded. For example, if we compare the italicized words in "They are *eating apples*," it is not clear whether the sentence is describing the act of consuming apples or if it is describing a type of apple, that is, eating apples as opposed to cooking apples. We can disambiguate the sentence if we precede the sentence in the following manner: "What are the children eating? They are eating apples." Or we can ask: "What kind of apples are these? They are eating apples." It is clear now that the first context leads to a decision indicating that we are describing the act of children consuming a fruit, while the second context is describing a type of apple.

The final observation offered by Rumelhart relates to the fact that our interpretation of what we read depends upon the context in which a text segment is embedded. For example, in the sentence, "The statistician was certain the difference was significant since all the figures on the right-hand side of the table were larger than any of those on the left," our interpretation of the word "figures" is that of numerals, whereas in the sentence, "The craftsman charged more for the carvings on the right since all the figures on the right-hand side of the table were larger than any of those on the left," the term relates to a wood or ceramic figure. Similarly, our interpretation of the ambiguous statement, "The shooting of the hunters was terrible," can be altered by prior context. For example, contrast the statement, "Their marksmanship was awful. In fact, the shooting of the hunters was terrible" with the statement, "Their cruelty was awful. In fact, the shooting of the hunters was terrible." We can observe in these examples that meaning is not constructed just from the particular text segment we are processing but from its surrounding environment.

Components of Rumelhart's model

The examples that have been presented in the previous paragraphs have illustrated how syntactic, semantic, lexical, and orthographic information can influence our perceptions. In each of the illustrations, our higher-order knowledge influenced the processing at a lower stage of analysis. Consequently, Rumelhart's model of reading, as seen in Figure 1, has each of these knowledge sources exerting influence upon the text processing and our ultimate interpretation of the text.

As seen in Rumelhart's model, information from syntactic, semantic, lexical, and orthographic sources converge upon the pattern synthesizer. These knowledge sources are providing input simultaneously and a mechanism must be provided which can accept these sources of information, hold the information, and redirect the information as needed. The mechanism which can accomplish these tasks is the message center.

The message center has several functions. As each of the knowledge sources feeds in information about the text being processed, the center holds this information in a temporary store. Each of the knowledge sources may use the information provided by one or more of the other sources. For example, lexical knowledge may search for information about spelling patterns or there may be a check for information about syntax. Rumelhart states:

The message center keeps a running list of hypotheses about the nature of the input string. Each knowledge source constantly scans the message center for the appearance of hypotheses relevant to its own sphere of knowledge. Whenever such a hypothesis enters the message center, the knowledge source in question evaluates the hypothesis in light of its own specialized knowledge. As a result of its analysis, the hypothesis may be confirmed, disconfirmed and removed from the message center, or a new hypothesis can be added to the message center. This procedure continues until some decision can be reached. At that point the most probable hypothesis is determined to be the right one. (1977: 589–590)

By means of separate knowledge sources and a message center which permits these sources to communicate and interact with others, the

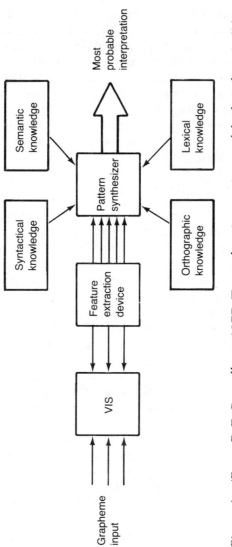

Figure 1 (From D.E. Rumelhart, 1977, Toward an interactive model of reading, in "Attention and performance," Vol. VI, S. Dornic (Ed.), p. 588. Hillsdale, N.J.: Erlbaum. Reprinted by permission.)

higher-order stages are able to influence the processing of lower-order stages. Thus, Rumelhart's model is able to accommodate the occurrences known to take place while reading which the linear models have difficulty accommodating. . . . ·

The Stanovich model

The Stanovich model (1980) integrates concepts from a variety of sources. He states (p. 32):

Interactive models of reading appear to provide a more accurate conceptualization of reading performance than do strictly top-down or bottom-up models. When combined with an assumption of compensatory processing (that a deficit in any particular process will result in a greater reliance on other knowledge sources, regardless of their level in the processing hierarchy), interactive models provide a better account of the existing data on the use of orthographic structure and sentence context by good and poor readers.

According to Stanovich, the earlier bottom-up reading models had a tendency to depict the information flow in a series of discrete stages, with each stage transforming the input and then passing the recorded information on to the next higher stage for additional transformation and recoding. Because the sequence of processing proceeds from the incoming data to higher-level encodings, these descriptions of the reading process are called bottom-up models. . . . [A]n important shortcoming of these models is lack of feedback, in that no mechanism is provided to allow for processing stages which occur later in the system to influence processing which occurs earlier in the system. Because of the lack of feedback loops in the early bottom-up models, it was difficult to account for sentence-context effects and the role of prior knowledge of text topic as facilitating variables in word recognition and comprehension. Stanovich states that because of this problem, "Samuels (1977) revised the LaBerge and Samuels (1974) model just for this reason" (p. 34)

Top-down models, on the other hand, conceptualize the reading process as one in which stages which are higher up and at the end of the information-processing sequence interact with stages which occur earlier in the sequence. More important, the higher-order stages seem to be driving and directing the process and are doing the lion's share of the work. In top-down processing, since the reader is only sampling text information in order to verify hypotheses and predictions, reading is viewed as being conceptually driven by the higher-order stages rather than by low-level stimulus analysis. One way to look at the difference between top-down and bottom-up models is that bottom-up models start with the printed stimuli and work their way up to the higher-level stages, whereas the top-down models start with hypotheses and predictions and attempt to verify them by working down to the printed stimuli.

Just as the bottom-up models have problems, so, too, do the top-down models. One of the problems for the top-down model is that for many texts, the reader has little knowledge of the topic and cannot generate predictions. A more serious problem is that even if a skilled reader can generate predictions, the amount of time necessary to generate a prediction may be greater than the amount of time the skilled reader needs simply to recognize the words. In other words, for the sake of efficiency, it is easier for a skilled reader to simply recognize words in a text than to try to generate predictions. Thus, while the top-down models may be able to explain beginning reading, with slow rates of word recognition, they do not accurately describe skilled reading behavior.

Stanovich has attempted to incorporate what is known about skilled and unskilled reading into the interactive-compensatory model. A key concept is that "a process at any level can compensate for deficiencies at any other level" (p. 36). Thus, if there is a deficiency at an early print-analysis stage, higher-order knowledge structures will attempt to compensate. For the poor reader, who may be both inaccurate and slow at word recognition but who has knowledge of the text topic, top-down processing may allow for this compensation. For example, if a beginning reader who is weak at decoding comes upon a word he does not know, such as *emerald* in the sentence "The jeweler put the green emerald in the ring," he may use sentence context and knowledge of gems to decide what the word is.

On the other hand, if the reader is skilled at word recognition but does not know much about the text topic, it may be easier to simply recognize the words on the page and rely on bottom-up processes. In essence, Stanovich states, "Interactive models...assume that a pattern is synthesized based on information provided simultaneously from several knowledge sources. The compensatory assumption states that a deficit in any knowledge results in a heavier reliance on other knowledge sources, regardless of their level in the processing hierarchy" (p. 63). The Stanovich model, then, is interactive in the sense that any stage, regardless of its position in the system, may communicate with any other stage, and it is compensatory in the sense that any reader may rely on better developed knowledge sources when particular, and usually more commonly used, knowledge sources are temporarily weak.

Stanovich has made a unique contribution to reading models, because he has allowed us to explain, from a theoretical viewpoint, the apparent anomaly in many particular research studies; that is, under certain conditions poor readers exhibit greater sensitivity to contextual constraints than do good readers. They do so in those circumstances where featural, orthographic, and/or lexical knowledge...sources are weak in comparison to syntactic and semantic knowledge. The reason good readers are sometimes less sensitive to contextual effects is that their knowledge sources for these lower-level processes are seldom weak. . . .

[In the original work, a section discussing the model of Just and Carpenter and the Kintsch Model is included at this point.]

Comparison of models

. . . Model evolution over time also makes comparison difficult. For example, additional studies since the LaBerge and Samuels model was first introduced have established the text conditions and the development levels of reading skill under which component and holistic processing of words operate. The LaBerge and Samuels model was originally formulated as a serial, linear model, with the higher-order stages unable to influence lower-order stages, which must do their work earlier in the processing sequence. However, the revisions outlined in this chapter clearly indicate that the LaBerge and Samuels model now allows interaction between stages in the model.

Despite these difficulties, there have been attempts to compare models along sets of common dimensions. For example, deBeaugrande (1981) has generated a set of sixteen categories for describing models of reading. Some of these categories include: the contributuion of the processor (Is it top-down or bottom-up?), memory storage (abstractive, constructive, or reconstructive), automatization (whether some processes require little or no attention), processing depth (how much processing is required as a function of the task), and serial versus parallel processing (whether only one task or several can be performed concurrently).

Mosenthal (1984) has argued, however, that the comparison of models needs to include social and political criteria as well as statistical and logical criteria. His argument is that the scope of models should be limited by their "partial specifications." A partially specified model consists of samples of the features, procedures, and criteria that approximate a fully specified model's features, and so on. This means that since models are less than complete, the implications should also be viewed as incomplete. Certainly, model builders have been less than likely to assume that their models can account for all reading phenomena.

Each of the builders of reading models is describing the process from a somewhat different perspective, with a different focus. If there are discrepancies among the empirical studies reported in support of a particular model, it is probably the result of differences in materials used in the studies, the task subjects had to perform, skill level of the experimental subjects, and the context of the studies.

While each model tends to draw upon conceptualizations of the reading process that have preceded it, it does not follow that the earlier models are no longer useful because each model describes a somewhat different aspect of reading. Thus, each model provides unique information about the reading process not found in the other models. In order to gain a more comprehensive view of reading, one should study each of the models. In fact, as one studies each of the models, one becomes impressed with how much experimental knowledge has been compressed with these few models.

Finally, we should recognize that our models have gaping holes in them. As we have developed some sophisticated ideas about how comprehension takes place and how metacognitive strategies are used to facilitate reading, the models have been slow to incorporate this information. It is as though there are separate knowledge entities in need of a cohesive force to integrate the disparate pieces of information into a unified model. However, before we attempt to build comprehensive models... it is important that we first establish partial models that can be tested and modified as the need arises. At our present stage of development, we need partial models which can be tested more than we need comprehensive models which are more difficult to test. It should be most fascinating in the years to come to see what changes will occur in our models of reading as new knowledge accumulates about this process.

References

Carroll, J. B. 1964. *Language and thought*. Englewood Cliffs, N.J.: Prentice-Hall.

Carver, R. P. 1977–8. Toward a theory of reading comprehension and reading. *Reading Research Quarterly* 13: 8–64.

Cattell, J. M. 1886. The time it takes to see and name objects. *Mind* 11: 63–65.

deBeaugrande, R. 1981. Design criteria for process models of reading. *Reading Research Quarterly* 16: 261–315.

Goodman, K. S. 1965. A linguistic study of cues and miscues in reading. *Elementary English* 42: 639–643.

1966. A psycholinguistic view of reading comprehension. In *New frontiers in college-adult reading* (15th Yearbook of the National Reading Conference), G. B. Schick and M. M. May (Eds.). Milwaukee, Wis.: National Reading Conference.

1970. Behind the eye: what happens in reading. In *Reading: process and program*, K. S. Goodman and O. S. Niles (Eds.). Urbana, Ill.: National Council of Teachers of English.

1976. Reading: a psycholinguistic guessing game. In *Theoretical models and processes of reading*, 2nd ed., H. Singer and R. Ruddell (Eds.). Newark, Del.: International Reading Association. (Originally published 1967.)

Gough, P. B. 1972. One second of reading. In *Language by ear and by eye*, J. F. Kavanagh and I. G. Mattingly (Eds.). Cambridge, Mass.: MIT Press.

Hockberg, J. 1970. Components of literacy: speculations and exploratory research. In *Basic studies on reading*, H. Levin and J. P. Williams (Eds.). New York: Basic Books.

Holmes. J. A. 1953. *The substrata-factor theory of reading*. Berkeley: California Book.

Huey, E. B. 1968. *The psychology and pedagogy of reading*. Cambridge, Mass.: MIT Press. (Originally published 1908).

Javal, E. 1879. Essai sur la physiologie de la lecture. *Annales d'oculistique* 82: 242–253.

Just, M. A., and P. A. Carpenter. 1980. A theory of reading: from eye fixations to comprehension. *Psychological Review* 87: 329–354.

Kintsch, W., and van Dijk, T. 1978. Toward a model of text comprehension and production. *Psychological Review* 85: 363–394.

LaBerge, D., and S. J. Samuels. 1974. Toward a theory of automatic information processing in reading. *Cognitive Psychology* 6: 293–323.

Levin, H., and E. L. Kaplan. 1970. Grammatical structure and reading. In *Basic studies on reading*, H. Levin and J. P. Williams (Eds.). New York: Basic Books.

Kolers, P. A. 1970. Three stages of reading. In *Basic studies on reading*, H. Levin and J. P. Williams (Eds.). New York: Basic Books.

Mackworth, J. F. 1972. Some models of the reading process: learners and skill readers. *Reading Research Quarterly* 7: 701–733.

Meyer, D. E., and R. W. Schvaneveldt. 1971. Facilitation in recognizing pairs of words: evidence of a dependence between retrieval operations. *Journal of Experimental Psychology* 90: 27–234.

Meyer, D. E., R. W. Schvaneveldt, and M. G. Ruddy. 1975. Loci of contextual effects on word recognition. In *Attention and performance V*, P. M. A. Rabbitt and S. Dornic (Eds.). New York: Academic Press.

Miller, G. A., J. S. Bruner, and L. Postman. 1954. Familiarity of letter sequences and tachistoscopic identification. *Journal of General Psychology* 50: 129–139.

Miller, G. A., and S. Isard. 1963. Some perceptual consequences of linguisic rules. *Journal of Verbal Learning and Verbal Behavior* 2: 217–228.

Mosenthal, P. 1984. The problem of partial specification in translating reading research into practice. *Elementary School Journal* 85: 199–227.

Ruddell, R. B. 1969. Psycholinguistic implications for a system of communication model. In *Psycholinguistics and the teaching of reading*, K. Goodman and J. Fleming (Eds.). Newark, Del.: International Reading Association.

Rumelhart, D. 1977. Toward an interactive model of reading. In *Attention and performance VI*, S. Dornic (Ed.). Hillsdale, N.J.: Erlbaum.

Samuels, S. J. 1977. Introduction to theoretical models of reading. In *Reading problems*, W. Otto (Ed.). Boston: Addison-Wesley.

Singer, H. 1983. The substrata-factor theory of reading and its history and conceptual relationship to interaction theory. In *Reading research revisited*, L. Gentiel, M. Kamil, and J. Blanchard (Eds.). Columbus, Oh.: Merrill.

Singer, H., and R. Ruddell (Eds.). *Theoretical models and processes of reading*, 2nd ed. Newark, Del.: International Reading Association.

Smith, F. 1971. *Understanding reading*. New York: Holt, Rinehart and Winston.

Stanovich, K. E. 1980. Toward an interactive-compensatory model of individual differences in the development of reading fluency. *Reading Research Quarterly* 16: 32–71.

Tulving, E., and C. Gold. 1963. Stimulus information and contextual information as determinants of tachistoscopic recognition of words. *Journal of Experimental Psychology* 66: 319–327.

Weber, R. M. 1970. First graders' use of grammatical context in reading. In *Basic studies on reading*, H. Levin and J. P. Williams (Eds.). New York: Basic Books.

3 A schema-theoretic view of basic processes in reading comprehension

Richard C. Anderson *and* P. David Pearson

> ...to completely analyze what we do when we read would almost be
> the acme of a psychologist's dream for it would be to describe very
> many of the most intricate workings of the human mind, as well as to
> unravel the tangled story of the most remarkable specific performance
> that civilization has learned in all its history. (Huey, 1908/1968, p. 8)

Huey's eloquent statement about the goals of the psychology of reading
is as relevant today as it was when he wrote it in 1908. The quotation
usually precedes an apology for how little we have learned in the past
75 years. We wish to break with that tradition and use Huey's statement
to introduce an essay in which we will try to demonstrate that while we
have not fully achieved Huey's goal, we have made substantial progress.

Our task is to characterize basic processes of reading comprehension.
We will not present a model of the entire reading process, beginning
with the focusing of the eye on the printed page and ending with the
encoding of information into long-term semantic memory or its subsequent retrieval for purposes of demonstrating comprehension to someone in the outer world. Instead, we will focus on one aspect of
comprehension of particular importance to reading comprehension: the
issue of how the reader's *schemata*, or knowledge already stored in
memory, function in the process of interpreting new information and
allowing it to enter and become a part of the knowledge store. Whether
we are aware of it or not, it is this interaction of new information with
old knowledge that we mean when we use the term comprehension. To
say that one has comprehended a text is to say that she has found a
mental "home" for the information in the text, or else that she has
modified an existing mental home in order to accommodate that new
information. It is precisely this interaction between old and new information that we address in this chapter.

Our plan for the chapter is straightforward. First, we will trace the
historical antecedents of schema theory. Then we will outline the basic
elements of the theory and point out problems with current realizations

of the theory and possible solutions. Next, we will consider the interplay between the abstracted knowledge embodied in schemata and memory for particular examples. Then we will decompose the comprehension process in order to examine components of encoding (attention, instantiation, and inference) and retrieval (retrieval plans, editing and summarizing, and reconstructive processes). Finally, we will evaluate the contributions of schema theory to our understanding of the comprehension process and speculate about the directions that future research should take.

History of the notion of a schema

While Sir Frederic Bartlett (1932) is usually acknowledged as the first psychologist to use the term schema in the sense that it is used today, historical precedence must surely be given to the Gestalt psychologists. The starting point for Gestalt psychology was a paper by Max Wertheimer in 1912 reporting research in which Wolfgang Kohler and Kurt Koffka served as assistants. These three became the principal figures in the Gestalt movement.

The term Gestalt literally means shape or form. Gestalt psychology emphasized holistic properties. It was the study of mental organization. The Gestalt movement was a reaction against the Zeitgeist at the turn of the century, which held that perception, thought, and emotion could be resolved into elemental sensations. According to Wilhelm Wundt, the dominant figure in psychology during that period, the business of psychology "was (1) the *analysis* of conscious processes into *elements*, (2) the determination of the manner of *connection* of these elements, and (3) the determination of their laws of connection" (cited in Boring 1950, p. 333). The popular metaphor was that psychology was "mental chemistry."

The insight of the Gestalt psychologists was that the properties of a whole experience cannot be inferred from its parts. Carrying the mental chemistry metaphor a step further, they liked to point out that the molecules of chemical compounds have emergent properties that cannot be predicted in a simple fashion from the properties of the constituent elements (see Kohler 1947: 115).

The basic principle of Gestalt psychology, called the Law of Pragnanz, is that mental organization will always be as good as prevailing conditions allow (see Koffka 1935: 110). In this definition, "good" embraces such properties as simplicity, regularity, and symmetry. The theory stresses that mental organization is "dynamic," which means that the tendency toward coherent organization is a spontaneous process that can happen without an external goad.

Figure 1   (From Wulf, 1922/1938, p. 140. By permission of Routledge & Kegan Paul, and Humanities Press International, Inc.)

Gestalt ideas were applied especially to visual perception. A notable example, which had a considerable influence on subsequent thinking, was Wulf's (1922/1938) research on memory for geometric designs. Subjects were asked to make drawings that reproduced the designs shortly after exposure, after 24 hours, and after a week. As the interval lengthened, Wulf observed characteristic changes in the reproductions that he termed "leveling" and "sharpening." Leveling means smoothing an irregularity. Sharpening means emphasizing or exaggerating a salient feature. The overall effect generally was to "normalize" reproductions. Wulf (1922/1938: 140) illustrated the process with the design shown in Figure 1.

Four subjects spoke of this as a "bridge," while another called it an "arch." In their reproductions of this figure, these subjects all lengthened the "supports." Wulf (1922/1938: 141) explained his results in these terms:

In addition to, or even instead of, purely visual data there were also general types or schemata in terms of which the subject constructed his responses... The schema itself becomes with time ever more dominant; visual imagery of the original disappears, ... details contained in the original are forgotten and incorrectly reproduced, yet even the last reproduction will usually show a steady progress towards representation of the type or schema originally conceived.

According to Bartlett in his classic book *Remembering* (1932: 201), the term "schema" refers to "an active organization of past reactions, or past experience." The term active was intended to emphasize what he saw as the constructive character of remembering, which he contrasted with a passive retrieval of "fixed and lifeless" memories. "The first notion to get rid of," Bartlett wrote (1932: 204), "is that memory is primarily or literally reduplicative, or reproductive.... It is with remembering as it is with the stroke in a skilled game [of tennis or cricket]. ... Every time we make it, it has its own characteristics."

Though he used phrases such as "mental set," "active organization," and "general impression" a great deal, Bartlett was never very clear about what he meant by them, other than to indicate a top-down influence:

an individual does not ordinarily take . . . a situation detail by detail and me-
ticulously build up the whole. In all ordinary instances he has an overmaster-
ing tendency simply to get a general impression of the whole; and, on the
basis of this, he constructs the probable detail. Very little of his construction
is literally observed. . . . But it is the sort of construction which serves to justify his general impression. (1932: 206)

Bartlett was vague about just how schemata work. For example, he
said several times that a central idea in his theory was "turning around
on one's schemata." He apparently meant deducing the way the past
must have been from one's current schema. But he never explicated the
idea. Indeed, he admitted, "I wish I knew exactly how it was done"
(1932: 206).

Bartlett's ideas resembled those of Gestalt psychology, and he even
described research of his own on memory for pictorial material that was
similar to Wulf's. Nevertheless, there is no indication that he was directly
influenced by the Gestalt tradition. The only Gestalt psychologist that
Bartlett cited was Kohler, and he in just a passing note that "recent
general psychological theories are still in a fluid state" (1932: 186). At
least one of the major Gestalt psychologists was aware of Bartlett's work.
In *Principles of Gestalt Psychology*, Koffka (1935: 519) complained that
he found Bartlett difficult to understand but acknowledged that there
was "a great affinity between Bartlett's theory of memory and our own."

With respect to empirical research, Bartlett is best remembered for his
study of the recall of the North American Indian folktale, *The War of
the Ghosts*. He reported that, especially after a long interval, subjects'
reproductions became simplified and stereotyped. Details that "fit in
with a subject's preformed interests and tendencies" (1932: 93) were
recalled. Other details were either omitted or "rationalized by linking
them together and so rendering them apparently coherent, or linking
given detail with detail not actually present . . . " (p. 94). As time passed,
elaborations, importations, and inventions appeared in subjects' reproductions with increasing frequency. Usually these intrusions could be
seen as contributing to the subject's rationalization of the text.

We turn now to a major figure in the recent history of education and
psychology, David P. Ausubel. He has had a direct influence on the
thinking of the current generation of educational research workers, including the present authors. His thinking, in turn, bears resemblances
to that of Bartlett, the Gestalt psychologists and, perhaps even more, to
nineteenth-century figures, such as Herbart, as Barnes and Clawson
(1975) have pointed out. However, Ausubel himself has emphatically
denied such intellectual debts (1978). It seems only fair to conclude that
he reinvented the ideas associated with his name and gave them a distinctive flourish.

According to Ausubel (Ausubel 1963; Ausubel and Robinson 1969), in meaningful learning, already-known general ideas "subsume" or "anchor" the new particular propositions found in texts. This happens only when the existing ideas are stable, clear, discriminable from other ideas, and directly relevant to the to-be-understood propositions. The reader has to be aware of which aspects of his knowledge are relevant. Sometimes this will be obvious. Sometimes the text will be explicit. When neither of these conditions holds or the reader's grasp of the required knowledge is shaky, an "advance organizer" may be prescribed. An advance organizer is a statement written in abstract, inclusive terms deliberately introduced before a text and intended to provide a conceptual bridge between what the reader already knows and the propositions in the text that it is hoped he will understand and learn.

Ausubel has not called his theory a schema theory, but it clearly is. Ausubel's own research and the research of those inspired by him has dealt mainly with advance organizers, which have proved to have facilitative effects (Luiten, Ames, and Ackerson 1980; Mayer 1979).

Among educators, something like schema theory has driven conceptions about reading. Take, for instance, Huey's (1908/1968) conclusion about whether we read letter by letter or in larger chunks:

So it is clear that the larger the amount read during a reading pause, the more inevitably must the reading be by suggestion and inference from clews of whatsoever kind, internal or external. In reading, the deficient picture is filled in, retouched, by the mind, and the page is thus made to present the familiar appearance of completeness in its details which we suppose to exist in the actual page. (p. 68)

Implicit, if not explicit, in the philosophy of Francis Parker when he ran the laboratory school at the University of Chicago at the turn of the last century was the importance of building knowledge structures through experience as a prerequisite to reading (see Mathews 1966). Ernest Horn (1937), famous for his work in spelling, recognized the active contribution of the reader: "[The author] does not really convey ideas to the reader; he merely stimulates him to construct them out of his own experience. If the concept is ... new to the reader, its construction more nearly approaches problem solving than simple association" (Horn 1937: 154). And, of course, William S. Gray recognized, both in his professional writing (1948) and in his suggestions for teachers in basal reader manuals, the necessity of engaging children's prior knowledge before reading.

But the full development of schema theory as a model for representing how knowledge is stored in human memory had to await the revolution in our conception of how humans process information spurred by the thinking of computer scientists doing simulations of human cognition (e.g., Minsky 1975; Winograd 1975). Hence, it was in the late 1970s that ambitious statements of schema theories began to emerge (Rumelhart 1980; Schank and Abelson 1977) and to be applied to entities like stories (e.g., Mandler and Johnson 1977; Rumelhart 1975; Stein and Glenn 1979) and processes like reading (see Adams and Collins 1979; R. C. Anderson 1977, 1978). Concurrently, schema-theoretic notions became the driving force behind empirical investigations of basic processes in reading. Much of this research is described later in this chapter. First, however, we attempt to elucidate schema theory as a model of human knowledge.

Some elements of schema theory

A schema is an abstract knowledge structure. A schema is abstract in the sense that it summarizes what is known about a variety of cases that differ in many particulars. An important theoretical puzzle is to determine just how much and what sort of knowledge is abstracted and how much remains tied to knowledge of specific instances. A schema is structured in the sense that it represents the relationships among its component parts. The theoretical issue is to specify the set of relationships needed for a general analysis of knowledge. The overriding challenge for the theorist is to specify the form and substance of schemata and the processes by which the knowledge embodied in schemata is used.

We will hang our discussion of these issues on a concrete case, the SHIP CHRISTENING schema. A possible representation of this schema is diagrammed in Figure 2. If for the sake of the argument, one takes this as a serious attempt to represent the average person's knowledge of ship christening, what does it say and what follows from it?

Figure 2 says that the typical person's knowledge of ship christening can be analyzed into six parts: that it is done to bless a ship, that it normally takes place in a dry dock, and so on. In the jargon of schema theory, these parts are called "nodes," "variables," or "slots." When the schema gets activated and is used to interpret some event, the slots are "instantiated" with particular information.

There are constraints on the information with which a slot can be instantiated. Presumably, for instance, the ⟨celebrity⟩ slot could be instantiated with a congressman, the husband or wife of a governor, the secretary of defense, or the Prince of Wales, but not a garbage collector or barmaid.

Suppose you read in the newspaper that,

Queen Elizabeth participated in a long-delayed ceremony in Clydebank, Scotland, yesterday. While there is still bitterness here following the protracted strike, on this occasion a crowd of shipyard workers numbering in the hundreds joined dignitaries in cheering as the HMS *Pinafore* slipped into the water.

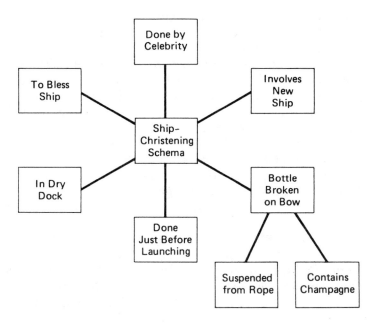

Figure 2

It is the generally good fit of most of this information with the SHIP CHRISTENING schema that provides the confidence that (part of the) message has been comprehended. In particular, Queen Elizabeth fits the ⟨celebrity⟩ slot, the fact that Clydebank is a well-known shipbuilding port and that shipyard workers are involved is consistent with the ⟨dry dock⟩ slot, the HMS *Pinafore* is obviously a ship and the information that it "slipped into the water" is consistent with the ⟨just before launching⟩ slot. Therefore, the ceremony mentioned is probably a ship christening. No mention is made of a bottle of champagne being broken on the ship's bow, but this "default" inference is easily made.

The foregoing informal treatment of the process of schema "activation" can be made more precise. Assume that words mentioning any component of a schema have a certain probability of bringing to mind the schema as a whole. Assume also that, once the schema is activated, there is a certain probability of being reminded of each of the other parts. It is not necessary to assume that the likelihood that a part will remind a person of the whole schema is the same as the likelihood that the schema will remind the person of that part. It seems likely, for example, that a person's SHIP CHRISTENING schema is more likely to activate the component concept of a celebrity than the mention of a celebrity is to activate the schema. The reason is that ⟨celebrity⟩ is a component of many schemata and SHIP CHRISTENING is not very prominent among them; therefore, the probability that words about a celebrity will activate SHIP CHRISTENING is low.

Some components of a schema are particularly salient; that is to say, words mentioning the component have a high probability of bringing to mind the schema and only that schema and, therefore, these words have great diagnostic value for the reader. One would suppose, for example, that words to the effect that a bottle was broken on the bow of a ship would be extremely likely to remind a person of ship christening.

A final assumption in this simple model of schema activation is that, when two or more components of a schema are mentioned, the aggregate probability of the whole schema being activated is a function of the sum of the probabilities that the individual components will activate the schema.

Ross and Bower (1981) worked out a formal, mathematical version of the schema-activation theory that has just been outlined and subjected it to experimental test. In one of their experiments, subjects studied 80 sets of four words, each related to a more or less obvious schema. For instance, one set was "driver," "trap," "rough," and "handicap," which relate to a GOLF schema. Another set was "princess," "mouth," "hold," and "dial," which relate to a TELEPHONE schema. After studying the word sets, subjects attempted to recall the words, given one or two words from each set as a cue. The schema model gave a good account of the recall patterns observed in this and two other experiments. In fact, it did better than a model based on S-R learning theory and traditional associationism.

To get a feeling for how a model of schema activation of this type might work with text, consider the following two sentences:

Princess Anne broke the bottle on the ship.
The waitress broke the bottle on the ship.

In the first case, the ⟨celebrity⟩ slot as well as the ⟨ship⟩ and ⟨bottle-breaking⟩ slots are matched and a ship christening interpretation is invited. If there is any hiatus over the end of the first sentence, it can be treated as elliptical for "broke the bottle on the bow of the ship." For most people, the second sentence does not suggest a ship christening but instead, perhaps, a scene in the ship's dining room. This intuition is consistent with the schema-activation model because a waitress will not fit in the ⟨celebrity⟩ slot and thus there is less evidence for a ship christening interpretation.

The simple model we are considering is likely to fail with the following sentence, though:

During the ceremony on the ship, Prince Charles took a swig from the bottle of champagne.

Here many slots in the schema are matched and the model cannot resist predicting activation of the SHIP CHRISTENING schema. How could the model be made smarter so that, like a person, it would not come to this conclusion?

First, consider a nonsolution. As a general rule people are unlikely to include in their schemata knowledge of the form, "in a ship christening the ceremony does *not* take place on board the ship" and "the celebrity does *not* drink from the bottle of champagne." The problem is that there are infinitely many things that are not true of any given type of event. Thus, it seems reasonable to suppose that what is *not* true of a type of event is "directly stored" only in special circumstances. For instance, one might store that a warbler does not have a thick beak if this is the critical feature that distinguishes it from the otherwise very similar song sparrow.

In general, though, determining what is *not* true requires an inference from what is true or is believed to be true. In the case of the Prince Charles sentence, the inference chain might look like the following:

1. A ship christening takes place on a platform on the dock next to the bow of the ship (from stored knowledge).
2. The celebrity playing the key role in the ceremony stands on this platform (from stored knowledge).
3. If Prince Charles were the celebrity taking the principal part in a ship christening ceremony, then he would have been standing on this platform (inference).
4. A platform on the dock next to the bow of a ship is not on the ship (inference).
5. During the ceremony, Prince Charles was on the ship (given in to-be-interpreted sentence).
6. During the ceremony, Prince Charles was not on a platform used for ship christening (inference).
7. The ceremony in which Prince Charles was participating was not a ship christening (inference).

Converging evidence that the sentence is not about a ship christening might come from analysis of the fact that Prince Charles took a swig of the champagne. In this case, the reader might make a lack-of-knowledge inference (Collins 1978), which would work something like the following:

1. I (the reader) do not have stored the information that the celebrity takes a swig from the bottle of champagne during a ship christening (computation based on stored knowledge).
2. I have many facts stored about ship christenings that are at the same level of detail as the information that the celebrity takes a swig from the bottle (computation based on stored knowledge).
3. If the celebrity's taking a drink from the bottle were a part of a ship christening, I would probably know that fact (inference).
4. A ceremony during which the celebrity takes a drink from a bottle of champagne is probably not a ship christening (inference).

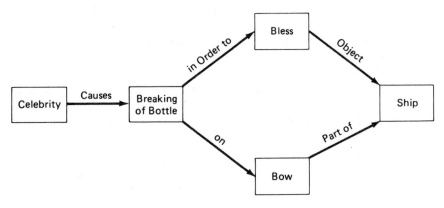

Figure 3

5. Prince Charles took a swig from a bottle of champagne (from the to-be-interpreted sentence).
6. The ceremony in which Prince Charles is participating is probably not a ship christening (inference).

Plainly, the representation of the SHIP CHRISTENING schema diagramed in Figure 2 is not adequate to support the chains of inference required to deal with the Prince Charles sentence. One problem is that some pieces of knowledge, such as that the christening takes place on a platform under the bow of the ship, are missing. But this is the least of the problems with the representation.

The fundamental problem with the representation is that it does not make explicit the temporal, causal, spatial, part–whole, and member–set relations among the components of a ship christening. For instance, the representation does not include the information that it is the celebrity who breaks the bottle on the bow of the ship and that the reason for the breaking of the bottle is to bless the ship. Figure 3 shows some of the relationships among these components. Such relational knowledge is necessary for inferencing and, as we have just seen, inferencing can be necessary to get the right schema activated.

Because the representation of the SHIP CHRISTENING schema portrayed in Figure 2 is impoverished, the relationships among the parts and between the parts and the whole are arbitrary and unmotivated. It can be predicted with some confidence on the basis of accumulated experimental evidence that a person who possessed the knowledge, and only the knowledge, represented in Figure 2 would not only have trouble making perspicuous inferences, but also (a) would have trouble learning similarly arbitrary additional facts about ship christening, (b) would be vulnerable to confusions when attempting to recall and use facts about ship christening, and (c) would be relatively slow to retrieve even well-known facts. Each of the preceding problems would grow more severe as the number of arbitrarily related facts that were known increased.

Every schema theorist has emphasized the nonarbitrary nature of knowledge. Notably, John Bransford (e.g., 1983) has stressed that "seeing the significance" of the parts in terms of the whole is the sine qua non of a schema-theoretic view of comprehension. In one of a number of experiments that Bransford and his colleagues have done which provide evidence for this claim, Stein and Bransford (1979) found that subjects were slightly worse at recalling core sentences, such as,

The fat man read the sign.

when the sentences were arbitrarily elaborated, as in,

The fat man read the sign that was 2-feet high.

In contrast, recall of the core sentences improved substantially when the core sentences were "precisely elaborated," as in,

The fat man read the sign warning of the thin ice.

A precise elaboration clarified the significance of the concepts in the core sentence and indicated how the concepts fit together.

Smith, Adams, and Schorr (1978; see also Clifton and Slowiaczek 1981 and Reder and Anderson 1980) have presented some strong evidence showing the benefits of integrating otherwise arbitrary information under the aegis of a schema. Subjects learned pairs of apparently unrelated propositions attributed to a member of some profession. For instance,

The banker broke the bottle.
The banker did not delay the trip.

Then, a third proposition was learned that either allowed the subject to integrate the three sentences in terms of a common schema or which was unintegratable with the other two sentences, as is illustrated below:

The banker was chosen to christen the ship.
The banker was asked to address the crowd.

Subjects required fewer study opportunities to learn the third sentence when it was readily integratable than when it was unintegratable. Most interesting was the fact that after all of the sentences had been learned to a high criterion of mastery, it took subjects longer to verify that sentences from the unintegratable sets were ones they had seen.

The explanation for this subtle finding is that, in an unintegrated set, all of the propositions fan out from a single common node representing, for instance, "the banker." This means that each new proposition added to the set increases the burden of memory search and verification and, therefore, causes an increase in memory search time called the "fanning effect" (J. R. Anderson 1976). In contrast, the interconnections among the concepts in integrated sets facilitate retrieval and verification; thus, adding a proposition to an integrated set causes little or no increase in search time.

Most discussions of schema theory have emphasized the use of schemata to assimilate information. Here, instead, we will deal with how a schema may be modified to accommodate new information. Obviously, a person may modify a schema by being told new information. For instance, a person might add to his or her SHIP CHRISTENING schema upon being informed that the platform on which the ceremony takes place is typically draped with bunting displaying the national colors.

Presumably, a logical person will check to make sure new information is consistent with the information already stored and, if it is not, will either reject the new information or modify the old. Presumably, a careful person will evaluate whether the source of new information is creditable or the evidence is persuasive before changing a schema. Lipson (1983) has evidence that suggests that even young readers will reject text information if it is inconsistent with an already possessed interpretation that they believe to be correct.

A primary source of data for schema change and development is experience with particular cases. In a process that is still not well understood, even though thinkers have wrestled with how it happens since the time of the ancient Greeks, people make inductive generalizations based on perceptible or functional features or patterns of particular cases. Traditional psychological theories envisioned a slow, grinding process of generalization, so slow and uncertain that the wonder was that anyone acquired the knowledge of a five-year-old. Current theories envision powerful inferential heuristics and generalization from a few cases or even a single case. Now the wonder is how people avoid filling their heads with all sorts of inaccurate and farfetched beliefs. How, for instance, is the nonexpert in ship christening, upon reading the newspaper describing the putative christening of the HMS *Pinafore*, to be restrained from inferring that the purpose of a ship christening is to celebrate the end of a labor dispute?

We turn now to the question of the relationship between the knowledge embodied in schemata and the knowledge of particular scenes, happenings, or messages. An attractive theory is that a schema includes just the propositions that are true of every member of a class. For instance, a BIRD schema may be supposed to include the information that birds lay eggs, have feathers, have wings, and fly, that the wings enable flying, and so on.

Collins and Quillian (1969) proposed the interesting additional assumption that, for reasons of "cognitive economy," propositions about

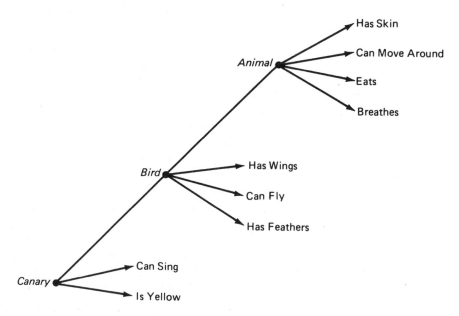

Figure 4   (From Collins and Quillian 1969, p. 241. By permission of Academic Press.)

the general case are not included in the representation for particular cases. So, the representation for a robin is supposed to include propositions about distinctive features of robins: that they have red breasts, but not that they fly or lay eggs. These facts can be deduced from the fact that a robin is a bird and that a robin has any property ascribed to all birds. Similarly, the bird representation does not directly include the information that birds breathe since birds are animals and breathing is a property of all animals.

Collins and Quillian theorized that knowledge is organized in semantic networks that permit graphical representations of the type illustrated in Figure 4. Notice that there is an increasingly long path in the network from the canary node to the information (or predicate) in each of the following sentences:

Canaries are yellow.
Canaries lay eggs.
Canaries can breathe.

It is a straightforward prediction that the greater the distance in the network that must be traversed to find the stored information, the longer it will take to verify the proposition. This prediction has been confirmed many times in many laboratories.

The appeal of the cognitive-economy hypothesis is that, while long-term human memory capacity is no doubt very large, it is not infinite. People could save a lot of memory space if they stored information at the most inclusive possible levels in their knowledge representations. Furthermore, most people have probably never seen a canary lay an egg or a giant condor fly, so there is little reason to suppose that this information would be directly stored in their canary or condor representations.

But what about the information that a robin can fly? Surely the typical person has seen countless flying robins. It would be an odd theory of human information processing that could explain why this fact was not stored directly in a person's robin representation. To do so would require postulating a mental librarian who, when the senses return information about flying robins, steadfastly files it on a higher shelf.

Current theories of concepts posit that the information represented in specific concepts, such as robin, overlaps with the information in general concepts, such as bird (Smith and Medin 1981). In fact, robin is a "good" example of a bird since the overlap is large, while penguin is a "poor" example because the overlap is small.

What is the best way in a theory of knowledge representations to cope with exceptional cases? In the first place, people probably place an implicit hedge on all the facts they think they know, of the form, "This proposition is true in only normal states of the world." At the very least, such a hedge helps fend off philosophers who ask questions like, "If a dog *is* a four-legged animal, what is a creature that has three legs but is otherwise a *dog*?"

The real theoretical problem, however, is not with abnormal cases such as dogs with three legs and hens that do not lay eggs, but with more mundane exceptions: most birds fly, however some, such as penguins, do not; canaries are often domesticated, however many more are wild; cups tend to be used to hold liquids, but they can be used to hold solids.

The classical issue in concept analysis was to specify the features that were individually necessary and jointly sufficient before a thing could rightly be called an instance of a concept. For example, following Katz (1972), some of the necessary features of bachelor are said to be ⟨male⟩, ⟨adult⟩, ⟨human⟩, and ⟨unmarried⟩. If a feature is *necessary*, then *all* instances of the concept display that feature. However, a feature that all instances possess may not be a necessary one. It may be safe to assume that every bachelor has a nose, but ⟨having a nose⟩ is not a necessary feature. If an unmarried, adult, human male without a nose did turn up, no one would be reluctant to call him a bachelor. In contrast, calling a married man a bachelor would be regarded as a non sequitur (or a joke or a metaphor). Thus, ⟨having a nose⟩ is a characteristic feature, while ⟨unmarried⟩ is a necessary feature, even though, by hypothesis, every bachelor displays both features.

The very idea that concepts or schemata (there is no principled distinction between the two) have necessary features has come under lethal attack in recent years. Wittgenstein (1953) noticed that it can be difficult, if not impossible, to specify the necessary features of most ordinary concepts. His famous analysis of games suggested that there are no features common to all games and that the relationship among games is most aptly characterized as one of "family resemblance." Putnam (1975; see also Kripke 1972) has shown that features of ordinary concepts that at first glance might seem to be necessary are really only characteristic. For instance, ⟨precious⟩ cannot be a necessary feature of gold because gold would no longer be precious if large quantities of it were discovered somewhere.

If there are few ordinary concepts with clearly necessary features and, indeed, not many with characteristic features true of all cases, the basis for positing that knowledge consists of abstract summaries of particular cases begins to erode. And this leads one to consider granting a greater role to memories for particular cases. It could be that much that passes for general knowledge is actually derived as needed by retrieving specific cases and making calculations based on what is known about them.

Let's do a thought experiment. What kind of nests do birds build? Try to pause before reading on and notice how your mind works as you answer this question.

Probably you answered the question by thinking of particular types of birds and then trying to remember occasions when you saw the nests of these birds, either in nature or in books. Probably, you began your search with a familiar, typical bird, such as a robin. If you know quite a bit about birds, your search probably turned up diverse kinds of nests, such as those of ducks, Baltimore orioles, barn swallows, and bald eagles.

Your intuitions were no doubt consistent with the hypothesized process of searching memories of specific cases. Experimental evidence, which does not rely on intuition, is also consistent with the hypothesized process. Walker (1975) asked subjects to accept or reject as quickly as possible propositions about a wide variety of things with quantifiable dimensions, such as the following:

A large dog could weigh 12 pounds.

Subjects quickly rejected this proposition and also quickly rejected sentences that ascribed an extremely heavy weight, such as 400 pounds, to a large dog. Furthermore, subjects quickly accepted statements ascribing a weight rated as typical of a large dog, such as 100 pounds. However, subjects were slow to accept or reject weights rated at the boundaries of a large dog, say 40 to 60 pounds.

It is very difficult to accommodate Walker's findings to a theory that says that people have directly stored as part of their general concept of a large dog that large dogs weigh from, say, 51 to 140 pounds. Such a theory would have to predict that people would be equally fast at accepting any weight between 51 and 140 pounds and equally fast at rejecting any weight outside this range. Moreover, the theory that people directly store as part of their knowledge of a class of objects generalizations about the range on each dimension along with the objects can be classified is highly implausible. Objects vary in innumerable dimensions. If a person has stored the range of weights of large dogs, why not the widths of their ears and the lengths of their tails? The more plausible and parsimonious theory, then, is that people make use of knowledge of specific cases in calculations such as the foregoing.

It is well established that words can have different meanings in different contexts, even when the words are being used in the same sense (Anderson et al. 1976; Anderson and Shiffrin 1980). This fact poses a grave problem for any theory along the lines that the meaning of a compound is the product of the general meanings of the constituent words. This conventional theory does work in some cases. For instance, it seems to work in the case of the compound, *red dress*. The dress can be construed as having a typical shade of red.

Now consider the following compounds, however: *red strawberry, red barn, red sunset,* and *red hair.* The red visualized is different in each of these cases, as Halff, Ortony, and Anderson (1976) have demonstrated empirically. To explain this effect, we propose that specific memories of, for instance, red hair are retrieved and the range of hues calculated. We further suggest that the hue of the compound is predicted on the basis of the generic concept of red and the generic concept of the object only when the person has not experienced this combination before or when an indeterminate range of hues is possible.

Stating the foregoing theory in general form, word meanings are context sensitive because people treat words and phrases as instructions to locate specific examples in memory. The sense and reference of the terms are then refined on the basis of these examples. When specific examples representing the intersection of the sets of examples signified by the terms cannot be located, then the default inference of a typical meaning is made, based on the general schemata that the terms represent.

How are the phrases, "a particular case" and "a specific example," to be interpreted? A robin is a specific example of a bird, but notice that ROBIN is itself an abstracted and generic schema. Still more specific is the-robin-I-saw-nesting-in-the-hawthorne-tree-outside-my-front-door-this-morning. Following Smith and Medin (1981), we assume that people have knowledge represented at various levels of specificity. Nothing about our thinking requires people always to get back to memories of cases experienced at particular moments in time and space.

In summary, the three main points of this section were that an adequate account of the structure of schemata will include information about the relationships among components, that a complete theory of schema activation will include a major role for inference, and that, during language comprehension, people probably rely on knowledge of particular cases as well as abstract and general schemata.

References

Adams, M. J., and A. M. Collins. 1979. A schema-theoretic view of reading. In *Discourse processing: multidisciplinary perspectives*, R. O. Freddle (Ed.). Norwood, N.J.: Ablex.

Anderson, J. R. 1976. *Language, memory and thought*. Hillsdale, N.J.: Erlbaum.

Anderson, R. C. 1977. The notion of schemata and the educational enterprise. In *Schooling and the acquisition of knowledge*, R. C. Anderson and R. J. Spiro (Eds.). Hillsdale, N.J.: Erlbaum.

1978. Schema-directed processes in language comprehension. In *Cognitive psychology and instruction*, A. Lesgold, J. Pelligreno, S. Fokkema, and R. Glaser (Eds.). New York: Plenum.

Anderson, R. C., J. W. Pichert, E. T. Goetz, D. L. Schallert, K. V. Stevens, and S. R. Trollip. 1976. Instantiation of general terms. *Journal of Verbal Learning and Verbal Behavior* 15: 667–679.

Anderson, R. C., and Z. Shiffrin. 1980. The meaning of words in context. In *Theoretical issues in reading comprehension*, R. J. Spiro, B. C. Bruce, and W. F. Brewer (Eds.). Hillsdale, N.J.: Erlbaum.

Ausubel, D. P. 1963. *The psychology of meaningful verbal learning*. New York: Grune and Stratton.

1978. In defense of advance organizers: a reply to the critics. *Review of Educational Research* 48: 251–258.

Ausubel, D. P., and F. G. Robinson. 1969. *School learning*. New York: Holt, Rinehart and Winston.

Barnes, B. R., and E. U. Clawson. 1975. Do advance organizers facilitate learning? Recommendations for further research based on an analysis of 32 studies. *Review of Educational Research* 45: 637–659.

Bartlett, F. C. 1932. *Remembering*. Cambridge: Cambridge University Press.

Boring, E. G. 1950. *A history of experimental psychology*. New York: Appleton-Century-Crofts.

Bransford, J. 1983. Schema-activation–schema acquisition. In *Learning to read in American schools*, R. C. Anderson, J. Osborn, and R. C. Tierney (Eds.). Hillsdale, N.J.: Erlbaum.

Clifton, C. Jr., and M. L. Slowiaczek. 1981. Integrating new information with old knowledge. *Memory and Cognition* 9: 142–148.

Collins, A. M. 1978. Fragments of a theory of human plausible reasoning. In *Theoretical issues in natural language processing*, Vol. 2, D. L. Waltz (Ed.). Urbana-Champaign: University of Illinois.

Collins, A. M., and M. R. Quillian. 1969. Retrieval time from semantic memory. *Journal of Verbal Learning and Verbal Behavior* 8: 240–247.

Gray, W. S. 1948. *On their own in reading.* Glenview, Ill.: Scott, Foresman.

Halff, H. M., A. Ortony, and R. C. Anderson. 1976. A context-sensitive representation of word meaning. *Memory and Cognition* 4: 378–383.

Horn, E. 1937. *Methods of instruction in the social studies.* New York: Scribners.

Huey, E. B. 1968. *The psychology and pedagogy of reading.* Cambridge, Mass.: MIT Press.

Katz, J. J. 1972. *Semantic theory.* New York: Harper and Row.

Koffka, K. 1935. *Principles of Gestalt psychology.* New York: Harcourt, Brace.

Kohler, W. 1947. *Gestalt psychology.* New York: Liveright.

Kripke, S. 1972. Naming and necessity. In *Semantics of natural languages,* D. Davidson and G. Harman (Eds.). Dordrecht: Reidel.

Lipson, M. Y. 1983. The influence of religious affiliation on children's memory for text information. *Reading Research Quarterly* 18: 448–457.

Luiten, J., W. S. Ames, and G. Ackerson. 1980. A meta-analysis of the effects of advance organizers on learning and retention. *American Educational Research Journal* 17: 211–218.

Mandler, J. M., and N. S. Johnson. 1977. Remembrance of things parsed: story structure and recall. *Cognitive Psychology* 9: 111–151.

Mathews, M. 1966. *Teaching to read: historically considered.* Chicago: University of Chicago Press.

Mayer, R. E. 1979. Can advance organizers influence meaningful learning? *Review of Educational Research* 49: 371–383.

Minsky, M. 1975. A framework for representing knowledge. In *The psychology of computer vision,* P. Evinston (Ed.). New York: Winston.

Putnam, H. 1975. The meaning of "meaning." In *Mind, language and reality,* H. Putnam (Ed.). Cambridge: Cambridge University Press.

Reder, L. M., and J. R. Anderson. 1980. A partial resolution of the paradox of interference: the role of integrating knowledge. *Cognitive Psychology* 12: 447–472.

Ross, B. H., and G. H. Bower. 1981. Comparisons of models of associative recall. *Memory and Cognition* 9: 1–16.

Rumelhart, D. E. 1975. Notes on a schema for stories. In *Representation and understanding: studies in cognitive science,* D. G. Bobrow and A. M. Collins (Eds.). New York: Academic Press.

　　 1980. Schemata: the building blocks of cognition. In *Theoretical issues in reading comprehension,* R. J. Spiro, B. C. Bruce, and W. F. Brewer (Eds.). Hillsdale, N.J.: Erlbaum.

Schank, R. C., and R. Abelson. 1977. *Plans, scripts, goals and understanding.* Hillsdale, N.J.: Erlbaum.

Smith, E. E., N. Adams, and D. Schorr. 1978. Fact retrieval and the paradox of interference. *Cognitive Psychology* 10: 438–474.

Smith, E. E., and D. C. Medin. 1981. *Categories and concepts.* Cambridge, Mass.: Harvard University Press.

Stein, B. S., and J. D. Bransford. 1979. Constraints on effective elaboration: effects of precision and subject generation. *Journal of Verbal Learning and Verbal Behavior* 18: 769–777.

Stein, N., and C. G. Glenn. 1979. An analysis of story comprehension in elementary school children. In *New directions in discourse processing*, R. Freedle (Ed.). Norwood, N.J.: Ablex.

Walker, J. H. 1975. Real-world variability, reasonableness judgments, and memory representations for concepts. *Journal of Verbal Learning and Verbal Behavior* 14: 241–252.

Wertheimer, M. 1912. Experimentalle Studien über das Sehen von Bewegung. *Zeitschrift f. Psych.* 16: 161–265.

Wilson, P. T., and R. C. Anderson. 1986. What they don't know will hurt them: the role of prior knowledge in comprehension. In *Reading comprehension: from research to practice*, J. Orasanu (Ed.). Hillsdale, N.J.: Erlbaum.

Winograd, T. 1975. Frame representations and the declarative-procedural controversy. In *Representation and understanding: studies in cognitive science*, D. G. Bobrow and A. M. Collins (Eds.). New York: Academic Press.

Wittgenstein, L. 1953. *Philosophical investigations*. New York: Macmillan.

Wulf, F. 1938. [Über die Veränderung von Vorstellungen (Gedächtnis und Gestalt).] In *A source book of Gestalt psychology* (trans. and condensed), W. D. Ellis (Ed.). London: Routledge and Kegan Paul.

4 Reassessing the term "interactive"

William Grabe

Throughout much of the ESL reading literature the use of the word *interactive* proliferates. Such a proliferation, however, has tended to obscure the importance that should be attributed to its more technical uses. The purpose of this chapter is to clarify relationships among the uses of the term *interactive* as it occurs in ESL reading research, first language reading research, and research on written texts. Later sections of this chapter will establish a distinction between the concepts "interactive process" and "interactive model" as they are used in reading research. Lastly, I will introduce a somewhat more exploratory use of the notion of interaction, that of "textual interaction," as it is being developed in a number of research studies by Biber and Grabe. How productive these distinct conceptions of the word *interactive* become depends, in large part, on future research.

Reading as an interactive process

In the last ten years, the accepted theory of ESL reading has changed dramatically, from a serial (or bottom-up) model, to "reading as an interactive process." Widdowson (1979) has discussed reading in this light as the process of combining textual information with the information a reader brings to a text. In this view the reading process is not simply a matter of extracting information from the text. Rather, it is one in which the reading activates a range of knowledge in the reader's mind that he or she uses, and that, in turn, may be refined and extended by the new information supplied by the text. Reading is thus viewed as a kind of dialogue between the reader and the text. Carrell and Eisterhold (1983, reprinted as Chapter 5 in this volume), reviewing the state of ESL reading, similarly concluded that our understanding of reading is

I would like to thank A. Cohen, C. Chapelle, J. Devine, D. Eskey, M. Haynes, R. Kaplan, F. Stoller, and J. Zukowski/Faust for reading and commenting on earlier versions of this chapter.

best considered as the interaction that occurs between the reader and the text, an interpretive process.

Such a perspective on reading has evolved out of the reading research of Goodman (1970, 1976) and Smith (1982), as well as from the development of schema theory (e.g., Adams and Collins 1985; Anderson and Pearson 1984, reprinted as Chapter 3 in this volume; Carrell 1983b; Rumelhart 1980, 1984). The general view espoused by Goodman and others is that reading is primarily concept driven. We sample the text as necessary to confirm hypotheses and form new hypotheses. This view of reading has been called the psycholinguistic guessing game, and is often referred to as a top-down approach to reading (as noted in Downing and Leong 1982; Gough 1984; Mitchell 1982; Rumelhart 1977; Samuels and Kamil 1984, reprinted as Chapter 2 in this volume; Stanovich 1980; and Weber 1984, among others).

This approach to reading has had a powerful impact on ESL reading theory and practice, and has led to a resurgent interest in reading, as evidenced by Clarke and Silberstein (1977), Coady (1979), Carrell (1983a, b, 1984b), Carrell and Eisterhold (1983), Johnson (1981, 1982), Hudson (1982, reprinted as Chapter 13 in this volume), as well as numerous good practical textbooks. Goodman's approach has led to extensive research on how conceptual knowledge, inference, and background information all affect the reading process, particularly in ESL reading. (See Carrell 1983a, 1984a, b for reviews.)

While the research and practical instruction generated has had a strong positive impact on the field, a number of problems created by this approach have been generally ignored until recently. In the 1970s, Eskey (1973), Coady (1979), and Clarke (1979) all raised questions about the psycholinguistic model for the ESL reader. There are, for example, questions about how and to what degree literate second language readers employ lower-level processing strategies, and how these skills interact with higher-level (top-down) strategies. There is also the problem of whether second language readers actually conform to assumptions of the psycholinguistic model of reading (i.e., to what extent a model of the fluent reader adequately characterizes such readers).

Second language readers invoke a unique set of constraints: (1) They may or may not read in their first language; there is, in fact, surprisingly little current information on how, why, and what students read in other cultures. (2) If second language students do have literacy training, we still do not know how they approach reading in their first language as a social phenomenon; that is, do they view reading as a major academic, professional, and entertainment activity, or do they read much less, for far fewer purposes? (3) Second language readers are often assumed to transfer readily their first language reading abilities to the second language context (Hudelson 1981); however, as Alderson (1984) argues, there is no adequate empirical evidence for assuming such a strong position. (4) Second language students coming from different ortho- graphic traditions do appear to be affected by differing orthographic conventions, depending on their stage of reading skills acquisition (Tzeng and Hung 1981; Taylor and Taylor 1983). (5) Second language readers do not begin reading English with the same English language knowledge available to English-speaking children. As Singer (1981) notes:

The language ability of most children at age 6 is already well developed.
They have attained sophisticated control over their syntax, they possess a
vocabulary of about 5000 words, and they have a phonological system that
can adequately communicate their needs. (p. 295)

Certainly, we cannot assume the same for students learning to read English.

This last distinction strongly separates first and second language read- ing students. For ESL reading, we cannot assume that a large vocabulary or basic syntactic structures are already available. Both Eskey (1973, 1986) and Clarke (1979) have characterized these limitations as a lan- guage ceiling, or threshold, which ESL students must surpass if they are to develop fluent reading abilities. Syntax-based difficulties are also dis- cussed in Cohen et al. (1979, reprinted as Chapter 11 in this volume) and Berman (1984). The importance of vocabulary knowledge for ESL reading is discussed in Cooper (1984) and Saville-Troike (1984).

Because of the dominance of "reading as an interactive process" in ESL reading theory, these issues have not received the attention they deserve. The only systematic attempt to discuss a more complete range of ESL reading difficulties is found in Carrell (Chapter 7 in this volume), in which she identifies the two basic kinds of difficulties – overreliance on text-bound processing and overreliance on context-bound processing. The need for a more encompassing approach to reading, particularly for ESL, is indicated by the present general disregard for lower-level pro- cessing and its relationship to higher-level processing in reading.

In the last ten years, beginning with Rumelhart (1977), researchers have proposed interactive models of reading which argue that lower- level and higher-level processes work together interactively as parts of the reading process. This view of reading should not be considered as an alternate version of "reading as an interactive process." The issue is not the relation of the reader to the text but the processing relations among various component skills in reading. Weber (1984), for example, has noted that

[The top-down perspective] fails to accommodate important empirical
evidence adequately. The interactive models, attempting to be more
comprehensive, rigorous and coherent, give emphasis to the interrelations
between the graphic display in the text, various levels of linguistic knowledge
and processes, and various cognitive activities. (p. 113)

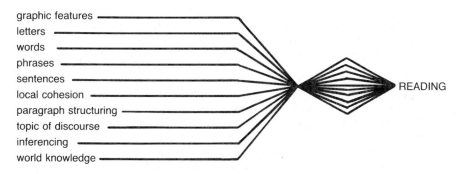

Figure 1   A simplified Interactive Parallel Processing sketch

Research on interactive models of reading may allow us to incorporate the insights gained thus far from earlier approaches, and, at the same time, address continuing weaknesses in ESL reading theory.

Interactive models of reading

As a starting point, interactive models of reading assume that skills at all levels are interactively available to process and interpret the text. Figure 1 suggests a simplified graphic perspective on this definition.

On the left are various processing levels for reading skills; on the right is the process of reading. Models of this type are often referred to as Interactive Parallel Processing models because the processing is distributed over a range of parallel systems simultaneously (Griffin and Vaughn 1984; Waltz and Pollack 1985). In their simplest forms such models incorporate both top-down and bottom-up strategies. The models incorporate within themselves the implications of "reading as an interactive process." At the same time they also incorporate notions of rapid and accurate feature recognition for letters and words, spreading activation of lexical forms and the concept of automaticity in processing such forms – that is, a processing that does not depend on active attentional context for primary recognition of linguistic units.

There are several reasons why ESL researchers should be interested in interactive models. First, there have been a number of studies in the ESL literature that note linguistic deficiencies as inhibiting factors in reading (Carrell, Chapter 7 in this volume; Clarke 1979; Cohen et al. 1979). Second, researchers have noted the need for extensive vocabulary for reading (Alderson and Urquhart 1984a; Singer 1981). Third, there is a need to account for poor readers who do guess extensively (Carrell, Chapter 7 in this volume; Haynes 1984). Fourth, evidence from first language research indicates that good readers are not good simply because they are better predictors, or make better use of context (e.g., Stanovich and West 1983; Perfetti 1985).

These issues are perhaps best addressed by van Dijk and Kintsch (1983):

> The full complex nature of the interaction between these top-down and bottom-up processes becomes apparent if one looks at the contrast between good and poor readers in these terms. What exactly distinguishes a good reader from a poor reader? ...
>
> The greatest facilitation of word recognition by meaningful context is observed with poor readers, not with good readers. Furthermore, it is simply not true that good readers take decoding lightly; they fixate almost every content word ... It has been found over and over again that the best discriminator between good and poor readers is performance on simple letter and word identification tasks. What is really wrong with poor readers is that they recognize isolated words inaccurately and too slowly, and compensate for their lack in decoding skills with context-dependent guessing or hypothesis testing ... Good readers with their superior decoding skills can decode letters and words rapidly in a bottom-up fashion, and therefore do not normally need to resort to guessing strategies ... What is really at issue are the speed and accuracy of context-free word recognition operations. (pp. 23–24)

There is no single interactive model. Rather, interactive models include any model that minimally tries to account for more than serial processing and that does so assuming that any parallel or array processing will interact. A key issue for all interactive models is how to account for the numerous word recognition studies in the literature that run counter to top-down assertions. It is consistently found that good readers are able to recognize lexical forms at a processing speed faster than the time required to activate context effects and conscious predicting (Balota, Pollatsek, and Rayner 1985). While this concern is not the only one addressed by interactive models, it represents a major distinction from the earlier, concept-driven (top-down) approaches.

Five models that appear to be useful for our understanding of the reading process are McClelland and Rumelhart's (1981) interactive-activation model, Stanovich's (1980) interactive-compensatory model, Taylor and Taylor's (1983) bilateral cooperative model, LaBerge and Samuels's (1974; see also Samuels 1977) automatic-processing model, and Perfetti's (1985, 1986a, b) verbal efficiency model. LaBerge and Samuels's model was originally considered a bottom-up model, but it has since been modified by feedback loops to make it interactive (Samuels and Kamil 1984). The sketches of these models which follow should be taken as no more than an indication of their respective approaches.

The interactive-activation model (McClelland and Rumelhart 1981) is at present based primarily on word recognition research. It follows largely from the logogen model of mental activation and information retrieval (Morton 1969, 1979). This theory is concisely summarized by Lesgold and Perfetti (1981a):

Morton proposed that for each word one is able to recognize, there is a re-sponse unit, called a logogen, that is sensitive to the set of auditory, visual and semantic features associated with that word. When the number of fea-tures that are currently active (being looked at or recently thought about) ex-ceeds the logogen threshold, that unit is automatically activated, and all the features are made available to the rest of the cognitive apparatus. Because logogen activation is automatic and does not require attention, the logogen theory is a theoretical forerunner of automaticity theories of reading. (p. 389)

To simplify, the process of activation is essentially one in which in-dividual features, letters, clusters, context, syntax, semantics, topic of discourse, background knowledge, etc., all excite (or activate) groups of lexical candidates for meaning, or comprehension selection. As excita-tion increases from more sources, the candidates not excited are blocked, or inhibited, leaving only one or two words to pass a consciousness threshold. This process happens at a rate more rapid than the time needed for conscious guessing. Generally speaking, the automaticity of this pro-cessing allows us to concentrate on comprehension rather than on active selection or prediction of words (see also van Dijk and Kintsch 1983; Downing and Leong 1982; Posner and Snyder 1975; Rumelhart and McClelland 1982; Stemberger 1982; Taylor and Taylor 1983).

The interactive-compensatory model of Stanovich (1980, 1984) is similarly based on many issues of word recognition processes. This ap-proach explains many complex results of research on good and poor readers in a comprehensive way. The basic premise, not unlike Carrell's (Chapter 7 in this volume), is that reading involves an array of processes. Readers who are weak in one strategy will rely on other processes to compensate for the weaker process. Good readers will have a larger repertoire of compensating strategies to draw upon than will poorer readers. In this way, Stanovich's approach accounts for a wide variety of experimental results. As Stanovich himself states:

A compensatory-interactive model of processing hypothesizes that a pattern is synthesized based on information provided simultaneously from all knowl-edge sources and that a process at any level can compensate for deficiencies at any other level. Compensatory-interactive models appear to be the only type of theorizing that can render certain findings in the reading literature non-paradoxical, such as the fact that poorer readers have been found to display larger contextual facilitation effects. (1981: 262)

Stanovich has also incorporated the concept of spreading activation, by means of which related lexical forms (that is, closely related in some way in the mental organization of the lexicon) become automatically available in reading. This concept, growing out of the logogen recog-nition theory, also allows us to consider schemata selection as a more manageable process. Stanovich (1981: 245) argues that semantically related memory locations, nearby in the network, are made available, or activated automatically. Those memory locations not automatically activated remain unaffected. Automatic spreading activation is fast acting and does not use attentional capacity; it is a type of context effect not controlled by the reader. (For further discussion, see also Briggs, Austin, and Underwood 1984; Collins and Loftus 1975; van Dijk and Kintsch 1983; Gough 1984; Samuels and Kamil 1984; Stanovich 1981; Stanovich and West 1983; Taylor and Taylor 1983.)

Taylor and Taylor's bilateral cooperation model combines features of the Stanovich and Rumelhart/McClelland models, along with a range of neurolinguistic research. It sets up parallel processing strategies at a number of levels of text information. The parallel processing operates both rapid and slow mechanisms for processing according to the needs of the reader and the difficulties imposed by either the task or the text. A brief summary from Taylor and Taylor indicates the distinctness of this model.

The bilateral cooperative model postulates two tracks of processes that complement one another at each of several stages in understanding text. The processes of one track are fast and global and attempt to find similarities between their inputs and familiar patterns. The processes of the other are slow and analytic and sort their inputs into elements in an attempt to find differences. The RIGHT (global) recognition is primarily template matching using a lax criterion to accept a match. The LEFT (analytic) recognition may use any of a variety of methods, including template matching and syntactic rules. (1983: 266)

The fourth model, LaBerge and Samuels's automatic-processing model, was initially a serial (bottom-up) processing approach. In Samuels (1977) feedback loops were added that allowed the reader to move back and forth between higher and lower levels of processing as needed. The original model made a strong argument for automatic processing of words, at no cost to conscious processing capacities. Simply put, the automatic processing of forms frees cognitive space for thinking about the meaning of what is being read. Thus, their claim is that fluent readers automatically recognize most words. (See also Downing and Leong 1982.)

The final model of importance to this discussion is Perfetti's (1985, 1986a, b) verbal efficiency model. This model argues that reading should be defined more narrowly than it is in many other models, interactive or otherwise. For Perfetti, reading comprehension should not be equated with thinking and its concomitant general inferential/problem-solving strategies, but more narrowly with processes specific to reading. He therefore proposes that processes of lexical access, proposition integration, and text model building form the core of his verbal efficiency model, with lexical access receiving primary emphasis. Using these three processing skills specific to reading, Perfetti is able to explain a wide range of variation in reading ability. For this reason, his approach, much like Stanovich's, may be more adaptable to issues in second language reading.

Each of the five models reviewed here takes a somewhat different perspective, and all have gaps that have not been adequately addressed. However inadequate any of these models might be – and most admit to being partial models – they represent improvements on basically top-down, or concept-driven, models, improvements widely recognized in the reading and psychology literature.

A number of important implications for ESL reading research follow from an acceptance of interactive models. First, reading as an interactive process, as described at the beginning of this chapter, remains an important part of the overall reading models; that is, the very nature of interactive models suggests that higher-level processing abilities play a significant role. Exactly how these processes interact – how such notions as background knowledge, topic of discourse, inferencing, and schemata all affect the overall reading model – is a question for future research. At the same time, we should not consider these top-down processes, central to "reading as an interactive process," to be the whole of the reading process (Eskey 1986).

Second, interactive models strongly imply that many lower-level processing skills are basic to good reading. Such a view suggests that methods of instruction for rapid visual recognition, for extensive vocabulary development, and for syntactic pattern recognition should become major pedagogical research concerns. Suggestions for recognition and vocabulary instruction can be found in Stoller (1984, 1986), McKeown et al. (1985), and Nagy, Herman, and Anderson (1985).

The third implication is the need for a massive receptive vocabulary that is rapidly, accurately, and automatically accessed – a fact that may be the greatest single impediment to fluent reading by ESL students. This concern may be particularly relevant for students in advanced level ESL courses. Students studying English for academic purposes are, for example, seldom tested specifically for their reading abilities. But many of these students are, in fact, weak in this language skill essential for academic success (cf. Grabe 1986a; Johns 1981; Ostler 1980; Robertson 1983).

A fourth implication follows from issues raised in Carrell (Chapter 7 in this volume). The apparent overreliance on text or on context noted by Carrell might best be explained by Stanovich's interactive-compensatory approach. That is, certain students may overcompensate for a lack of relevant schemata by reading in a slow text-bound manner; other students may overcompensate by guessing. In contrast, students who are not capable of rapid low-level processing may compensate by persevering word by word, or they may overcompensate by guessing too often. This somewhat more complex perspective on students' reading difficulties is welcome. Simple analyses of student difficulties which explain all problems as word-boundedness, or as unwillingness to guess or take chances, are not justified by the range of empirical studies in the literature.

The fifth and final implication is that the development of reading abilities may be viewed more profitably if seen in terms of stages of skills development. Chall (1983) has proposed a five-stage theory of reading acquisition that could account for different types of overcompensation noted in ESL students. The stages she discusses are prereading, initial reading or decoding, confirmation and fluency, reading for new information, multiple viewpoints, and construction and reconstruction. Of particular interest for this discussion are the references Chall makes to various types of processing that occur at each stage, with interactive processing beginning by stage three. While such a multistage approach would have to be modified to meet the specific conditions of the ESL reading context, it does hold out some promise for considering reading skills development in ESL students.

Textual interaction

There is a third type of interaction that should also be considered in reading research: the interactive nature of the text that is being read. An important part of the reading process is the ability to recognize text genres and various distinct text types, even within a major genre (e.g., expository prose). Recent research by Biber (1984, 1985, 1986, in press) and Grabe (1984, 1986b) indicates that the linguistic elements of texts combine interactively to help create the "textuality" (i.e., what makes a text a text as opposed to a collection of individual sentences – see Carrell, Chapter 7 in this volume) that must be processed by the reader. In the research cited, factor analytic studies, employing numerous linguistic variables, were performed on large text samples. The results in Grabe's (1984) study, for example, suggested that at least four textual dimensions exist within the range of expository prose texts examined, each of these dimensions represented by the interactive co-occurrence of certain linguistic features that were found to load on four of the factors analyzed.

For the purposes of this discussion, however, the findings of the research are of less concern than are certain implications that may be drawn from such an approach to text-type research. For linguistic variables to converge and define textual parameters suggests that these parameters are consistently employed, or created, by writers. It is suggested that writers purposefully use and manipulate different combinations of linguistic variables in different text types and genres. This interaction is what I have termed *textual interaction* – the interaction of linguistic forms to define textual functions.

A further claim can be made from the research. If these parameters are consistently present in various text types, it suggests that writers deliberately exploit them (to what extent they do so consciously is another question). The converse of this would then also hold – that readers must be able to recognize these textual parameters at some level as part of their comprehension abilities, probably at the level of intentions or genre information. Such a suggestion is reasonable since writers are also readers during the writing process.

This discussion of textual interaction returns the study of text as product to its rightful place as an equal partner with the text process, whether the research goal is to explore comprehension or production. Careful study of the text product will allow researchers to define multidimensional form–function relations expressed in that product.

This sort of interaction also has implications for ESL reading research and pedagogy. For research, textual interaction suggests that earlier reading research studies with a limited, or experimentally created, text sample may not tap into particular genre or linguistic information that is available to readers when processing longer text segments. For pedagogy, textual interaction suggests that certain linguistic structures and vocabulary be taught in combination as they might co-occur in types of expository prose. This option would be more reasonable than teaching structures and vocabulary derived from some linguistic model or simply as they happen to occur in the text.

While this analysis of textual interaction is admittedly exploratory, it nevertheless points out that the product within which reading occurs, the text itself, involves a sort of complex form–function interaction that is not simply the interactive process of reading (i.e., text–reader relations) as usually discussed, nor can it be simply represented by interactive models of reading (i.e., interaction of various component skills), which are essentially process oriented.

Conclusion

The term *interactive* may take on a number of meanings for reading researchers. In the case of the first two uses of the term – as process and as model – a clear distinction exists, one that should be recognized in all ESL reading research. With the third use of the term, as textual interaction or interaction among the elements of a text product, the discussion is somewhat more speculative. While textual interaction might

66 *William Grabe*

be considered part of either of the two former types of interaction, it has never been so considered to my knowledge. Neither considers the importance of multidimensional form–function interaction as part of its description. Whether this third type of interaction deserves independent treatment remains to be seen; further research may decide the issue.

In exploring new theoretical positions, there is always the danger of the bandwagon effect, as new theories come into vogue; thus, a note of caution is appropriate. At the same time, newer approaches necessarily broaden our perspectives on research issues when they address problems and inadequate explanations in a currently accepted approach. Interactive models and textual interaction may not provide all the answers we seek, but they do extend the range of our inquiry, and that is to be welcomed.

References

Adams, M. J., and A. Collins. 1985. A schema-theoretic view of reading. In *Theoretical models and processes of reading*, 3rd ed., H. Singer and R. Ruddell (Eds.), 404–425. Newark, Del.: International Reading Association.

Alderson, J. C. 1984. Reading in a foreign language: a reading problem or a language problem? In Alderson and Urquhart (Eds.), 1984b, 1–27.

Alderson, J. C., and A. H. Urquhart. 1984a. Introduction: What is reading? In Alderson and Urquhart (Eds.), 1984b, xv–xxviii.

Alderson, J. C., and A. H. Urquhart. 1984b. *Reading in a foreign language.* New York: Longman.

Anderson, R. C., and P. D. Pearson. 1984. A schema-theoretic view of the basic processes in reading comprehension. In Pearson (Ed.), 255–292. [Reprinted as Chapter 3 in this volume.]

Balota, D., A. Pollatsek, and K. Rayner. 1985. The interaction of contextual constraints and parafoveal visual information in reading. *Cognitive Psychology* 17: 364–390.

Berman, R. 1984. Syntactic components of the foreign language reading process. In Alderson and Urquhart (Eds.), 1984b, 139–159.

Biber, D. 1984. A model of textual relations within the written and spoken modes. Ph.D. diss., University of Southern California.

1985. Investigating macroscopic textual variation through multifeature/multidimensional analysis. *Linguistics* 23: 337–360.

1986. Spoken and written textual dimensions in English: Resolving the contradictory findings. *Language* 62: 384–414.

In press. *Textual relations in speech and writing.* New York: Cambridge University Press.

Briggs, P., S. Austin, and G. Underwood. 1984. The effects of sentence context in good and poor readers: a test of Stanovich's interactive-compensatory model. *Reading Research Quarterly* 20: 54–61.

Carrell, P. L. 1983a. Three components of background knowledge in reading comprehension. *Language Learning* 33: 183–208.

1983b. Background knowledge in second language comprehension. *Language Learning and Communication* 2: 25–34.

1984a. Inferencing in ESL: presuppositions and implications of factive and implicative predicates. *Language Learning* 34: 1–21.

1984b. Evidence of a formal schema in second language comprehension. *Language Learning* 34: 87–112.

1984c. Review of "Introduction to text linguistics." *Language Learning* 34: 111–118.

Carrell, P. L., and J. C. Eisterhold. 1983. Schema theory and ESL reading pedagogy. *TESOL Quarterly* 18: 553–573. [Reprinted as Chapter 5 in this volume.]

Chall, J. 1983. *Stages of reading development.* New York: McGraw-Hill Book Co.

Clarke, M. 1979. Reading in Spanish and English: Evidence from adult ESL learners. *Language Learning* 29: 121–150.

Clarke, M., and S. Silberstein. 1977. Toward a realization of psycholinguistic principles in the ESL reading class. *Language Learning* 27: 135–154.

Coady, J. 1979. A psycholinguistic model of the ESL reader. In *Reading in a second language*, R. Mackay, B. Barkman, and R. Jordan (Eds.), 5–12. Rowley, Mass.: Newbury House.

Cohen, A. D., H. Glasman, P. R. Rosenbaum, J. Ferrara, and J. Fine. 1979. Reading English for specialized purposes: discourse analysis and the use of students. *TESOL Quarterly* 13: 551–564. [Reprinted as Chapter 11 in this volume.]

Collins, A. M., and E. Loftus. 1975. A spreading activation theory of semantic processing. *Psychological Review* 82: 407–428.

Cooper, M. 1984. Linguistic competence of practiced and unpracticed non-native readers of English. In Alderson and Urquhart (Eds.), 1984b, 122–135.

Dijk, T. A. van, and W. Kintsch. 1983. *Strategies of discourse comprehension.* New York: Academic Press.

Downing, J., and C. K. Leong. 1982. *Psychology of reading.* New York: Macmillan.

Eskey, D. 1973. A model program for teaching advanced reading to students of English as a foreign language. *Language Learning* 23: 169–184.

1986. Theoretical foundations. In *Teaching second language reading for academic purposes*, F. Dubin, D. Eskey, and W. Grabe (Eds.), 3–23. Reading, Mass.: Addison-Wesley.

Goodman, K. 1970. Behind the eye: what happens in reading. In *Reading: process and program*, K. Goodman and O. Niles (Eds.). Urbana, Ill.: National Council of Teachers of English.

1976. Reading: a psycholinguistic guessing game. In *Theoretical models and processes of reading*, 2nd ed., H. Singer and R. Ruddell (Eds.), 497–505. Newark, Del.: International Reading Association.

Gough, P. 1984. Word recognition. In Pearson (Ed.), 225–254.

Grabe, W. 1984. Toward defining expository prose within a theory of text construction. Ph.D. diss., University of Southern California.

1986a. The transition from theory to practice in second language reading. In *Teaching second language reading for academic purposes*, F. Dubin, D. Eskey, and W. Grabe (Eds.), 25–48. Reading, Mass.: Addison-Wesley.

1986b. Contrastive rhetoric and text-type research. In *Writing across cultures*, U. Connor and R. B. Kaplan (Eds.), 115–137. Reading, Mass.: Addison-Wesley.

Griffin, P., and B. Vaughn. 1984. The nature of the interactive model of reading. Paper presented at the 18th Annual TESOL Convention, Houston, April.

Haynes, M. 1984. Patterns and perils of guessing in second language reading. In *On TESOL '83*, J. Handscombe, R. A. Orem, and B. P. Taylor (Eds.), 163–176. Washington, D.C.: TESOL.

Hudelson, S. (Ed.). 1981. *Learning to read in different languages*. Linguistics and literacy, Series 1. Arlington, Va.: Center for Applied Linguistics.

Hudson, T. 1982. The effects of induced schemata on the "short circuit" in L2 reading: non-decoding factors in L2 reading performance. *Language Learning* 32: 1–31. [Reprinted as Chapter 13 in this volume.]

Johns, A. 1981. Necessary English: a faculty survey. *TESOL Quarterly* 15: 51–57.

Johnson, P. 1981. Effects on reading comprehension of language complexity and cultural background of a text. *TESOL Quarterly* 15: 169–181.

1982. Effects on reading comprehension of building background knowledge. *TESOL Quarterly* 16: 503–516.

LaBerge, D., and S. J. Samuels. 1974. Toward a theory of automatic information processing in reading. *Cognitive Psychology* 6: 293–323.

Lesgold, A., and C. Perfetti. 1981a. Interactive processes in reading: where do we stand. In Lesgold and Perfetti (Eds.), 1981b, 387–407.

Lesgold, A., and C. Perfetti (Eds.). 1981b. *Interactive processes in reading*. Hillsdale, N.J.: Erlbaum.

McClelland, J., and D. Rumelhart. 1981. An interactive activation model of the effect of context in perception. *Psychological Review* 88: 375–407.

McKeown, M., I. Beck, R. Omanson, and M. Pople. 1985. Some effects of the nature and frequency of vocabulary instruction on the knowledge and use of words. *Reading Research Quarterly* 20: 522–535.

Mitchell, D. C. 1982. *The process of reading*. New York: Wiley.

Morton, J. 1969. Interaction of information in word recognition. *Psychological Review* 76: 165–178.

1979. Facilitation in word recognition: experiments causing change in the logogen model. In *Processes of visible language*, Vol. 1, P. Kolers, M. Wrolstad, and H. Bouma (Eds.), 259–268. New York: Plenum Press.

Nagy, W., P. Herman, and R. Anderson. 1985. Learning words from context. *Reading Research Quarterly* 20: 233–253.

Ostler, S. 1980. A survey of acadmic needs for advanced ESL. *TESOL Quarterly* 14: 489–502.

Pearson, P. D. (Ed.). 1984. *Handbook of reading research*. New York: Longman.

Perfetti, C. A. 1985. *Reading ability*. New York: Longman.

1986a. Cognitive and linguistic components of reading ability. In *Acquisition of reading skills*, B. Foosman and A. Siegel (Eds.), 11–40. Hillsdale, N.J.: Erlbaum.

1986b. Reading acquisition and beyond: decoding includes cognition. In *Literacy in American schools*, N. Stein (Ed.), 41–61. Chicago, Ill.: University of Chicago Press.

Posner, M., and C. R. Snyder. 1975. Attention and cognitive control. In *Infor-

mation processing and cognition, R. L. Solso (Ed.). Hillsdale, N.J.: Erlbaum.

Robertson, D. 1983. English language use, needs, and proficiency among foreign students at the University of Illinois at Champaign-Urbana. Ph.D. Diss., University of Illinois at Champaign-Urbana.

Rumelhart, D. 1977. Toward an interactive model of reading. In *Attention and performance*, Vol. VI, S. Dornic (Ed.), 573–603. New York, Academic Press.

    1980. Schemata: the building blocks of language. In *Theoretical issues on reading comprehension*, R. J. Spiro, B. Bruce, and W. Brewer (Eds.), 33–58. Hillsdale, N.J.: Erlbaum.

    1984. Understanding understanding. In *Understanding reading comprehension*, J. Flood (Ed.), 1–20. Newark, Del.: International Reading Association.

Rumelhart, D., and J. L. McClelland. 1982. An interactive activation model of the effects of context in perception. *Psychological Review* 89: 60–94.

Samuels, S. J. 1977. Introduction to theoretical models of reading. In *Reading Problems* , W. Otto (Ed.). Boston: Addison-Wesley.

Samuels, S., and M. Kamil. 1984. Models of the reading process. In Pearson (Ed.), 185–224. [Reprinted as Chapter 2 in this volume.]

Saville-Troike, M. 1984. What really matters in second language learning for academic achievement. *TESOL Quarterly* 18: 199–219.

Singer, H. 1981. Instruction in reading acquisition. In *Perception of print*, O. Tzeng and H. Singer (Eds.), 291–312. Hillsdale, N.J.: Erlbaum.

Smith, F. 1982. *Understanding reading. 3rd Ed.* New York: Holt, Rinehart and Winston.

Stanovich, K. 1980. Toward an interactive-compensatory model of individual differences in the development of reading fluency. *Reading Research Quarterly* 16: 32–71.

    1981. Attentional and automatic context effects. In Lesgold and Perfetti (Eds.), 1981b, 241–267.

    1984. The interactive-compensatory model of reading: A confluence of developmental, experimental, and educational psychology. *Remedial and Special Education* 5: 11–19.

Stanovich, K., and R. West. 1983. On priming by a sentence context. *Journal of experimental psychology: General* 112: 1–36.

Stemberger, R. 1982. Syntactic errors in speech. *Journal of Psycholinguistic Research* 11: 313–345.

Stoller, F. 1984. Implications of the interactive model of reading for recognition skills instruction. Paper presented at the 18th Annual TESOL Convention, Houston, Texas, April.

    1986. Reading lab: developing low level reading skills. In *Teaching second language reading for academic purposes*, F. Dubin, D. Eskey, and W. Grabe (Eds.), 51–76. Reading, Mass.: Addison-Wesley.

Taylor, I., and M. Taylor. 1983. *The psychology of reading*. New York: Academic Press.

Tzeng, O., and D. Hung. 1981. Linguistic determinism: a written language perspective. In *Perception of print*, O. Tzeng and H. Singer (Eds.), 237–255. Hillsdale, N.J.: Erlbaum.

Waltz, D., and J. Pollack. 1985. Massively parallel parsing: a strongly interactive model of natural language interpretation. *Cognitive Science* 9: 51–74.

Weber, R. 1984. Reading: United States. *Annual Review of Applied Linguistics* 4: 111–123.

Widdowson, H. 1979. The process and purpose of reading. In *Explorations in applied linguistics*, H. Widdowson (Ed.), 171–183. New York: Cambridge University Press.

PART II:
INTERACTIVE APPROACHES TO SECOND LANGUAGE READING – THEORY

The chapters in this section present and discuss the implications of interactive models of second language reading from theoretical perspectives. The chapter by Carrell and Eisterhold pursues the implications of an interactive view of the relation between reader and text for second language readers, especially in the context of second language readers coping with culture-specific texts for which they need to possess and activate the appropriate culture-specific schemata.

The chapter by Eskey emphasizes the particular importance of the need for adequate decoding skills in second language reading. In light of recent emphasis on top-down processing, Eskey is concerned that second language reading not neglect the needs of second language readers for the language skills they need in bottom-up processing.

Carrell's chapter explores some of the causes for failure of second language readers to process text interactively. In terms of schema activation, schema availability, skill deficiencies, conceptions about reading, and cognitive style, Carrell identifies and discusses some things that may interfere with second language readers' interactive processing of text and cause them to process texts unidirectionally, in either totally top-down or bottom-up processing directions.

Part II concludes with Clarke's chapter on the so-called short circuit hypothesis in second language reading. Clarke points to second language proficiency as a potential limiting factor in the transfer of good reading skills from native to second language reading. Clarke argues that failure to read effectively and efficiently in a second language, that is, interactively, may be due to inadequate language skills in the second language.

Thus, all of the chapters in this section deal not only with the notion of interactive reading in a second language but with unique aspects of second language reading that may interfere with the interaction.

Questions for the reader to bear in mind while reading the chapters in this section include: (1) What are the unique aspects of reading in a *second* language that make it different from reading in a *first* language? (2) How are these unique aspects of second language reading manifested in interactive models of second language reading? (3) Why are language skills, as opposed to reading skills, particularly crucial in second language reading? (4) What kinds of factors may have deleterious effects on interactive second language reading?

5 Schema theory and ESL reading pedagogy

Patricia L. Carrell *and* Joan C. Eisterhold

> Every act of comprehension involves one's knowledge of the world as well. (Anderson et al. 1977:369)

The idea expressed by the above quote is certainly not new, but it is one worth reminding ourselves of when we consider comprehension in a second or foreign language, and specifically reading comprehension in EFL/ESL. If, as Immanuel Kant claimed as long ago as 1781, new information, new concepts, new ideas can have meaning only when they can be related to something the individual already knows (Kant 1781/ 1963), this applies as much to second language comprehension as it does to comprehension in one's native language. Yet, traditionally in the study of second language comprehension (as much as, if not more so than, in the study of first language comprehension), the emphasis has been almost exclusively on the language to be comprehended and not on the comprehender (listener or reader). In this perspective, each word, each well-formed sentence, and every well-formed text passage is said to "have" a meaning. Meaning is often conceived to be "in" the utterance or text, to have a separate, independent existence from both the speaker or writer and the listener or reader. Also in this view, failures to comprehend a nondefective communication are always attributed to language-specific deficits – perhaps a word was not in the reader's vocabulary, a rule of grammar was misapplied, an anaphoric cohesive tie was improperly coordinated, and so on.

Recent empirical research in the field which has come to be known as *schema theory* has demonstrated the truth of Kant's original observation and of the opening quote from Anderson et al. Schema theory research has shown the importance of background knowledge within a psycholinguistic model of reading. The purpose of this chapter is two-fold. Our first goal is to give a brief overview of schema theory as part

From "Schema theory and ESL reading pedagogy" by Patricia L. Carrell and Joan C. Eisterhold, 1983, *TESOL Quarterly, 17* (4), pp. 553–73. Copyright 1983 by Teachers of English to Speakers of Other Languages. This article grew out of the authors' portions of a workshop entitled "Reading in ESL: Insights and Applications from Research," presented at the 16th Annual TESOL Convention in Honolulu, Hawaii, May 1, 1982.

of a reader-centered, psycholinguistic processing model of EFL/ESL reading. This goal is addressed in the first part of the chapter, in which we discuss how EFL/ESL reading comprehension involves background knowledge which goes far beyond linguistic knowledge. Our second purpose is to explore the relationship of culture-specific background knowledge and EFL/ESL reading methodology and is taken up in the second part of the chapter, where we review this relationship as it has been discussed in the extant methodology literature. We illustrate this discussion of the culturally based and culturally biased nature of background knowledge with sample reading passages which have actually caused comprehension problems for EFL/ESL students. Finally, we suggest a variety of techniques and classroom activities for accommodating this phenomenon in a reader-centered EFL/ESL reading program.

The psycholinguistic model of reading

During the past decade, EFL/ESL reading theory has come under the influence of psycholinguistics and Goodman's (1967, 1971, 1973a) psycholinguistic model of reading (see also Smith 1971). Goodman has described reading as a "psycholinguistic guessing game" (1967) in which the "reader reconstructs, as best as he can, a message which has been encoded by a writer as a graphic display" (1971:135). Goodman views this act of the construction of meaning as being an ongoing, cyclical process of sampling from the input text, predicting, testing and confirming or revising those predictions, and sampling further. In this model, the reader need not (and the efficient reader *does* not) use all of the textual cues. The better the reader is able to make correct predictions, the less confirming via the text is necessary, that is, the less visual perceptual information the reader requires:

> ...the reader does not use all the information available to him. Reading is a process in which the reader picks and chooses from the available information only enough to select and predict a language structure which is decodable. It is not in any sense a precise perceptual process. (Goodman 1973b:164)

These views are by now generally well known and widely accepted in our field.

Coady (1979) has elaborated on this basic psycholinguistic model and has suggested a model in which the EFL/ESL reader's background knowledge interacts with conceptual abilities and process strategies, more or less successfully, to produce comprehension (see Figure 1).

By *conceptual ability*, Coady means general intellectual capacity. By *processing strategies*, Coady means various subcomponents of reading ability, including many which are also more general language processing

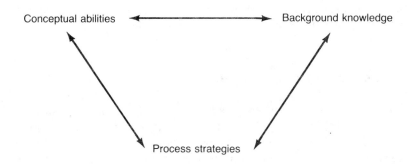

Figure 1 Coady's (1979) Model of the ESL Reader

skills which also apply to oral language (e.g., grapheme-morphophoneme correspondences, syllable-morpheme information, syntactic information [deep and surface], lexical meaning, and contextual meaning). Coady says little more about the role of *background knowledge* other than to observe that

background knowledge becomes an important variable when we notice, as many have, that students with a Western background of some kind learn English faster, on the average, than those without such a background. (Coady 1979:7)

Coady also suggests that background knowledge may be able to compensate for certain syntactic deficiencies:

The subject of reading materials should be of high interest and relate well to the background of the reader, since strong semantic input can help compensate when syntactic control is weak. The interest and background knowledge will enable the student to comprehend at a reasonable rate and keep him involved in the material in spite of its syntactic difficulty. (Coady 1979:12)

It is this third factor, background knowledge, that has been the most neglected in EFL/ESL reading. Even though the psycholinguistic model of reading is seen as an interaction of factors, it has generally failed to give sufficient emphasis to the role of background knowledge. Recent research indicates that what the reader brings to the reading task is more pervasive and more powerful than the general psycholinguistic model suggests:

More information is contributed by the reader than by the print on the page. That is, readers understand what they read because they are able to take the stimulus beyond its graphic representation and assign it membership to an appropriate group of concepts already stored in their memories... The reader brings to the task a formidable amount of information and ideas, attitudes and beliefs. This knowledge, coupled with the ability to make linguistic predictions, determines the expectations the reader will develop as he reads. Skill

in reading depends on the efficient interaction between linguistic knowledge
and knowledge of the world. (Clarke and Silberstein 1977:136–137)

The schema theory model

The role of background knowledge in language comprehension has been
formalized as *schema theory* (Bartlett 1932; Rumelhart and Ortony
1977; Rumelhart 1980), which has as one of its fundamental tenets that
text, any text, either spoken or written, does not by itself carry meaning.
Rather, according to schema theory, a text only provides directions for
listeners or readers as to how they should retrieve or construct meaning
from their own, previously acquired knowledge. This previously acquired knowledge is called the reader's *background knowledge*, and the
previously acquired knowledge structures are called *schemata* (Bartlett
1932; Adams and Collins 1979; Rumelhart 1980).[1] According to schema
theory, comprehending a text is an interactive process between the reader's background knowledge and the text. Efficient comprehension requires the ability to relate the textual material to one's own knowledge.
Comprehending words, sentences, and entire texts involves more than
just relying on one's linguistic knowledge. As the opening quote from
Anderson et al. points out, "every act of comprehension involves one's
knowledge of the world as well" (Anderson et al. 1977:369).

According to schema theory, the process of interpretation is guided
by the principle that every input is mapped against some existing schema
and that all aspects of that schema must be compatible with the input
information. This principle results in two basic modes of information
processing, called *bottom-up* and *top-down* processing. Bottom-up processing is evoked by the incoming data; the features of the data enter
the system through the best fitting, bottom-level schemata. Schemata are
hierarchically organized, from most general at the top to most specific
at the bottom. As these bottom-level schemata converge into higher level,
more general schemata, these too become activated. Bottom-up pro-

---

1 Other closely related concepts, which are technically distinct from *schemata* but
which may be thought of as part of the same general, cognitive approach to text
processing, are *scripts*, *plans*, and *goals* (Schank and Abelson 1977), *frames* (Minsky 1975; Fillmore 1976; Tannen 1979), *expectations* (Tannen 1978), and *event
chains* (Warren, Nicholas, and Trabasso 1979). All of these terms emanate from
basic research at the intersection of artificial intelligence, cognitive psychology, and
linguistics in the new discipline called *cognitive science*. These terms are not identical or even interchangeable; however, they may all be broadly characterized as part
of a schema-theoretical orientation to text processing.
    Carrell (1983a) gives an extensive overview of schema theory and the relevant
theoretical literature as well as the empirical research in first language processing
(children and adults) and second language processing (adults).

cessing is, therefore, called *data-driven*. Top-down processing, on the other hand, occurs as the system makes general predictions based on higher level, general schemata and then searches the input for information to fit into these partially satisfied, higher order schemata. Top-down processing is, therefore, called *conceptually driven*.

An important aspect of top-down and bottom-up processing is that both should be occurring at all levels simultaneously (Rumelhart 1980). The data that are needed to *instantiate*, or fill out, the schemata become available through bottom-up processing; top-down processing facilitates their assimilation if they are anticipated by or consistent with the listener/reader's conceptual expectations. Bottom-up processing ensures that the listeners/readers will be sensitive to information that is novel or that does not fit their ongoing hypotheses about the content or structure of the text; top-down processing helps the listeners/readers to resolve ambiguities or to select between alternative possible interpretations of the incoming data.

To illustrate the effects of background knowledge, schematic interpretation, and the simultaneity of top-down and bottom-up processing, consider the following mini-text (originally from Collins and Quillian 1972; discussed in Rumelhart 1977:267):

The policeman held up his hand and stopped the car.

In the process of trying to understand this sentence, we try to relate it to something familiar, some schema which will account for the event described. There are many schemata possible, but perhaps the most likely is the one involving a traffic cop who is signaling to a driver of a car to stop. Notice that when we interpret this mini-text against that schema, a number of related concepts come to the fore which are not literally mentioned in the text. In particular, we imagine that the car has a driver and that the policeman got the car to stop through signaling to the driver, who then put on the brakes of the car, which, in turn, caused the car to stop. The proximal cause of the car's stopping is, in this interpretation, the operation of the car's brakes. Further, the significance of the policeman's holding up his hand is that of a signal to the driver to stop. This fact is neither stated in the sentence nor is it even in the direct visual perception of such a situation, but is rather a fact in our prior cultural knowledge about the way traffic police are known to communicate with automobile drivers. Notice how the interpretation of the text would change if the policeman were known to be Superman and the car were known to be without a driver. A completely different schema would be required to understand the text. Notice how the relationship of the policeman's holding up his hand and the car's stopping takes on an entirely different interpretation when the text is interpreted against the Superman schema. Now, holding up the hand is not interpreted as a signal at all, but rather the direct physical mechanism for stopping the car. In this interpretation, the hand actually comes into physical contact with the car and is the proximal physical cause of the car's halting. The brakes of the car do not come into play in this schema.

Notice how sets of inferential reading comprehension questions would receive diametrically opposed answers depending upon which of the two schemata was activated in the mind of the reader:

QUESTION	ANSWER	
	Traffic cop schema	*Superman schema*
a) Did the policeman's hand touch the car?	No	Yes
b) Were the car's brakes applied?	Yes	No

Now let us consider a slightly longer text from Rumelhart:

Mary heard the ice cream man coming down the street. She remembered her birthday money and rushed into the house ... (1977:265)

Upon reading just these few lines, most readers are able to construct a rather complete interpretation of the text. Presumably, Mary is a little girl who heard the ice cream man coming and wanted to buy some ice cream from this ice cream man. Buying ice cream costs money, so she had to think quickly of a source of funds. She remembered some money which she had been given for her birthday and which, presumably, was in the house. So she hurried into the house to try to get the money before the ice cream man arrived. Of course, the text does not say all of this; we readers are inferring a lot of this in giving the text an interpretation. Other interpretations are also possible. Yet, most readers will probably give this text an interpretation quite similar to the one suggested here, and most readers will retain this interpretation unless some contradictory information is encountered. Notice what happens if the reader next encounters the phrase:

... and locked the door.[2]

The reader is unable to fit this new piece of textual input information into the developing interpretation. The reader is forced to revise the interpretation in such a way as to make this new information compatible with the previous information – to make the whole text cohere. If there were no such thing as schemata guiding the developing interpretation in a top-down processing mode, causing the reader to make conceptual predictions about the meaning of the text, then why would encountering

2 This example was offered by Charles J. Fillmore in a class lecture at the University of California, Berkeley, in 1980.

the added phrase cause the reaction it does in the reader? What has happened, we claim, is that as long as the incoming information being processed through bottom-up processing and the conceptual predictions being made through top-down processing are compatible, we have a satisfactory interpretation of the text. When we encounter a mismatch between the top-down predictions and the bottom-up information, we are forced to revise the interpretation in such a way as to make the two compatible once again. In this example, we must revise our interpretation to accommodate the information about Mary's locking the door. Perhaps we infer that for some reason Mary is afraid that the ice cream man might steal her birthday money and that she locks the door to protect it and herself. We believe these two examples vividly demonstrate the existence and operation of schemata in the process of text interpretation.

Thus, it seems clear that readers activate an appropriate schema against which they try to give a text a consistent interpretation. To the extent that they are successful, we may say that they have comprehended the text. However, one potential source of reading difficulties may be that the reader has a consistent interpretation for the text, but it may not be the one intended by the author. Nonetheless, the basic point is that much of the meaning understood from a text is really not actually in the text, per se, but in the reader, in the background or schematic knowledge of the reader. What is understood from a text is a function of the particular schema that is activated at the time of processing (i.e., reading) the text.

In seeking to understand the role of background knowledge in reading comprehension, it is often useful to draw a distinction between *formal* schemata (background knowledge of the formal, rhetorical organizational structures of different types of texts) and *content* schemata (background knowledge of the content area of a text) (Carrell 1983b). In other words, one type of schema which readers are said to possess is background knowledge about, and expectations of, differences among rhetorical structures, such as differences in genre, differences in the structure of fables, simple stories, scientific texts, newspaper articles, poetry, and so forth. Our schema for simple stories, for example, includes the information that the story should have, minimally, a setting, a beginning, a development, and an ending. Also for simple stories, Mandler (1978) distinguishes between schemata for causally connected and temporally connected stories. For expository texts, Meyer and her colleagues (Meyer 1975, 1977, 1981; Meyer and Rice 1982; Meyer and Freedle 1984) recognize five different types of expository rhetorical organization: *collection* – list, *causation* – cause and effect, *response* – problem and solution, *comparison* – comparison and contrast, and *description* – attribution. Each of these types, they say, represents a different abstract schema of ways writers organize and readers understand topics.

In schema theory research, this type of *formal* schematic knowledge is usually contrasted with *content* schematic knowledge, which is claimed to be background knowledge about the content area of a text, such as a text about washing clothes, celebrating New Year's Eve in Hawaii or Halloween in Carbondale, or about the economy of Mexico, the history of Canada, problems of nuclear breeder reactors, and so forth.

A reader's failure to activate an appropriate schema (formal or content) during reading results in various degrees of noncomprehension. This failure to activate an appropriate schema may either be due to the writer's not having provided sufficient clues in the text for the reader to effectively utilize a bottom-up processing mode to activate schemata the reader may already possess, or it may be due to the fact that the reader does not possess the appropriate schema anticipated by the author and thus fails to comprehend. In both instances there is a mismatch between what the writer anticipates the reader can do to extract meaning from the text and what the reader is actually able to do. The point is that the appropriate schemata must exist and must be activated during text processing.

One of the most obvious reasons why a particular content schema may fail to exist for a reader is that the schema is culturally specific and is not part of a particular reader's cultural background. Studies by Steffensen, Joag-dev, and Anderson (1979), Johnson (1981), and Carrell (1981) have shown that the implicit cultural content knowledge presupposed by a text interacts with the reader's own cultural background knowledge of content to make texts whose content is based on one's own culture easier to read and understand than syntactically and rhetorically equivalent texts based on a less familiar, more distant culture.

Other research has shown general effects of content schemata on EFL/ESL reading comprehension. Johnson (1982) has shown that a text on a familiar topic is better recalled by ESL readers than a similar text on an unfamiliar topic. Hudson (1982, reprinted as Chapter 13 in this volume) reports a study showing an interaction between overall linguistic proficiency in ESL and content-induced schematic effects in ESL reading comprehension. Specifically, that study demonstrates the facilitating effects on comprehension of explicitly inducing content schemata through pre-reading activities, especially at the beginning and intermediate proficiency levels, as compared to two other methods of inducing content schemata (through vocabulary activities and read-reread activities). Finally, Alderson and Urquhart (1985, reprinted as Chapter 12 in this volume) have found a discipline-specific effect of content background knowledge in measuring reading comprehension in ESP/EST.

Several recent studies have shown the effects of formal, rhetorical schemata in EFL/ESL. In a study by Carrell (1984), two groups of university-bound, intermediate-level ESL subjects each read a different type of simple story – one type well structured according to a simple story schema structure and the other type deliberately violating the story schema structure. Results showed that when stories violating the story schema are processed by second language learners, both the quantity of recall and the temporal sequences of recall are affected. In other words, when the content is kept constant but the rhetorical structure is varied, second language reading comprehension is affected.

Recent studies done in the area of contrastive rhetoric (Kaplan 1966) also demonstrate the effects of formal schemata on both the comprehension and production of written texts in a second language (Ostler and Kaplan 1982). In particular, Hinds's research (1983a, b) shows the contrasting effects on different groups of readers of typical Japanese rhetorical organization and typical English rhetorical organization. Burtoff (1983) has found differences among the typical rhetorical patterns of expository prose produced by writers with different formal schemata according to their native-language/native-culture backgrounds.

Thus, a growing body of empirical research attests to the role of both content and formal schemata in EFL/ESL reading comprehension and to the potential cultural specificity of both types of schemata. In the following sections, we focus on the implications of the cultural specificity of content schemata for EFL/ESL readers and EFL/ESL reading methodology.

Implications for EFL/ESL readers

Given the role of content schemata in reading comprehension, there are obvious implications for the EFL/ESL reader. The background knowledge that second language readers bring to a text is often culture-specific. Hudson notes that

the reading problems of the L_2 reader are not due to an absence of attempts at fitting and providing specific schemata ... Rather, the problem lies in projecting appropriate schemata. (Hudson 1982:9)

Second language readers attempt to provide schemata to make sense of texts, and they do so persistently. However, these efforts will fail if the reader cannot access the appropriate existing schemata, or if the reader does not possess the appropriate schemata necessary to understand a text.

Most commonly, accessing appropriate content schemata depends initially on textual cues; the graphic display must be somehow reconstructed by the reader as meaningful language. At this point, general language processing skills are most important. For second language readers, then, obviously *some* language proficiency is required to activate relevant schemata, and it is not surprising that failures to access appropriate schemata (i.e., comprehend) are often interpreted solely as deficiencies in language processing skills. Consequently, poor readers are encouraged to expand their vocabularies and to gain greater control over complex syntactic structures in order to improve reading comprehension. Indeed, some reading problems are related to such language skill deficiencies. However, as we have noted, reading comprehension depends crucially on the reader's being able to relate information from the text to already existing background knowledge.

In the EFL/ESL classroom, we must be particularly sensitive to reading problems that result from the implicit cultural knowledge presupposed by a text. A review of the literature in EFL/ESL methodology shows that the role of cultural knowledge as a factor in reading comprehension has been an issue for some time. Fries (1945, 1963) talked about meaning at the social-cultural level – that is, the meaning that transcends the language code and is related to the background knowledge of the native speakers of that code. Reading comprehension occurs when the total meaning of a passage is fitted into this network of information organized in ways meaningful to a society. The following passage from an ESL reading text[3] illustrates Fries's concept of social-cultural meaning:

By voting against mass transportation, voters have chosen to continue on a road to ruin. Our interstate highways, those much praised golden avenues built to whisk suburban travelers in and out of downtown have turned into the world's most expensive parking lots. That expense is not only economic – it is social. These highways have created great walls separating neighborhood from neighborhood, disrupting the complex social connections that help make a city livable. (Baudoin et al. 1977:159)

In reading this passage, some ESL students fail to perceive the connection between mass transportation and highways. In the United States, where individual ownership of cars results in an overabundance of highways and a reduced need for mass transportation, this passage makes sense. Sometimes, however, students perceive that highways are built *for* mass transportation, which renders this passage (and especially the critical reading question which asks whether the author supports the idea of mass transportation) at best illogical, at worst incomprehensible.

The social-cultural meaning in this passage relates to the culture-

---

3 The passages chosen to illustrate reading problems related to culture-specific background information are all drawn from *Reader's choice* (Baudoin et al. 1977), a widely used and widely respected ESL reading text. The difficulties noted with the passages from this text are in no way intended as a criticism of the book, which we consider an excellent text based on psycholinguistic principles. Rather, these passages were chosen because they caused actual classroom problems and because they illustrate often subtle or hidden problems which we, as EFL/ESL teachers, may find difficult to identify.

specific schema of the cars/mass transportation opposition. Furthermore, comprehension can also be related to semantic associations available when a schema is accessed. The notion of interstate highways, here referred to narrowly as those in urban areas, invites the semantic associations of crowding, congestion, and rush hour traffic. The meaning of the phrase *the world's most expensive parking lots* is associated with, and can only be understood with reference to, this specific *urban* highway subschema.

Elsewhere in the EFL/ESL methodology literature, Rivers (1968) recommends that the strong bond between culture and language must be maintained for the student to have a complete understanding of the meaning of language. She believes that differences in values and attitudes are one of the main sources of problems in foreign language learning. Culture-specific values can be a significant factor in comprehension if the values expressed by the text differ from the values held by the reader. Devout Muslim students, for example, tend to have problems with the following passage:

There is a question about the extent to which any one of us can be free of a prejudiced view in the area of religion. (Baudoin et al. 1977:185)

While this sentence is excellent for developing critical reading skills, the mention of religion in this context does not coincide with Islamic values. A subsequent exercise requires the student to analyze the relation of the original text to the following sentence: *Because we can't be free of prejudice in the area of religion, we should not practice a religion.* One student refused to even consider the premise of this sentence; his only comment: "For me, it's false."

More recently, Rivers and Temperley (1978) have emphasized the importance of providing background information, explaining high-frequency but culturally loaded terms, and using illustrations with reading passages to provide additional meaning to texts. The important point is that problems with individual lexical items may not be as pervasive as problems related to the absence of appropriate generalized information assumed by the writer and possessed by a reader sharing that writer's cultural background.

The relevance of appropriate generalized, underlying information is illustrated by the following text:

Although housewives still make up the majority of volunteer groups, male participation is reported on the rise nationwide as traditional distinctions between men's work and women's work begin to fade. (Baudoin et al. 1977:184)

The phrase *volunteer groups* requires appropriate underlying information before this sentence can be understood. Although the lexical items *volunteer* and *groups* were clearly understood by one student, the concept of *volunteer groups* (predominantly female, unpaid social workers) was clearly not understood since he wondered if these women had volunteered to be housewives.

Paulston and Bruder (1976) also discuss covert information and reading. Proficient readers, they say, must draw on their own experience in order to supply a semantic component to a message. They argue that texts with familiar settings and even specialized low-frequency vocabulary are appropriate (even though the texts may "feel" as if they are not appropriate) because they are relevant to the students' world (and are, thus, easier to read). Robinett (1978) agrees that covert cultural information is a factor in reading performance and suggests that the teacher facilitate reading by providing specific background experience.

When covert information is assumed by the writer, it must be supplied by the reader and is sometimes done so erroneously.

I saw by the clock of the city jail that it was past eleven, so I decided to go to the newspaper immediately. (Baudoin et al. 1977:83)

After reading this sentence, one student was convinced that the writer had been in jail at the time because, as he said, "an outside clock is only on a church." He had concluded that the only place the writer could have seen *the clock of the city jail* was from inside the jail itself. If this sentence merely "sets the scene," then this misinterpretation is insignificant. However, if the misreading causes the reader to consider such a scene significant (when it is not), or to dismiss it as *in*significant (when it is not), then a serious comprehension problem has resulted.

Finally in the methodology literature, Marquardt's work (1967, 1969) is representative of the pedagogical approach that holds that reading should be in the literature of the target culture for the express purpose of teaching that culture to foreign students. Such literature, however, must be chosen carefully. Consider the following passage from *Cheaper by the Dozen*:

Mother the psychologist and Dad the motion study man and general contractor decided to look into the new field of the psychology of management, and the old field of psychologically managing a houseful of children. They believed that what would work in the home would work in the factory, and what would work in the factory would work in the home.

Dad put the theory to a test shortly after we moved to Montclair. The house was too big for Tom Grieves, the handyman, and Mrs. Cunningham, the cook, to keep in order. Dad decided we were going to have to help them, and he wanted us to offer the help willingly. He had found that the best way to get cooperation out of employees in a factory was set up a joint employer-employee board, which would make work assignments on a basis of personal choice and aptitude. He and Mother set up a Family Council, patterned after the employer-employee board. The Council met every Sunday afternoon, immediately after dinner. (Baudoin et al. 1977:91)

This text would require considerable background teaching before the text itself could teach anything (even if we considered what it has to teach to be culturally relevant). Using literature to teach *culture* may be the most direct way to teach culture, but it certainly implies thorough background preparation and may, in fact, not be the best way to teach *language.*

There is much in these methods that is of value, but in light of the broad message behind the schema-theoretic view of reading, are they sufficiently sensitive to cross-cultural interference at all levels of meaning? The factors noted above are important not just to "ground" words and phrases for the reader. Rather, notions such as *social-cultural meaning, culture-specific values,* and *covert information* refer to different aspects of the same problem, and that is how to deal with reading difficulties caused by the mismatch of the background knowledge presupposed by the text and the background knowledge possessed by the reader. A schema-theoretic view of reading suggests the pervasive effects of such a mismatch and requires our being sensitive to these reading difficulties on a more global level.

Classroom activities

Our immediate goal as EFL/ESL reading teachers is to minimize reading difficulties and to maximize comprehension by providing culturally relevant information. Goodman puts the issue into focus when he says that

even highly effective readers are severely limited in comprehension of texts by what they already know before they read. The author may influence the comprehensibility of a text particularly for specific targeted audiences. But no author can completely compensate in writing for the range of differences among all potential readers of a given text. (Goodman 1979:658)

Since no author can compensate for the individual variation among readers, especially readers from different cultural backgrounds, this is one of the roles of the teacher in the EFL/ESL reading classroom. As teachers we can approach this problem by manipulating either one of the two variables: the text and/or the reader.

Text

What can we do with texts to minimize cultural conflicts and interference and to maximize comprehension? For the beginning reader, the Language Experience Approach (LEA) (Rigg 1981) is an excellent way to control vocabulary, structure, and content. The basic LEA technique uses the students' ideas and the students' own words in the preparation of beginning reading materials. The students decide what they want to say and how to say it, and then dictate to the teacher, who acts as a scribe. LEA works when the students' beginning reading materials, developed by them with the teacher's help, have the student's ideas in their own words. LEA works because students tend to be able to read what they have just said. The students, in effect, write their own texts, neutralizing problems of unfamiliar content.

Another way to minimize interference from the text is to encourage narrow reading, as suggested by Krashen (1981). Narrow reading refers to reading that is confined to a single topic or to the texts of a single author. Krashen suggests that "narrow reading, and perhaps narrow input in general, is more efficient for second language acquisition" (Krashen 1981:23). Reading teachers usually provide short and varied selections which never allow students to adjust to an author's style, to become familiar with the specialized vocabulary of the topic, or to develop enough context to facilitate comprehension. Rather, such selections force students to move from frustration to frustration.

However, students who read either a single topic or a single author find that the text becomes easier to comprehend after the first few pages. Readers adjust either to the repeated vocabulary of a particular topic or to the particular style of a writer. Furthermore, repetitions of vocabulary and structure mean that review is built into the reading. The significant advantage from the schema-theoretic point of view is that schemata are repeatedly accessed and further expanded and refined, resulting in increased comprehension.

The third possibility of text facilitation is to develop materials along the lines of those proposed by Paulston and Bruder (1976). As we have noted, they suggest using texts with local settings and specialized low-frequency vocabulary. These materials might be student or local newspapers, pamphlets, brochures, or booklets about local places of interest. English travel guides or *National Geographic*-type articles from the students' own countries are also good sources for the EFL/ESL reader.

Finally, Sustained Silent Reading (SSR) is an excellent activity for ESL readers. Through silent reading of texts, students become self-directed agents seeking meaning. To be effective, however, an SSR program must be based on student-selected texts so that the students will be interested in what they are reading. Students select their own reading texts with respect to content, level of difficulty, and length. What is important, from our point of view, is that readers tend to be interested in reading texts that are relevant to their own experiences. Students who choose their own texts are, in effect, also providing their own appropriate background knowledge for understanding the text.

Reader

Instead of, or in addition to, text control, we also need to consider what we can do with the readers themselves. Providing background information and previewing content for the reader seem to be the most obvious strategies for the language teacher. We want to avoid having students read material "cold." Asking students to manipulate both the linguistic and cultural codes (sometimes linguistically easy but culturally difficult, and vice versa) is asking too much.

Providing background information and previewing are particularly important for the less proficient language student (see the findings of Hudson 1982). These readers are more word-bound, and meaning tends to break down at the word level. Thus, less proficient students tend to have vocabulary acquisition emphasized and, as such, are encouraged to do a lot of specific (and less efficient) word-by-word processing exclusively in a bottom-up processing mode. Readers who are more proficient in a language tend to receive content previews because they are no longer as susceptible to vocabulary and structure difficulties in reading. As a result, these more proficient students are encouraged to do more global, predictive (and more efficient) processing in the top-down processing mode. One thing we surely want to remind ourselves of, however, is that less proficient readers also need familiar content selections and/or content preview as much as, if not more than, more proficient readers. Illustrations may be particularly appropriate for students with minimal language skills. Providing the semantic content component for low-level readers will free them to focus on vocabulary and structure expressive of that content.

Previewing is an important activity in the reading classroom, but it is not necessarily a process of simply providing a preliminary outline of what is to be read. Sometimes, it involves teaching a key concept which is culturally loaded, such as the one in the short story *The lottery* (Baudoin et al. 1977:140–145). If one does not understand the process or purpose of a lottery, then this short story about one woman who "wins" and is then killed by her neighbors will be totally incomprehensible. In this case, a discussion of lotteries before assigning the reading would be absolutely necessary.

Previewing can also include presenting specialized vocabulary and structures that the teacher predicts will cause difficulties. In the mass transportation passage cited earlier, students who could not come up with the appropriate background information also had difficulty with the phrase *road to ruin* (*a road for ruining*, as in *an apple to eat?*) and *expensive parking lots* (*parking will be expensive?*). Even a sentence that supposedly contains within it enough experiential context to explain the word *mildew* is often incomprehensible to many students from arid regions: *What could John expect? He had left his wet swimming trunks in the dark closet for over a week. Of course they had begun to mildew* (Baudoin et al. 1977:5).

Finally, by carefully listening to what our students say about the texts they are asked to read, we can become further sensitized to their hidden comprehension problems. As teachers, we should not respond to what the reader does (right/wrong) as much as to what the reader is *trying* to do. Given that the reader is trying to make sense of the text (construct meaning), a teacher who listens carefully and responds to a student's efforts will become aware of both the background knowledge and the cultural problems that students themselves bring to the text. In any case, the most valuable information is in our students' perceptions and not our own. This is the type of information that is gleaned through asking open-ended questions, probing for inferences from the text, and asking students to justify answers to more direct questions (for example, "Why do you think so?"). In addition, having students provide oral or written summaries will help teachers to discern problem areas in comprehension.

Conclusion

Thus, in achieving our immediate goals in the EFL/ESL reading classroom, we must strive for an optimum balance between the background knowledge presupposed by the texts our students read and the background knowledge our students possess. As we have shown by means of the foregoing classroom activities and techniques, this balance may be achieved by manipulating either the text and/or the reader variable.

Of course, our long-range goal as reading teachers is to develop independent readers outside the EFL/ESL classroom, readers whose purpose in learning to read in English as a foreign or second language is to *learn* from the texts they read.[4] But there, too, as Anderson notes, "without some schema into which it can be assimilated, an experience is incomprehensible, and therefore, little can be *learned* from it" (Anderson 1977:429; emphasis added). What makes the classroom activities and other techniques we have described valid is their applicability to the

---

4 We use the phrase "reading to *learn* from texts" in the broadest sense, including reading for academic purposes, reading for survival purposes or for purposes of functioning in society at various levels, and even reading for recreation or entertainment.

"real" world beyond the EFL/ESL reading classroom. Every culture-specific interference problem dealt with in the classroom presents an opportunity to build new culture-specific schemata that will be available to the EFL/ESL student outside the classroom. In addition, however, and possibly more importantly, the process of identifying and dealing with cultural interference in reading should make our EFL/ESL students more sensitive to such interference when they read on their own. By using the classroom activities and techniques we have described, our EFL/ESL readers should become more aware that reading is a highly interactive process between themselves and their prior background knowledge, on the one hand, and the text itself, on the other.

References

Adams, M. J., and A. Collins. 1979. A schema-theoretic view of reading. In *New directions in discourse processing*, R. O. Freedle (Ed.), 1–22. Norwood, N.J.: Ablex.

Alderson, J. C., and A. Urquhart. 1985. This test is unfair: I'm not an economist. In *Second language performance testing*, P. Hauptman, R. LeBlanc, and M. Bingham Wesche (Eds.), 25–43. Ottawa: University of Ottawa Press. [Reprinted as Chapter 12 in this volume.]

Anderson, R. C. 1977. The notion of schemata and the educational enterprise: general discussion of the conference. In *Schooling and the acquisition of knowledge*, R. C. Anderson, R. J. Spiro, and W. E. Montague (Eds.), 415–431. Hillsdale, N.J.: Erlbaum.

Anderson, R. C., R. E. Reynolds, D. L. Schallert, and E. T. Goetz. 1977. Frameworks for comprehending discourse. *American Educational Research Journal* 14(4): 367–381.

Bartlett, F. C. 1932. *Remembering: a study in experimental and social psychology.* Cambridge: Cambridge University Press.

Baudoin, E. M., E. S. Bober, M. A. Clarke, B. K. Dobson, and S. Silberstein. 1977. *Reader's choice: a reading skills textbook for students of English as a second language.* Ann Arbor: University of Michigan Press.

Burtoff, M. 1983. Organizational patterns of expository prose: a comparative study of native Arabic, Japanese and English speakers. Paper presented at the 17th Annual TESOL Convention, Toronto, Canada, March 1983.

Carrell, P. L. 1981. Culture-specific schemata in L2 comprehension. In *Selected papers from the ninth Illinois TESOL/BE annual convention, the first Midwest TESOL conference*, R. Orem and J. Haskell (Eds.), 123–132. Chicago: Illinois TESOL/BE.

1983a. Background knowledge in second language comprehension. *Language Learning and Communication* 2(1):25–34.

1983b. Some issues in studying the role of schemata, or background knowledge, in second language comprehension. *Reading in a Foreign Language* 1(2):81–92.

1984. Evidence of a formal schema in second language comprehension. *Language Learning* 34(2):87–112.

Clarke, M. A., and S. Silberstein. 1977. Toward a realization of psycholinguistic principles in the ESL reading class. *Language Learning* 27(1):135–154.

Coady, J. 1979. A psycholinguistic model of the ESL reader. In *Reading in a second language*, Ronald Mackay, Bruce Barkman, and R. R. Jordan (Eds.), 5–12. Rowley, Mass.: Newbury House.

Collins. A. M., and M. R. Quillian. 1972. How to make a language user. In *Organization of memory*, E. Tulving and W. Donaldson (Eds.), 310–351. New York: Academic Press.

Fillmore, C. J. 1976. The need for a frame semantics within linguistics. In *Statistical methods in linguistics*, 5–29. Stockholm: Sprakforlaget Skriptor.

Fries, C. C. 1945. *Teaching and learning English as a foreign language*. Ann Arbor: University of Michigan Press..

    1963. *Linguistics and reading*. New York: Holt, Rinehart and Winston.

Goodman, K. S. 1967. Reading: a psycholinguistic guessing game. *Journal of the Reading Specialist* 6(1):126–135.

    1971. Psycholinguistic universals in the reading process. In *The psychology of second language learning*, P. Pimsleur and T. Quinn (Eds.), 135–142. Cambridge: Cambridge University Press.

    1973a. On the psycholinguistic method of teaching reading. In *Psycholinguistics and reading*, F. Smith (Ed.), 177–182. New York: Holt, Rinehart and Winston.

    1973b. Analysis of oral reading miscues: applied pyscholinguistics. In *Psycholinguistics and reading*, F. Smith (Ed.), 158–176. New York: Holt, Rinehart and Winston.

    1979. The know-more and the know-nothing movements in reading: a personal response. *Language Arts* 55(6):657–663.

Hinds, J. 1983a. Contrastive rhetoric: Japanese and English. Paper presented at the 16th Annual TESOL Convention, Honolulu, Hawaii, May 1982.

    1983b. Retention of information using a Japanese style of presentation. *Text* 3:183–195.

Hudson, T. 1982. The effects of induced schemata on the "short circuit" in L2 reading: non-decoding factors in L2 reading performance. *Language Learning* 32(1):1–31. [Reprinted as Chapter 13 in this volume.]

Johnson, P. 1981. Effects on reading comprehension of language complexity and cultural background of a text. *TESOL Quarterly* 15(2):169–181.

    1982. Effects on reading comprehension of building background knowledge. *TESOL Quarterly* 16(4):503–516.

Kant, I. 1963. *Critique of pure reason* (1st ed. 1781, 2nd ed. 1787, N. Kemp Smith, translator.) London: Macmillan.

Kaplan, R. B. 1966. Cultural thought patterns in inter-cultural education. *Language Learning* 16(1–2):1–20.

Krashen, S. D. 1981. The case for narrow reading. *TESOL Newsletter* 15(6):23.

Mandler, J. M. 1978. A code in the node: the use of a story schema in retrieval. *Discourse Processes* 1(1):14–35.

Marquardt, W. F. 1967. Literature and cross-culture communication in the course in English for international students. *The Florida Foreign Lanaguage Reporter* 5(1):9–10.

    1969. Creating empathy through literature between members of the mainstream culture and disadvantaged learners of the minority cultures. *The Florida Foreign Language Reporter* 7(1):133–141, 157.

Meyer, B. J. F. 1975. *The organization of prose and its effects on memory.* Amsterdam: North-Holland.

1977. The structure of prose: effects on learning and memory and implications for educational practice. In *Schooling and the acquisition of knowledge,* R. C. Anderson, R. J. Spiro, and W. E. Montague (Eds.), 179–208. Hillsdale, N.J.: Erlbaum.

1981. Basic research on prose comprehension: a critical review. In *Comprehension and the competent reader: inter-specialty perspectives,* D. F. Fisher and C. W. Peters (Eds.), 8–35. New York: Praeger.

Meyer, B. J. F., and R. O. Freedle. 1984. The effects of different discourse types on recall. *American Educational Research Journal* 21(1):121–143.

Meyer, B. J. F., and G. E. Rice. 1982. The interaction of reader strategies and the organization of text. *Text* 2(1–3):155–192.

Minsky, M. 1975. A framework for representing knowledge. In *The psychology of computer vision,* P. H. Winston (Ed.), 211–277. New York: McGraw-Hill.

Ostler, S. E., and R. B. Kaplan. 1982. Contrastive rhetoric revisited. Paper presented at the 16th Annual TESOL Convention, Honolulu, Hawaii, May 1982.

Paulston, C. B., and M. N. Bruder. 1976. *Teaching English as a second language: techniques and procedures.* Cambridge, Mass.: Winthrop.

Rigg, P. 1981. Beginning to read in English the LEA way. In *Reading English as a second language: moving from theory,* C. W. Twyford, W. Diehl, and K. Feathers (Eds.), 81–90. Monographs in Language and Reading Studies 4. Bloomington: Indiana University Press.

Rivers, W. M. 1968. *Teaching foreign language skills.* University of Chicago Press.

Rivers, W. M., and M. S. Temperley. 1978. *A practical guide to the teaching of English as a second or foreign language.* New York: Oxford University Press.

Robinett, B. W. 1978. *Teaching English to speakers of other languages.* New York: McGraw-Hill.

Rumelhart, D. E. 1977. Understanding and summarizing brief stories. In *Basic processes in reading: perception and comprehension,* D. LaBerge and S. J. Samuels (Eds.), 265–303. Hillsdale, N. J.: Erlbaum.

1980. Schemata: the building blocks of cogniton. In *Theoretical issues in reading comprehension,* R. J. Spiro, B. C. Bruce, and W. E. Brewer (Eds.), 33–58. Hillsdale, N. J.: Erlbaum.

Rumelhart, D. E., and A. Ortony. 1977. The representation of knowledge in memory. In *Schooling and the acquisition of knowledge,* R. C. Anderson, R. J. Spiro, and W. E. Montague (Eds.), 99–135. Hillsdale, N.J.: Erlbaum.

Schank, R. C., and R. P. Abelson. 1977. *Scripts, plans, goals and understanding.* Hillsdale, N.J.: Erlbaum.

Smith, 1971. *Understanding reading: a psycholinguistic analysis of reading and learning to read.* New York: Holt, Rinehart and Winston.

Steffensen, M. S., C. Joag-dev, and R. C. Anderson. 1979. A cross-cultural perspective on reading comprehension. *Reading Research Quarterly* 15(1):10–29.

Tannen, D. 1978. The effect of expectations on conversation. *Discourse Processes* 1(2):203–209.

1979. What's in a frame? Surface evidence for underlying expectations. In *New directions in discourse processing*, R. O. Freedle (Ed.), 137–181. Norwood, N.J.: Ablex.

Warren, W. H., D. W. Nicholas, and T. Trabasso. 1979. Event chains and inferences in understanding narratives. In *New directions in discourse processing*, R. O. Freedle (Ed.), 23–52. Norwood, N.J.: Ablex.

6 Holding in the bottom: an interactive approach to the language problems of second language readers

David E. Eskey

During the past fifteen years or so, we have witnessed something like a revolution in the way that researchers understand and describe the process of reading. The work of psycholinguists like Goodman and Smith (e.g., Goodman 1967, 1970; Smith 1982) is familiar to, and very widely accepted by, reading specialists everywhere, now including researchers, writers of texts, and even teachers of reading in a *second* language. Goodman's well-known characterization of reading as "a psycholinguistic guessing game" has largely carried the day in our field, as in others.

I take it as almost axiomatic that this "top-down" revolution has resulted in major improvements in both our understanding of what good and many not so good readers do, and in the methods and materials that we now employ. We have come a long way in the right direction since the audiolingual reinforcement-of-oral-language (Fries 1945) days, thanks in large part to the work of these scholars.

But top-down models do have some limitations. They tend to emphasize such higher-level skills as the prediction of meaning by means of context clues or certain kinds of background knowledge at the expense of such lower-level skills as the rapid and accurate identification of lexical and grammatical forms. That is, in making the perfectly valid point that fluent reading is primarily a cognitive process, they tend to *de*emphasize the perceptual and decoding dimensions of that process. The model they promote is an accurate model of the skillful, fluent reader, for whom perception and decoding have become automatic, but for the less proficient, developing reader – like most second language readers – this model does not provide a true picture of the problems such readers must surmount (see Clarke 1979; 1980, reprinted as Chapter 8 in this volume).

More recently, however, a newer and perhaps even more insightful model of the reading process has been proposed (by Rumelhart 1977, and further developed by Rumelhart and others: McClelland and Rumelhart 1981; Lesgold and Perfetti 1981) which seems to strike a better balance among the various subprocesses of reading and also may account for some empirical research that appears to conflict with certain top-down assumptions. Unlike the top-down model, this so-called *interactive* model does not presuppose the primacy of top-down processing skills – the gradual replacing of painful word-by-word decoding with educated guessing based on minimal visual cues – but rather posits a constant interaction between bottom-up and top-down processing in reading, each source of information contributing to a comprehensive reconstruction of the meaning of the text. In this view, good readers are both good decoders and good interpreters of texts, their decoding skills becoming more automatic but no less important as their reading skill develops.

One reason that I am attracted to this model is that it addresses – successfully, in my opinion – certain reservations that I have always had (especially in the context of *second* language reading) about the Goodman/Smith model (Eskey 1973:172). The thrust of these top-down advocates has always been to downgrade the perceptual dimension of reading and the simple decoding of the language of the text,[1] and to promote higher-order cognitive skills, like prediction based on knowledge of both texts and the world, as the means of achieving true fluency in reading. I have no quarrel with the latter, but I also believe that simple language decoding has a major role to play in the process – that good reading is a more language-structured affair than the guessing-game metaphor seems to imply.

A simple way to explain my position would be to say that I think the rapid and accurate decoding of language is important to any kind of reading and especially important to second language reading. Good readers know the language: They can decode, with occasional exceptions, both the lexical units and syntactic structures they encounter in texts, and they do so, for the most part, not by guessing from context or prior knowledge of the world, but by a kind of automatic identification that requires no conscious cognitive effort. It is precisely this "automaticity" that frees up the minds of fluent readers of a language to think about and interpret what they are reading – that is, to employ higher-level, top-down strategies like the use of schemata and other kinds of background knowledge (Neely 1977). Good decoding skills are therefore one of the causes, and not merely a result, as Goodman has argued (1981; but the empirical evidence is overwhelming here: see Stanovich 1980 for citations), of fluent (both rapid *and* accurate) reading. No doubt the whole process is reciprocal, but that is exactly what an interactive model would predict.

A second reason that I favor the interactive model is that it plausibly

---

1 Goodman's "miscue analysis," for example, is particularly good at ferreting out readers addicted to bottom-up strategies – readers who seem to think that reading is converting individual letters to sounds or bursts of print into isolated words. Since it only deals with miscues, however, it tells us much less about what readers do when they decode accurately.

accounts for much empirical research which appears to conflict with basic top-down assumptions. At the level of word recognition, for example, many studies suggest that fluent readers are no more likely than poor ones to rely on orthographic or sentence context effects for the simple identification of words. Nor does prediction increase speed of recognition. "Reading rate," according to Stanovich, "is more dependent on the speed with which a reader can recognize words and construct a representation," that is, on bottom-up skills, "than on the ability to use predictions" (1980:44), that is, on the basic top-down strategy. As a rule, then, "fluent readers do not use conscious expectancies to facilitate word recognition" (1980:35).

Even more to the point, many studies have shown that poor readers are just as likely as good ones to rely on prior knowledge in deciphering texts, and that the use of this top-down strategy is not, as top-down theorists would have us believe, the hallmark of good reading in every situation. In this respect, it is important to distinguish between the use of prior knowledge (top-down processing) to facilitate the simple recognition of words, and the use of such knowledge to facilitate higher-level interpretations of texts. The latter *is* characteristic of good readers, but the former is not. Frequent use of top-down strategies at word level suggests a simple failure to decode properly. Good readers, as Allington has observed, are "more reliant on context for fluency and poor readers more reliant on context for accuracy" (Stanovich 1980:51). To properly achieve both, developing readers must therefore work at perfecting both their bottom-up recognition skills and their top-down interpretation strategies. Good reading – that is, fluent and accurate reading – can result only from a constant interaction between these processes.

Despite the emergence of interactive models, I am therefore concerned that much of the second language reading literature continues to exhibit a strongly top-down bias.[2] One reason may be that in the context of reading, the word *interactive* is ambiguous, pointing as it does to two independent (though related) bodies of research. The first – and, so far, the better publicized – deals with the interaction between the mind of the reader and external texts. This approach draws a sharp distinction between information provided by the text itself (bottom-up?) and in-

---

2 Carrell (Chapter 7 in this volume) provides a more balanced view, but for the last few years second language researchers have almost exclusively focused on such top-down concerns as the role of culture-specific assumptions or subject-matter schemata in second language reading (see, for example, practically everything published on reading in the *TESOL Quarterly* between the years 1981 and 1984, e.g.: Carrell and Eisterhold 1983, reprinted as Chapter 5 in this volume; Carrell 1984; Perkins 1983; Johnson 1981, 1982). This research has resulted in many useful insights, but the lack of attention to decoding problems has, I think, produced a somewhat distorted picture of the true range of problems second language readers face.

formation provided by the reader's mind (top-down?). By means of the latter, readers can, as they read, reconstruct a plausible meaning for the text by relating what it says to what they already know about its subject matter and the world in general.

As a broad description of reading comprehension, this is perfectly sound and a useful corrective to the commonsense notion that the meaning of a text is somehow self-contained (that the writer has simply put so much meaning in for the readers to take back out as they read). But this particular version of reader–text interaction may also foster the illusion that texts themselves *are* information, when in fact they are merely marks on a page, which readers must convert into language/ information as they engage in the complex process of reading. Successful reading is much more than simple decoding, but decoding is a cognitive process too, involving bottom-up as well as top-down skills, and successful comprehension cannot be achieved without it. For me, a Chinese text contains no information, and neither my best top-down reading strategies nor any amount of background knowledge on its subject will make me a successful reader of that text unless I take the trouble to learn to decode Chinese script. Few of our students are as helpless when faced with texts written in English as I am when faced with texts written in Chinese, but many are far from efficient decoders, and we must not ignore this dimension of the process.

Knowledge of the language of a text must be an integral part of whatever background knowledge is required for the full comprehension of that text. Language is a kind of schema too, albeit one that for fluent native users may be activated automatically, and there is no easy top-down route around the fact that fluent reading entails bottom-up perceptual and linguistic skills as well as higher-order cognitive processes.

Thus I am more attracted to the somewhat different version of the word *interactive* which derives from the way that readers make internal use of several kinds of knowledge in simultaneously decoding and interpreting texts. In this model, *interactive* refers to the interaction between information obtained by means of bottom-up decoding and information provided by means of top-down analysis, *both* of which depend on certain kinds of prior knowledge and certain kinds of information-processing skills. Among readers and categories of readers, there will of course be individual differences. The mix of skills and knowledge (bottom-up and top-down) will naturally vary from reader to reader (and even for one reader in moving from text to text), but the model can account for and accommodate this. It can, for example, accommodate the problems of developing, less-than-fluent readers, such as second language readers, who seem to need as much help in "holding in the bottom" (that is, in simple decoding) as they do in performing higher-level interpretations of texts.[3]

In practical terms, my concern is thus to keep the language in the teaching of second language reading. That may not sound very controversial, but I think that in promoting higher-level strategies – like predicting from context or the use of schemata and other kinds of background knowledge – some researchers have been sending a message to teachers that the teaching of reading to second language readers is mostly just a matter of providing them with the right background knowledge for any texts they must read, and encouraging them to make full use of that knowledge in decoding those texts. Though that is certainly important, it is also, I think, potentially misleading as a total approach.

We must not, I believe, lose sight of the fact that language *is* a major problem in second language reading, and that even educated guessing at meaning is no substitute for accurate decoding.

Let me give you an example of what I mean. In their groundbreaking study of cohesion in English, Halliday and Hasan (1976) cite the following two lines of text from a cookbook:

Wash and core six cooking apples. Put them into a fireproof dish.

They note that the pronoun *them* in this example functions as a simple cohesive device: it refers to the noun phrase *six cooking apples* and thus helps to link the second sentence to the first. All this seems straightforward enough, but a leading second language reading researcher (Carrell 1982) rejects it, citing Morgan and Sellner (1980), who approach the comprehension of written texts as a purely top-down phenomenon. Carrell notes that Morgan and Sellner ask how we can know what *them* refers to in this text:

What leads to the conclusion that *them*, in fact, is intended to refer to the apples and not, say, the author's children, or the pages of the cookbook, or anything else for that matter? It is our background knowledge of cooking and of the author's purpose, as well as our ability to reason, and the assumption that the recipe is coherent. Without this latter assumption, there would be no way of knowing what *them* is intended to refer to. As Morgan and Sellner argue, it is precisely because we assume the text is coherent that we infer that *them* is intended to refer to apples. Halliday and Hasan have misconstrued all their examples in exactly the same way, say Morgan and Sellner, by taking certain aspects of linguistic form as the cause, and not the effect, of coherence. (Carrell 1982: 483–484)

But I find this line of thought unconvincing in its total disregard for the extent to which the rules of language structure meaning. The notion

---

3 I am indebted to Peg Griffin for the phrase and my title.

that simple pronoun reference is determined by a series of pragmatic inferences seems to me a clear example of overrating the importance – or at least the scope – of top-down cognitive processes. It is also, I think, fairly easy to refute. Consider, for example, this very similar text. I can provide you with no context since I have none in mind:

Take three stiggles. Stick them in your ear.

Since none of us, including me, knows what a *stiggle* is, and there is virtually no context to provide us with a hint, we have no extra-linguistic motivation for assuming that the pronoun *them* refers to *stiggles*, but we all know that it does because we all know the language, and the structure of the language *dictates* that it does. Or consider this:

Slowly sinking in the west, we admired the blood-red sun.

So-called dangling participles like this one would not elicit smiles if all we had to do was assign the participle to whatever noun our knowledge of the world tells us is the right one. In this case, two sources of the knowledge we need (knowledge of the grammar and knowledge of the real world) to comprehend this short text bump into each other instead of interacting, thereby generating the humorous effect. However, for me at least, the grammar comes through first, which suggests that the structure of the language of the text contributes much more to the reader's reconstruction of meaning than strictly top-down theorists would have us believe.

What all this adds up to may be summarized as follows. Fluent reading entails both skillful decoding and relating the information so obtained to the reader's prior knowledge of the subject and the world. Thus the fluent reader is characterized by *both* skill at rapid, context-free word and phrase recognition and, at higher cognitive levels, the skillful use of appropriate comprehension strategies. For the proper interpretation of texts the latter skills are crucial, but such lower-level skills as the rapid and accurate identification of lexical and grammatical forms are not merely obstacles to be cleared on the way to higher-level "guessing game" strategies, but skills to be mastered as a necessary means of taking much of the guesswork out of reading comprehension. An interactive model of reading provides the most convincing account of this reciprocal perceptual/cognitive process.

For second language teachers, this interactive model has important implications in relation to curriculum, methods, and materials – implications we have just begun to explore. If we can no longer afford to teach reading as a kind of linguistic analysis, we also cannot afford to teach it as a kind of cued speculation. One practical problem that remains, in any case, is that no model can determine what mix of skills and strategies second language readers in general employ, let alone the mix for particular readers. These are empirical questions of the kind that neither models nor research can ever fully resolve — the kind of questions that good teachers learn to work around, in the absence of perfect knowledge of their students, by means of patience, concern, and good judgment, in helping those students to learn how to help themselves. A major virtue of the interactive model, however, is that it does direct our attention to *both* the top-down and bottom-up skills that fluent and accurate reading demands.

References

Carrell, P. L. 1982. Cohesion is not coherence. *TESOL Quarterly* 16: 479–488.
    1984. The effects of rhetorical organization on ESL readers. *TESOL Quarterly* 18: 441–469.
Carrell, P. L., and J. C. Eisterhold. 1983. Schema theory and ESL reading pedagogy. *TESOL Quarterly* 17: 553–573. [Reprinted as Chapter 5 in this volume.]
Clarke, M. A. 1979. Reading in Spanish and English: evidence from adult ESL students. *Language Learning* 29: 121–150.
    1980. The short circuit hypothesis of ESL reading. *Modern Language Journal* 64: 203–209. [Reprinted as Chapter 8 in this volume.]
Eskey, D. E. 1973. A model program for teaching advanced reading to students of English as a foreign language. *Language Learning* 23: 169–184.
Fries, C. C. 1945. *Teaching and learning English as a foreign language.* Ann Arbor: University of Michigan Press.
Goodman, K. S. 1967. Reading: a psycholinguistic guessing game. *Journal of the Reading Specialist* 4: 126–135.
    1970. Psycholinguistic universals in the reading process. *Journal of Typographic Research* 4: 103–110.
    1981. Letter to the editor. *Reading Research Quarterly* 16: 477–478.
Halliday, M. A. K., and R. Hasan. 1976. *Cohesion in English.* London: Longman.
Johnson, P. 1981. Effects on reading comprehension of language complexity and cultural background of a text. *TESOL Quarterly* 15: 169–181.
    1982. Effects on reading comprehension of building background knowledge. *TESOL Quarterly* 16: 503–516.
Lesgold, A. M., and C. A. Perfetti (Eds.). 1981. *Interactive processes in reading.* Hillsdale, N.J.: Erlbaum.
McClelland, J. L., and D. E. Rumelhart. 1981. An interactive activation model of context effects in letter perception. *Psychological Review* 88: 375–407.
Morgan, J. L., and M. B. Sellner. 1980. Discourse and linguistic theory. In *Theoretical issues in reading comprehension,* R. J. Spiro, B. C. Bertram, and W. F. Brewer (Eds.). Hillsdale, N.J.: Erlbaum.
Neely, J. H. 1977. Semantic priming and retrieval from lexical memory roles of inhibitionless spreading activation and limited capacity attention. *Journal of Experimental Psychology: General* 106: 226–254.
Perkins, K. 1983. Semantic constructivity in ESL reading comprehension. *TESOL Quarterly* 17: 19–27.

Rumelhart, D. E. 1977. Toward an interactive model of reading. In *Attention and performance*, Vol. VI, S. Dornic (Ed.), 573–603. New York: Academic Press.

Smith, F. 1982. *Understanding reading*, 3rd ed. New York: Holt, Rinehart and Winston.

Stanovich, K. E. 1980. Toward an interactive-compensatory model of individual differences in the development of reading fluency. *Reading Research Quarterly* 16: 32–71.

7 Some causes of text-boundedness and schema interference in ESL reading

Patricia L. Carrell

Recent developments in the theory of knowledge representation, going under the general rubric of *schema theory* (Bartlett 1932; Anderson 1977; Adams and Collins 1979; Rumelhart and Ortony 1977; Rumelhart 1980), have had a pervasive influence on current thinking about text comprehension. Through an emphasis on the role of preexisting knowledge structures in providing information left implicit in text, schema-theoretic approaches have made possible the fairly detailed modeling of many of the active, constructive processes necessary to comprehension (e.g., Schank and Abelson 1977). Within the schema-theoretic framework, text comprehension, or more specifically for our purposes, reading comprehension, is characterized as involving an interaction of text-based processes and knowledge-based processes, the latter related to the reader's existing background or schemata (Adams and Collins 1979; Anderson 1977; Rumelhart 1977, 1980; Rumelhart and Ortony 1977; Carrell and Eisterhold 1983, reprinted as Chapter 5 in this volume; and Anderson and Pearson 1984, reprinted as Chapter 3 in this volume).

Schema-theory research has shown that the most efficient processing of text is interactive – a combination of top-down and bottom-up processing modes (Rumelhart 1977, 1980). Top-down processing is the making of predictions about the text based on prior experience or background knowledge, and then checking the text for confirmation or refutation of those predictions. Bottom-up processing is decoding individual linguistic units (e.g., phonemes, graphemes, words) and building textual meaning from the smallest units to the largest, and then modifying preexisting background knowledge and current predictions on the basis of information encountered in the text. Skilled readers constantly shift their mode of processing, accommodating to the demands of a particular text and a particular reading situation; less skilled readers tend to overrely on processes in one direction, producing deleterious effects on comprehension (Spiro 1978, 1979).

This chapter explores the bidirectionality of text-based and knowledge-based processing of text in ESL reading comprehension. Specifically, some factors are discussed that may interfere with efficient bidirectional text processing and cause overreliance on one or the other mode of processing, which may, in turn, result in comprehension problems. Overreliance on text-based or bottom-up processing will be referred to as *text-biased* processing or *text-boundedness*, and overreliance on knowledge-based or top-down processing as *knowledge-biased* processing, or *schema interference.*

In order to illustrate overreliance on text-based processing and knowledge-based processing, consider the following sample text from Fillmore (1981). Imagine the reader who encounters the following minitext:

The princess ate some jam.
The queen slapped her.
The princess began to cry.

The text-based processing of this text involves decoding the individual words and their lexical meanings, and decoding the syntactic structures of each sentence and their grammatical-functional meanings as subjects, direct objects, etc. Fillmore calls this the E–0 level of envisionment, E–0 level processing. If this text-based processing were the only kind of processing going on, one would understand from this text only that somebody who is a princess ate some jam, and someone who is a queen slapped a female being, and somebody who is a princess cried. If, however, in reading the three sentences, knowledge-based processing is successfully invoked, readers would assume that they were dealing with a cohesive, coherent text, rather than three separate sentences. Fillmore calls this level E–1 of envisionment. So readers might assume that the princess in sentences 1 and 3 and the *her* in sentence 2 all refer to the same person. If the readers engage in yet further knowledge-based processing, they might invoke a royal family schema and assume the queen in sentence 2 is the princess's mother. At a still higher level of knowledge-based processing, Fillmore's level E–2 of envisionment, readers might interpret the text in terms of their knowledge of human goals, institutions, and human nature. They might make sense of what is going on in the text by assuming that the queen's act of slapping the princess is related to the princess's having eaten the jam (e.g., as punishment), and assume the princess's tears are in response to the slap (e.g., showing pain, remorse, shame). So far, these knowledge-based assumptions about the text seem well-motivated by the text and general, conventional knowledge about human behavior. In fact, they seem to be the kinds of knowledge-based assumptions we feel the writer must have intended the readers to make in order to understand the text. However, readers might do additional knowledge-based processing of the text (Fillmore's level E–3 envisionment) and fill in details not motivated by the text itself or by general conventional knowledge. Readers might inject their own personal experiences or assumptions about human behavior and assume, for example, that the queen was selfish and had wanted the jam herself, or that the jam was plum-flavored. If readers engage in much of this latter type of knowledge-based processing, we have an overreliance on knowledge-based processing. To summarize, Fillmore's various levels of envisionment appear to correspond as follows to different kinds of processing:

E–0   text-based processing only
E–1 and E–2   text-based processing and knowledge-based processing
E–3   knowledge-based processing only

Recent studies of ESL reading (Carrell 1983a; Carrell and Wallace 1983) have found that ESL readers may not effectively utilize knowledge-based processes; specifically they may not utilize contextual information they are supplied with, to facilitate comprehension. They seem to engage almost exclusively in text-based processing to the detriment of comprehension.

By contrast, other studies of ESL reading have found what appears to be evidence of overreliance on or interference from top-down or knowledge-based processes. Relevant here are studies by Steffensen, Joag-dev, and Anderson (1979), Johnson (1981), and Carrell (1981) which have shown the effects of culturally biased content schemata.

What causes such unidirectional biases in text processing, especially in reading in a second language? Although we do not know the answer to this question with much certainty, some causes can be hypothesized for the breakdown of bidirectional processing and the overreliance on unidirectional processing in ESL reading. In the remainder of this chapter, these causes are grouped and discussed under the following headings: (1) schema availability, (2) schema activation, (3) skill deficiencies, including deficiencies in reading skills, as well as linguistic deficiencies, (4) misconceptions about reading, specifically about reading in a second language and especially in a second language classroom where reading evaluation is involved, and (5) individual differences in cognitive styles. Identifying and discussing these five causes of overreliance on text-based or knowledge-based reading is not intended to imply that this list is exhaustive or that the causes are mutually exclusive.

Schema availability

The most obvious cause of overreliance on the text in comprehension is the absence of relevant knowledge structures to utilize in top-down processing; if the schemata do not exist for the reader they cannot be used. However much the vocabulary and syntax of a highly technical or scientific text are simplified, it is unlikely that any reader (adult, child, native or nonnative) will comprehend it without first acquiring the requisite background of scientific knowledge. (Isn't this why my psycholinguistics students say they really understand their textbook only after they've had the whole course? They understand the early chapters much better after they've gotton more background from the entire course. And how many of us can say that we really understood Chomsky's *Aspects* [1965] until after the second or third reading?)

In seeking to understand the role of schema availability in ESL reading comprehension, it is often useful to draw a distinction between *formal* schemata (background knowledge of the formal rhetorical organizational structure of the text) and *content* schemata (background knowledge of the content area of the text) (Carrell 1983b). In other words, one type of schema a reader needs to possess in order to comprehend a text is background knowledge about rhetorical organization, for example, differences in the structure of fables, short stories, newspaper articles, poetry, and expository text types. The other type of schema a reader needs to possess is background knowledge about the content area of a text, for example, information about physics, Greek mythology, Black American culture, or the political situation in Afghanistan.

As Carrell and Eisterhold (1983) argue, one of the most obvious reasons a particular content schema may fail to exist for a reader is that the schema is culture-specific. Studies by Steffensen et al. (1979), Johnson (1981), and Carrell (1981) have all shown that implicit cultural content knowledge presupposed by a text and a reader's own cultural background knowledge of content interact to make texts whose content is based on one's own culture easier to read and understand than syntactically and rhetorically equivalent texts based on a less familiar, distant culture.

Other research has shown general effects of content schemata on ESL reading comprehension. Johnson (1982) has shown that a text on a familiar topic is better recalled by ESL readers than a similar text on an unfamiliar topic. Alderson and Urquhart (1985, reprinted as Chapter 12 in this volume) have found a discipline-specific effect of familiar versus unfamiliar content background knowledge in measuring reading comprehension in English for specific purposes (ESP), in particular, English for science and technology (EST).

Fewer studies have been done showing the effects of formal schemata in ESL reading. However, some of the studies done in the area of contrastive rhetoric (Ostler and Kaplan 1982) reveal the effects of formal schemata on both the comprehension and production of written text in a second language. In particular, Hinds's research (1983a, b) shows the contrasting effects on different groups of readers of texts organized with a typical Japanese pattern and those organized with a typical American

English pattern. Carrell (1984) has shown the effects of different types of rhetorical organization of English expository prose on ESL readers of different native language backgrounds. The results in that study indicated that certain types of English rhetorical organization are more facilitative of recall for nonnative readers in general, but also that there are differences among the texts for the different native language groups targeted in the study: Spanish, Arabic, and Oriental (Korean and Chinese). It is speculated in that article – and I admit it is only speculation at this point – that one of the causes of these differences may be the absence of some of the different formal schemata among the different groups of ESL readers.

Thus, to summarize this section on schema availability, a number of empirical studies have shown that the absence of the content and formal schemata appropriate to a particular text can result in processing difficulties with that text. If ESL readers are not able to engage successfully in an appropriate degree of knowledge-based processing because they lack the appropriate content and/or formal schemata, they will resort to other strategies. Either they will overrely on text-based processes, and try to construct the meaning totally from the textual input (a virtual impossibility, because no text contains all the information necessary for its comprehension), or they will substitute the closest schema they possess and will try to relate the incoming textual information to that schema, resulting in schema interference. In either case, comprehension and recall suffer.

Schema activation

Of course, schema availability alone is not a sufficient condition for adequate comprehension. Relevant schemata must be activated (Carrell and Eisterhold 1983), although the processes by which schemata are evoked are not well understood.

The Carrell (1983a) and Carrell and Wallace (1983) studies previously mentioned showed that ESL reading comprehension may be affected not because the ESL readers lack the appropriate schema, but because they fail to activate the appropriate schema. In one part of the Carrell and Wallace (1983) study, advanced ESL readers were faced with a text about a familiar topic ("Brushing Your Teeth"), which did not contain sufficient textual (i.e., lexical) cues to signal the appropriate schema to be activated. (Such texts are called "opaque.") In postexperimental debriefing of subjects, prior familiarity with the text topic was determined to be 4.9 on a 5.0 scale; thus, we are certain that subjects possessed the appropriate schema for this text. However, for the advanced ESL readers of this text, there were no differences in their reading recall performance

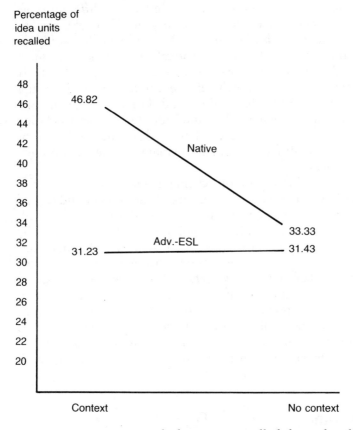

Figure 1   Percentage of idea units recalled from familiar but opaque texts by native and advanced ESL readers in context and no-context conditions (Carrell and Wallace 1983)

whether they were told the topic before reading or not (i.e., context or no context) (see Figure 1). That is, the vast majority of the ESL readers possessed the appropriate schema, and those in the context condition were even told which schema to activate. Yet, because the text itself failed to signal the appropriate schema, not only did those without context engage in text-based processing – the only possibility for that condition – but even those who were given the context before reading failed to access it to make the appropriate bidirectional linkages between the text and the context.[1]

---

1 Bransford, Stein, and Vye (1982) describe an interesting training/intervention technique they've used successfully to show fifth grade native readers of English that

Skill deficiencies

Two different but potentially related types of skill deficiencies may cause the inefficient interaction of text-based and knowledge-based processing in ESL reading: (1) linguistic deficiencies and (2) reading skill deficiencies. The important role of language competence in English for successful ESL reading is too obvious to warrant extended discussion here (see Eskey, Chapter 6 in this volume). Obviously, text-based processing cannot take place at all without appropriate skill levels in decoding the syntactic structures, and possibly more important, the content vocabulary of a text. More significant in this regard, Clarke's (1979; 1980, reprinted as Chapter 8 in this volume) research on native Spanish and ESL reading showed that second language proficiency may limit the transference of good L1 reading skills to reading in the second language. Thus, we must recognize the crucial role of English language skills in text-based processing. Without these skills, efficient interaction between text-based and knowledge-based processing cannot occur. However, as Hudson's (1982, reprinted as Chapter 13 in this volume) research showed, efficient knowledge-based processing can often compensate for lower proficiency levels in language.

Given the role of linguistic deficiencies, how might reading skills in the second language and the way these reading skills are manifested in a reading comprehension style affect efficient bidirectional interaction with text? Spiro (1978) argues for a two-level approach to this question. The first level concerns the various component skills of reading comprehension and deficiencies among these component skills; the second level concerns how reading skill deficiencies manifest themselves in a reading comprehension "style" (see Figure 2). Spiro argues that there is no determinate effect of the first level on the second; that is, different skill deficiencies may result in the same comprehension style, or one skill deficiency may result in differing comprehension styles. At the first level, reading problems may involve skills that are either predominantly text-based (e.g., decoding) or knowledge-based (e.g., pragmatic inferencing). Spiro reasons that two options are open to readers confronted with a skill problem of one of these two types: They may persevere in the problem area (with detrimental effects on the other process), or they may escape from the problem by shifting processing resources in an effort to compensate for the problem. For example, consider readers who are laborious, effortful decoders. They may persevere with their

knowledge activation can be a significant help in reading comprehension and in later recall from memory.

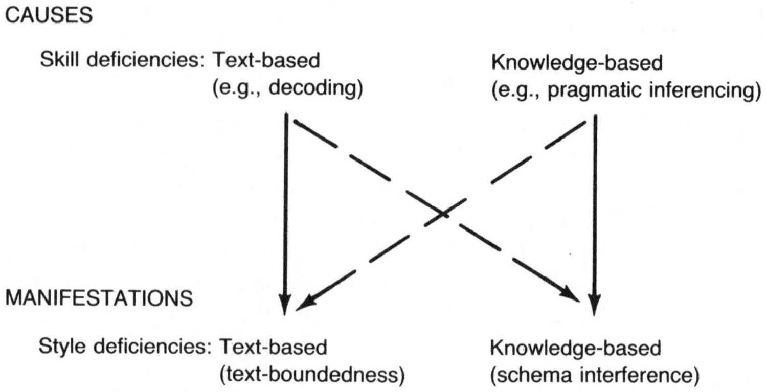

CAUSES

Skill deficiencies: Text-based   Knowledge-based
(e.g., decoding)   (e.g., pragmatic inferencing)

MANIFESTATIONS

Style deficiencies: Text-based   Knowledge-based
(text-boundedness)   (schema interference)

*Figure 2   Reading skill and reading style deficiencies. Solid lines =
perseverate; dashed lines = opt out.*

decoding efforts. However, given the limitations on information-processing capacity and short-term memory, this behavior soon produces a log-jam in the system – the reader attempts to store too many separate pieces of information without any higher-order relationship among them. In this style, higher-order knowledge-based processes are neglected. On the other hand, readers who are effortful decoders may seek (not necessarily consciously) to avoid the unpleasant decoding task. One way to do that would be to rely on prior knowledge to infer or guess what is likely to be in the text rather than actually sampling or processing much of the text. In this style, text-based processing is neglected in favor of wild guessing about the text's content. Thus, the same skill deficiency (effortful decoding) may lead to either one of two totally different comprehension styles – text-biased or knowledge-biased – depending on what the reader does in either persevering in the problem area or trying to escape from it. What this means is that the manifestation of a unidirectional reading comprehension style (text-biased or knowledge-biased) may be caused by two diametrically opposite reading skill deficiencies. The manifestation does not equal the cause.

Conceptions about reading

Some of the work with native English-speaking children's reading, especially in classroom and evaluative settings, suggests that children seem to think that knowledge-based processing is not an appropriate activity in reading (Fillmore 1981; Spiro 1979). They fail to correctly answer questions about text that require extra-textual knowledge. When informally interrogated, they are perfectly able to answer the same questions. If they are asked why they did not utilize the same knowledge to answer correctly after reading, they respond with remarks indicating they thought they were not supposed to. They suffer from what has been called a "meaning is in the text" fallacy (Spiro 1979). It is also interesting to note that for some children, this fallacy seems to apply only to their reading for school.

It is purely conjecture, for I know of no research on this question, but I wonder whether many of our ESL readers suffer from the same misconceptions about reading in ESL, especially in classroom settings where reading is often done for the teacher's purposes and not the students', and where reading comprehension is usually tested by question answering? And, if many ESL readers do misconceive ESL reading as primarily a bottom-up process, what causes such misconceptions? Possible candidates include overemphasis on decoding skills, and on the code in general, especially in early language and reading instruction; reading passages that are insular and lacking in relevance to existing knowledge and reader interests; and tests of reading that stress literal text content rather than its integration with related prior knowledge.

Cognitive style

Under the rubric of *cognitive style* I shall briefly mention one other possible cause of unidirectional processing. For some readers who underutilize prior knowledge in understanding text, the problem may transcend reading. It may be a matter of cognitive style. Similar to the way Brown (1987) has described the relationship of cognitive style to second language "learning" or "acquisition" style, cognitive style may relate to "comprehension" style. A reader's reading style may be part of a general cognitive style of processing any incoming information, regardless of the type of information or its modality of transmission. Text is an external stimulus with a structure; interactive reading requires that relevant internal knowledge structures be superimposed on the text. Those who are overly text-bound in reading situations may tend to be stimulus-bound in general.

Spiro (1978; Spiro and Tirre 1979) has studied the relationship between cognitive styles and reading comprehension for native English readers, using an embedded figures test. In an embedded figures test, a memorized geometric shape (an internal structure) must be located within a complex line and shading configuration in the visual field (an external stimulus structure). Spiro claims to have shown that those who have difficulty fitting the memorized internal structure onto the external stimulus structure in an embedded figures test also underutilize internal knowledge structures in reading comprehension (Spiro 1978; Spiro and Tirre 1979).

Kimmel and MacGinitie (1984) have identified a reading strategy they call "perseverative text processing," wherein native English readers make an interpretation prematurely based on only an initial sampling of the text, and neglect to revise it in line with further information. They fail to reevaluate their initial hypothesis. Such readers experience great difficulty with inductively organized material (main idea last). Based on their reading rates, however, it does not seem that these readers are reading only the first part of the text and failing to sample the rest of the text. They are able to recall as many words as nonperseverative readers, but their recalls show they have missed the main idea. They also exhibit this behavior on oral language comprehension tasks. Kimmel and MacGinitie have speculated that this behavior may be related to a more general construct underlying differences in the evaluation of hypotheses, namely an impulsivity-reflection dimension (Kagan 1965). That we may be encountering the same types of individual differences in ESL reading comprehension styles is suggested by the research of Hewett (1983, 1986). In her earlier research, Hewett (1983) found a relationship between reflectivity-impulsivity and second language reading; subjects who rated themselves more reflective than impulsive achieved significantly better reading scores. Her latest research (Hewett 1986) shows that of four possible components of the reflectivity-impulsivity construct, a component related to *persistence* appears to account for a significant amount of the variance. Furthermore, Hewett finds this encouraging, since persistence is one component of reflectivity-impulsivity that is subject to intervention and change.

Conclusion

In this chapter I have suggested five different kinds of causes for over-reliance on text-based or knowledge-based processing in ESL reading. Some of these have been more or less securely grounded in both theory and empirical research; others have been based on conjecture and supposition from schema theory and have yet to be empirically studied.

As researchers and educators it is important that we be aware not only that there are different maladaptive styles of reading comprehension – text-biased and knowledge biased – but it is even more important that we be aware of the *causes* of these styles. If the same reading comprehension style (text-biased or knowledge-biased) can be attributed to a multiplicity of causes across individuals (bearing in mind that the extent to which causes co-occur for individuals has not yet been determined), then how we approach instruction should most logically be determined by the cause and not by its manifestation. As in some aspects of health care, this would be a situation in which we would need to treat the underlying causes, not the overt symptoms. What is likely to help an ESL reader with a text bias that results from insufficient background knowledge (schema unavailability) will probably be different from what will help other readers with similar text biases that result from a misconception about ESL reading, or from a decoding problem, or from cognitive style biases.

References

Adams, M. J., and A. Collins. 1979. A schema-theoretic view of reading. In *New directions in discourse processing*, Roy O. Freedle (Ed.), 1–22. Norwood, N.J.: Ablex.

Alderson, J. C., and A. Urquhart. 1985. This test is unfair: I'm not an economist. In *Second language performance testing*, P. Hauptman, R. LeBlanc, and M. Bingham Wesche (Eds.), 25–43. Ottawa: University of Ottawa Press. [Reprinted as Chapter 12 in this volume.]

Anderson, R. C. 1977. The notion of schemata and the educational enterprise: general discussion of the conference. In *Schooling and the acquisition of knowledge*, R. C. Anderson, R. J. Spiro, and W. E. Montague (Eds.), 415–431. Hillsdale, N.J.: Erlbaum.

Anderson, R. C., and P. D. Pearson. 1984. A schema-theoretic view of basic processes in reading comprehension. In *Handbook of reading research*, P. D. Pearson (Ed.), 255–291. New York: Longman. [Reprinted as Chapter 3 in this volume.]

Bartlett, F. C. 1932. *Remembering: a study in experimental and social psychology*. Cambridge: Cambridge University Press.

Bransford, J. D., B. S. Stein, and N. J. Vye. 1982. Helping students learn how to learn from written texts. In *Competent reader, disabled reader: research and application*, M. H. Singer (Ed.), 141–150. Hillsdale, N.J.: Erlbaum.

Brown, H. D. 1987. *Principles of language learning and teaching*, 2nd ed. Englewood Cliffs, N.J.: Prentice-Hall.

Carrell, P. L. 1981. Culture-specific schemata in L2 comprehension. In *Selected papers from the ninth Illinois TESOL/BE annual convention, the first midwest TESOL conference*, R. Orem and J. Haskell (Eds.), 123–132. Chicago: Illinois TESOL/BE.

1983a. Three components of background knowledge in reading comprehension. *Language Learning* 33(2): 183–207.

1983b. Some issues in studying the role of schemata, or background knowledge, in second language comprehension. *Reading in a Foreign Language* 1(2): 81–92.

1984. The effects of rhetorical organization on ESL readers. *TESOL Quarterly* 18(3): 441–469.

Carrell, P. L., and J. C. Eisterhold. 1983. Schema theory and ESL reading pedagogy. *TESOL Quarterly* 17(4): 553–573. [Reprinted as Chapter 5 in this volume.]

Carrell, P. L., and B. Wallace. 1983. Background knowledge: context and familiarity in reading comprehension. In *On TESOL '82*, M. Clarke and J. Handscombe (Eds.), 295–308. Washington, D.C.: TESOL.

Chomsky, N. 1965. *Aspects of the theory of syntax*. Cambridge, Mass.: MIT Press.

Clarke, M. A. 1979. Reading in Spanish and English: evidence from adult ESL students. *Language Learning* 29(1): 121–150.

1980. The short-circuit hypothesis of ESL reading – or when language competence interferes with reading performance. *Modern Language Journal* 64(2): 203–209. [Reprinted as Chapter 8 in this volume.]

Fillmore, C. J. 1981. Ideal readers and real readers. In *Georgetown University Roundtable on Languages and Linguistics 1981*, D. Tannen (Ed.), 248–270. Washington, D.C.: Georgetown University Press.

Hewett, N. M. 1983. *Cultural variables and impulsivity in second-language-reading acquisition*. Ann Arbor: University Microfilms.

1986. Reading and impulsivity: a look at some relationships in L2 acquisition – persistence pays. Paper presented at the 20th Annual Convention of TESOL, March 1986.

Hinds, J. L. 1983a. Retention of information using a Japanese style of presentation. Paper presented at the 17th Annual Convention of TESOL, Toronto, Canada, March 1983.

1983b. Contrastive rhetoric: Japanese and English. *Text* 3(2): 183–195.

Hudson, T. 1982. The effects of induced schemata on the "short circuit" in L2 reading: non-decoding factors in L2 reading performance. *Language Learning* 32(1): 1–31. [Reprinted as Chapter 13 in this volume.]

Johnson, P. 1981. Effects on reading comprehension of language complexity and cultural background of a text. *TESOL Quarterly* 15(2): 169–181.

1982. Effects on reading comprehension of building background knowledge. *TESOL Quarterly* 16(4): 503–516.

Kagan, J. 1965. Reflection-impulsivity and reading ability in primary grade children. *Child Development* 36(3): 609–628.

Kimmel, S., and W. H. MacGinitie. 1984. Identifying children who use a perseverative text processing strategy. *Reading Research Quarterly* 19(2): 162–172.

Ostler, S. E., and R. B. Kaplan. 1982. Contrastive rhetoric revisited. Paper presented at the 16th Annual Convention of TESOL, Honolulu, Hawaii, May 1982.

Rumelhart, D. E. 1977. Toward an interactive model of reading. In *Attention and performance*, Vol. VI, S. Dornic (Ed.), 573–603. New York: Academic Press.

1980. Schemata: the building blocks of cognition. In *Theoretical issues in reading comprehension*, R. J. Spiro, B. C. Bruce, and W. F. Brewer (Eds.), 33–58. Hillsdale, N.J.: Erlbaum.

Rumelhart, D. E., and A. Ortony. 1977. The representation of knowledge in memory. In *Schooling and the acquisition of knowledge*, R. C. Anderson, R. J. Spiro, and W. E. Montague (Eds.), 99–135. Hillsdale, N.J.: Erlbaum.

Schank, R. C., and R. P. Abelson. 1977. *Scripts, plans, goals, and understanding*. Hillsdale, N.J.: Erlbaum.

Spiro, R. J. 1978. Beyond schema availability. Paper presented at the Annual

Meeting of the National Reading Conference, St. Petersburg, December 1978.

1979. Etiology of reading comprehension style. In *Reading research: studies and applications*, M. L. Kamil and A. J. Moe (Eds.), 118–122. Clemson, S. C.: National Reading Conference.

Spiro, R. J., and W. C. Tirre. 1979. Individual differences in schema utilization during discourse processing. *Technical Report No. 111*. Champaign, Ill.: Center for the Study of Reading, University of Illinois.

Steffensen, M. S., C. Joag-dev, and R. C. Anderson. 1979. A cross-cultural perspective on reading comprehension. *Reading Research Quarterly* 15(1): 10–29.

8 The short circuit hypothesis of ESL reading – or when language competence interferes with reading performance

Mark A. Clarke

Reading is perhaps the most thoroughly studied and least understood process in education today. In spite of a multitude of books and journals devoted to the study and the teaching of reading, no theory of reading has won general acceptance. The quantity and variety of theoretical models of reading in the first language (L1) has resulted in a great amount of theoretical and pedagogical diversity among second language (L2) researchers and teachers (see, for example, Singer and Ruddell 1970). Recently a number of authors have cited the lack of a generally accepted theory of L2 reading as a major obstacle to teaching and testing ESL reading skills (see Eskey 1973; Harris 1976; Hatch 1973; Norris 1970; Robinett 1976). The following summary of ESL reading instruction is intended as a sampling of current practices rather than as an exhaustive account of the "state of the art."

In low-level ESL classes, students are presented with reading tasks only after they have oral/aural familiarity with the structures and vocabulary contained in the passages. Grammar and vocabulary work consumes most of the time and effort of teachers at this level. As students' command of English improves, they are usually eased into a familiar pattern of reading instruction characterized by: 1) an introduction to concepts, vocabulary, and structure contained in a reading, followed by 2) time (in or out of class) to read the assignment and answer comprehension questions, capped off by 3) class discussion/teacher explanation of the passage and comprehension exercises (see the following texts for typical recommendations: Finocchiaro 1974; Lado 1964; Mellgren and Walker 1973a, b; Slager 1966). Textbooks at the intermediate and advanced levels generally contain a wide variety of reading selections, but the tendency for exercises on vocabulary and grammar (see, for example, Baumwoll and Saitz 1965; Hirasawa and Markstein 1974) would seem to confirm Eskey's contention that ESL teaching at the intermediate and

Reprinted by permission from Mark A. Clarke, The short-circuit hypothesis of ESL reading–or when language competence interferes with reading performance, *Modern Language Journal* 64(2): 203–209. © *The Modern Language Journal.*

This paper is a revised and expanded version of a presentation given at the 1979 TESOL convention in Boston.

advanced levels is dominated by a "beginners model," one which emphasizes language instruction rather than reading instruction or, more accurately, language instruction through a medium of reading (Eskey 1973).

A number of articles and textbooks on ESL reading instruction have used psycholinguistic descriptions of the reading process as the foundation for methods and material development (Eskey 1973; Baudoin et al. 1977; Clarke and Silberstein 1977). Goodman's characterization of reading as a "psycholinguistic guessing game" is the most familiar description within this tradition (Goodman 1970). Goodman and others have adopted tenets of communication theory emphasizing the fact that proficient reading is an active process in which the reader produces hypotheses about the message of the text, then samples textual cues to confirm or reject those hypotheses (Cherry 1966; Miller 1967; Kolers 1969, 1973). These recent attempts to apply psycholinguistic principles to ESL reading instruction would seem to affirm Harris's and Yorkey's conviction that reading and study skills can be taught independently of language instruction (Harris 1966; Yorkey 1970). This approach to reading instruction relies on the (often implicit) assumption that reading is a process characterized by universals, that reading is basically the same in all languages.

The research reported here was developed, in part, to provide preliminary data on that assumption. The research questions addressed were: 1) Can the psycholinguistic perspective of reading explain the reading performance of proficient adult Spanish-speaking readers, reading in Spanish and English? 2) Do proficient L1 readers transfer their reading skills to the second language?

A detailed account of the research project is beyond the scope of this chapter; in the pages that follow, a summary of the results of two studies will be presented and implications for ESL reading teachers will be discussed (see Clarke 1978 for a detailed account of this research).

Reading in Spanish and English[1]

The two studies summarized here were developed as preliminary investigations into the reading behaviors of adults reading in two languages. Because of the detail with which the data were analyzed, it was not possible to study a large number of subjects; the results, therefore, are

---

1 The studies reported on here are part of a larger research project conducted while the author was at the University of Michigan. Special thanks for assistance in that project are due to H. Douglas Brown (now at San Francisco State University) and John A. Upshur.

suggestive rather than definitive. In the first study, the Spanish and English cloze test performances of good and poor L1 readers were examined. In the second study, the oral reading performances of a good and a poor L1 reader were analyzed. The former provide a description of group performance; the latter provide an in-depth analysis of the reading behaviors of individuals.

In the first study, twenty-one low-level ESL students (native Spanish speakers) were administered cloze tests in Spanish and in English.[2] "Good" and "poor" L1 readers were identified according to their performance on the Spanish cloze tests; the unacceptable cloze test responses (those responses receiving less than SYNAC 4, SEMAC 6) of these two groups of readers were then analyzed for syntactic and semantic acceptability according to the following scales:[3]

Syntactic Acceptability (SYNAC)

4: totally acceptable
3: acceptable in the sentence; the response satisfies sentence level constraints, but violates discourse constraints
2: acceptable only with the following portion of the sentence; from the response on, the sentence is syntactically acceptable
1: acceptable only with the preceding portion of the sentence; the sentence is syntactically acceptable up to and including the response
0: totally unacceptable

Semantic Acceptability (SEMAC)

6: totally acceptable
5: totally acceptable if minor syntactic constraints are ignored; the sentence and/or the response requires minor syntactic changes
4: acceptable in the sentence; the response violates passage-level meaning constraints
3: acceptable in the sentence if syntactic constraints are ignored; the sentence and/or the response require minor syntactic changes to become acceptable at the sentence level
2: acceptable only with the following portion of the sentence; from the response on, the sentence is semantically acceptable

2 "Low Level ESL students" were selected from sections 110 and 120 of the intensive English program of the English Language Institute, University of Michigan. Students are placed in these sections if they score between 0 and 30 on the *Michigan Placement Test*, M. Spaan and L. Strowe (Ann Arbor: Office of Testing and Administration, English Language Institute, Univ. of Michigan). The scores for the subjects of this study are provided in Clarke (1978: 126).
3 Space does not permit a detailed explanation of test development and administration, or of subsequent coding and analysis. A battery of three tests (taken from graded ESL readers) was used in order to provide a range of tasks on which each student could be expected to experience some success. Coding and analysis decisions were verified by independent judges. Details on research procedures are available in Clarke (1978). For details on code categories and coding instructions, see Clarke and Burdell (1977: 131–143).

TABLE 1. PERCENTAGE OF UNACCEPTABLE CLOZE TEST RESPONSES WHICH
WERE TOTALLY SYNTACTICALLY ACCEPTABLE (SYNAC 4)

	Spanish (%)	English (%)
Good L1 readers	35[a]	36[c]
Poor L1 readers	50[b]	36[d]

Note: Two pools of unacceptable responses were required for analysis. The best readers and the poorest readers were selected until two approximately equal pools of responses were identified for analysis. This procedure produced a Good Reader group of 8 subjects and a Poor Reader group of 6 subjects.
[a] 8 subjects, 68 responses
[b] 6 subjects, 124 responses
[c] 8 subjects, 124 responses
[d] 6 subjects, 157 responses

TABLE 2. PERCENTAGE OF UNACCEPTABLE CLOZE TEST RESPONSES WHICH
WERE SEMANTICALLY ACCEPTABLE WITH MINOR SYNTACTIC ERROR (SEMAC 5)

	Spanish (%)	English (%)
Good L1 readers	41[a]	22[c]
Poor L1 readers	25[b]	18[d]

Note: See note for Table 1; same procedures followed.
[a] 8 subjects, 68 responses
[b] 6 subjects, 124 responses
[c] 8 subjects, 129 responses
[d] 6 subjects, 157 responses

1: acceptable only with the preceding portion of the sentence; the sentence is semantically acceptable up to and including the response
0: totally unacceptable
9: doubtful; the response seems to fit the context, but it is impossible to determine the contextual motivation for it

The assumption was made that, in a cloze test, a response which is totally syntactically and semantically acceptable indicates that the subject has understood what s/he has read. Responses which are not acceptable provide evidence about the processes used by the reader in responding to a mutilated text. A second assumption was that good readers will use larger chunks of text in attempting to fill cloze test blanks than will poor readers, and that good readers will rely on semantic cues rather than syntactic cues (see Neville and Pugh 1976–7; Oller 1972, 1975). Finally, it was assumed that, given equivalent English proficiency, the difference between good and poor readers would be basically the same in both languages. Tables 1 and 2 present the results of the analysis of the unacceptable cloze test responses.

In their native language, the good readers seemed to rely on semantic

TABLE 3. PERCENTAGE OF MISCUES WHICH WERE TOTALLY SYNTACTICALLY
ACCEPTABLE (SYNAC 4)

	Spanish (%)	English (%)
Good L1 reader	52	54
Poor L1 reader	52	46
$n = 50$		

rather than syntactic cues. Forty-one percent of the unacceptable responses of the good readers were judged to be semantically acceptable with minor syntactic adjustments, compared to 25% for the poor readers. Table 1 shows that the poor readers relied on syntactic cues more than did the good readers (50% versus 35% syntactically acceptable).

In English, however, the picture changed. The use of syntactic cues by both good and poor readers was equal (36% – Table 1), and the advantage enjoyed by the good readers in producing semantically acceptable responses shrunk from 16 to 4 percentage points (41% and 25% in Spanish versus 22% and 18% in English – Table 2). The difficulties of reading in a second language seem to have reduced the distinction between good readers and poor readers.

In the second study, the oral reading performance in Spanish and English of a good L1 reader and a poor L1 reader were compared using standard miscue research procedures (Goodman and Burke 1973; Allen and Watson 1976). Miscue research procedures require subjects to read a passage in its entirety and to relate as much as they can remember after they have finished. The errors produced during the reading are analyzed on a number of linguistic levels and their comprehension score is calculated from their retelling.

The results obtained from the oral reading of the two subjects were similar to those obtained from the cloze test results. The good reader produced fewer miscues than did the poor reader in both Spanish and English; his/her miscues (in both languages) were of higher quality (i.e., either semantically acceptable or subsequently corrected), and the good reader was evaluated by independent judges to have understood more of both readings than did the poor reader. However, in each of these categories, the difference between the good reader and the poor reader diminished considerably in English as compared to Spanish. Of particular interest is a comparison of the syntactic and semantic acceptability of the miscues generated by both readers in Spanish and in English. Tables 3 and 4 present these results.

Note that in Spanish, the two readers showed equal dependence on syntactic use (52% totally acceptable – Table 3), while the good reader produced a much higher percentage of semantically acceptable miscues

TABLE 4. PERCENTAGE OF MISCUES WHICH WERE SEMANTICALLY ACCEPTABLE[a]

	Spanish (%)	English (%)
Good L1 reader	80	46
Poor L1 reader	64	38
$n = 50$		

[a] Semantically acceptable here indicates those miscues which were totally semantically acceptable (SEMAC 6) or acceptable if minor syntactic constraints are ignored (SEMAC 5).

(80% versus 64% – Table 4). This indicates that the good reader focused on the meaning of the text; he seemed far less concerned with the syntactic acceptability of this oral reading than with the semantic acceptability. The poor reader, on the other hand, while producing the same percentage of syntactically acceptable miscues, did not produce as many semantically acceptable miscues.

In English, the picture changed dramatically. The good reader produced a higher percentage of syntactically acceptable miscues than did the poor reader (54% versus 46%) and his advantage in producing semantically acceptable miscues slipped from 16 percentage points in Spanish to 8 percentage points in English (80% and 64% in Spanish versus 46% and 38% in English). The good L1 reader appeared less able to focus on semantic cues in the target language than in the native language.

The short circuit hypothesis

The studies summarized here indicate that the psycholinguistic perspective of reading can account for the reading behaviors of proficient adult Spanish-speaking readers reading in Spanish and in English. In both languages, and in both cloze tasks and oral readings, these subjects seemed to utilize the same basic behaviors of sampling linguistic cues. For them, as for the subjects of previous studies (Goodman and Burke 1973; Rigg 1977; Sims 1972), reading is not an exact process which depends on accuracy at all levels of language but rather, it seems to be a process of hypothesizing, testing, confirming, rejecting.

With regard to the second research question addressed by the studies – do proficient L1 readers transfer their skills to the target language? – the results are not as conclusive. There is some transfer of skills, for the good readers perform better than the poor readers in both languages, but limited language proficiency appears to exert a powerful effect on the behaviors utilized by the readers. The results of these studies suggest that, while some form of the "universals hypothesis" may be justified, the role of language proficiency may be greater than has previously been assumed; apparently, limited control over the language "short circuits" the good reader's system causing him/her to revert to poor reader strategies when confronted with a difficult or confusing task in the second language. This suggests that it may be inaccurate to speak of "good readers" and "poor readers." Perhaps there are not "good readers" and "poor readers" but merely "good" and "poor" reading behaviors which characterize most readers at different times; when one is confronted with difficult reading (whether because of complex language or unfamiliar content) one is likely to revert to poor reading behaviors.

What implications does the "short circuit hypothesis" have for ESL reading teachers? The research summarized here would seem to support psycholinguistics as a model for curriculum planning and methods and materials development, at least for Spanish-speaking ESL students. It would seem justifiable to develop reading programs which this and previous research show to be characteristic of good readers. Among the behaviors which appear most productive and which might be effectively taught are: concentration on passage-level semantic cues; the formulation of hypotheses about the text before reading, then reading to confirm, refine or reject those hypotheses; the deemphasis of graphophonic and syntactic accuracy, that is, developing a tolerance for inexactness, a willingness to take chances and make mistakes.

On the other hand, the results of these studies underscore the importance of language skills for effective reading. This finding supports the activities of "traditional" teachers (Lado 1964; Finocchiaro 1974) whose approach to teaching reading emphasized grammar lessons and vocabulary instruction, as well as recent attempts to integrate reading skills and language development (Baudoin et al. 1977; Eskey 1973; Clarke and Silberstein 1977). The dilemma for ESL reading teachers is one of attempting to provide students with a "global" view of the task – by emphasizing the inexact nature of reading, the need for guessing, taking chances, etc. – while at the same time helping them to acquire the fundamental language skills to facilitate the process. Attempting to teach students to use the phonological, morphological, syntactic, semantic, and discourse cues of the language before they have learned what they are, how and when they occur, and their contexual variations, seems unrealistic. Yet, the familiar example of the student who knows all the words and grammatical structures of a sentence or paragraph and yet cannot comprehend what s/he has read is the result of learning the elements of the language without understanding the processes which one utilizes to communicate with those elements. In other words, ESL reading teachers must emphasize both the *psycho* and the *linguistic*.

Another implication of the "short circuit hypothesis" concerns the diagnosis of ESL readers' problems. It is possible that two students with comparable L2 proficiency could produce similar L2 reading behaviors for different reasons: one, because s/he is a poor reader and the other because s/he has not been able to transfer his/her L1 reading skills to the target language. Consider the cloze test at the end of this chapter and the responses produced by two subjects from the studies reported here. A teacher might give a test such as this to an ESL reading class for diagnostic and placement purposes. On the basis of the responses provided by Reader 1 and Reader 2, the teacher would seem justified in considering the two students as relatively equal in reading ability (their English proficiency test performance indicated comparable L2 competence), requiring, therefore, basically the same instruction. (Reader 1 received an exact score of 4/11 and an acceptable score of 8/11 if items 1, 7, 10, 11 are accepted. Reader 2 received an exact score of 5/11 and an acceptable score of 7/11 if items 7 and 11 are accepted.)

In fact, Reader 1 is the "good reader" in the miscue study summarized above and Reader 2 is the "poor reader." Their cloze test and oral reading performances in Spanish indicate that they are of vastly different L1 reading abilities, yet their ESL cloze performance fails to distinguish them. While both students require more language instruction, the nature of the reading instruction which each requires is markedly different. Reader 1 is a good reader in his native language; perhaps all he needs is to be "reminded" of reading strategies which he used in Spanish. Reader 2, on the other hand, would seem to require more fundamental instruction in how to read effectively.

It is unrealistic to suggest that the teacher produce different materials or methods for students such as these (providing, of course, that s/he was aware of the source of their respective problems), but an awareness of the potential explanations for students' reading problems would certainly increase the teacher's sensitivity and, therefore, increase the chances of helping the students overcome their difficulties. By systematically integrating language-focused instruction with reading-skills development the teacher would be most likely to meet the needs of both types of students.

Sample diagnostic cloze test

"Grandfather's Ride Home"[a]

Mrs. Brown's grandfather lives with her. Every morning he goes for a walk in the park. He comes home about noon to eat his lunch. One morning a police car

[a]Adapted from L. A. Hill, "Grandfather's Ride Home," in *Stories for Reproduction: Elementary* (London: Oxford University Press, 1965), p. 9.

122   *Mark A. Clarke*

stopped outside (1) _Mrs._ Brown's house at 12:00 and two (2) _policemen_
helped the old man to the house. (3) _One_ of the policemen said to Mrs.
Brown, "The poor (4) _old_ gentleman lost his way in the (5) _park_ and
telephoned the police station for help, so they (6) _sent_ us to bring him home."
Mrs. Brown was very (7) _surprised_ but she thanked the policemen and they
left.

"But (8) _Grandfather_," she said, "you have been to that (9) _park_ nearly
every day for twenty years. How (10) _did_ you get lost there?"

The old (11) _gentleman_ smiled, winked, and said, "I didn't exactly lose my
way. I just got tired and didn't want to walk home."

Reader 1[b]	*Reader 2[b]*
1. of	1.
2.	2. policeman
3.	3.
4.	4.
5. morning	5.
6. call	6. help
7. worried	7. worried
8.	8. after
9. for	9. 0
10. can	10.
11. father	11. man

References

Allen, D. P. and D. Watson. 1976. *Findings of research in miscue analysis.*
Champaign-Urbana: ERIC-NCTE.
Baudoin, E. M. G., M. A. Clarke, B. Dobson, and S. V. Silberstein. 1977. *Reader's choice: A reading skills textbook for students of English as a second language.* Ann Arbor: University of Michigan Press.
Baumwoll, D., and R. L. Saitz. 1965. *Advanced reading and writing.* New York: Holt, Rinehart.
Cherry, C. 1966. *On human communication.* Cambridge, Mass.: MIT Press.
Clarke, M. A. 1978. Reading in Spanish and English: the performance of selected adult ESL students, Ph.D. diss., University of Michigan.
1979. Reading in Spanish and English. *Language Learning* 29: 121–150.
Clarke, M. A., and L. Burdell. 1977. Shades of meaning: syntactic and semantic parameters of cloze test responses. In *Teaching and learning: trends in research and practice (On TESOL '77)*, H. D. Brown, C. A. Yorio, and R. H. Crymes (Eds.), 131–143. Washington, D.C.: TESOL.
Clarke, M. A., and S. V. Silberstein. 1977. Towards a realization of psycholinguistic principles in the ESL reading class. *Language Learning* 27: 135–154.

[b]Numbers that have no word next to them indicate that the subject produced the exact response for that blank. The symbol 0 indicates no response provided by the subject.

Eskey, D. E. 1973. A model program for teaching advanced reading to students of EFL. *Language Learning* 23: 169–184.

Finocchiaro, M. 1974. *English as a second language: from theory to practice.* New York: Regents.

Goodman, K. S. 1970. Reading: a psycholinguistic guessing game. In *Theoretical models and the process of reading*, H. Singer and R. B. Ruddell (Eds.), 259–271. Newark, Del.: International Reading Association.

Goodman, K. S., and C. Burke, 1973. *Theoretically based studies of patterns of miscues in oral reading performance.* Washington, D.C.: Department of HEW, Office of Education.

Harris, D. P. 1966. *Reading improvement exercises for students of English as a second language.* N.J.: Prentice-Hall.

1976. Testing reading comprehension in ESL: background and current state of the art. In *Papers in ESL: selected conference papers of the Association of TESL*, J. Morley (Ed.). Washington, D.C.: NAFSA.

Hatch, E. 1973. Research on reading a second language. *UCLA Workpapers in Teaching English as a Second Language* 7: 1–10.

Hirasawa, C., and L. Markstein. 1974. *Developing reading skills: advanced.* Rowley, Mass.: Newbury House.

Kolers, P. A. 1969. Reading is only incidentally visual. In *Psycholinguistics and the teaching of reading*, K. S. Goodman and J. T. Fleming (Eds.), 8–16. Newark, Del.: International Reading Association.

1973. Reading temporally and spatially transformed texts. In *The psycholinguistic nature of reading*, K. S. Goodman (Ed.), 29–40. Detroit: Wayne State University Press.

Lado, R. 1964. *Language teaching.* New York: McGraw-Hill.

Mellgren, L., and M. Walker. 1973a. Meet Don Rogers. In *New horizons*, Book 2. Menlo Park, Calif.: Addison-Wesley.

1973b. My summer vacation. In *New horizons*, Book 3. Menlo Park, Calif.: Addison-Wesley.

Miller, G. A. 1967. The magical number seven, plus or minus two: some limits on our capacity to process information. In *The psychology of communication*, 14–43. New York: Basic Books.

Neville, M. H., and A. K. Pugh. 1976–7. Context in reading and listening variations in approach to cloze tasks. *Reading Research Quarterly* 12: 13–31.

Norris, W. E. 1970. Teaching second language reading at the advanced level: goals, techniques, procedures. *TESOL Quarterly* 4: 17–35.

Oller, J. W. 1972. Scoring methods and difficulty levels for cloze tests of ESL proficiency. *Modern Language Journal* 56: 151–158.

1975. Cloze, discourse, and approximations to English. In *On TESOL '75*, M. K. Burt and H. C. Dulay (Eds.), 345–355. Washington, D.C.: TESOL.

Rigg, P. 1977. Reading in ESL. In *On TESOL '76*, J. Fanselow and R. Crymes (Eds.). Washington, D.C.: TESOL.

Robinett, B. J. W. 1976. Reading English as a second language. In *Papers in ESL: selected papers from the Association of TEFL*, 61–78. Washington, D.C.: NAFSA.

Sims, R. 1972. A psycholinguistic description of miscues generated by young readers during the oral reading of text material in black dialect and standard English. Ph. D. diss., Wayne State University.

Singer, H., and R. B. Ruddell (Eds.). 1970. *Theoretical models and processes of reading.* Newark, Del.: International Reading Association.

Slager, W. R. (Ed.). 1966. *English for today.* New York: McGraw- Hill.

Yorkey, R. C. 1970. *Study skills for students of English as a second language.* New York: McGraw-Hill.

PART III:
INTERACTIVE APPROACHES TO SECOND LANGUAGE READING – EMPIRICAL STUDIES

The chapters in this section present a number of empirical studies which have been conducted investigating various aspects of interactive second language reading. Devine's chapter investigates a theme presented in Carrell, Chapter 7, namely the role of the second language reader's conception, or "model," of reading and its relation to reading performance. Her study shows how the way a reader conceptualizes the reading process is directly related to different types of reading performance.

The chapter by Steffensen investigates the relationship between cohesion and coherence in terms of second language readers' recalls of culturally familiar and unfamiliar texts. The question explored is whether coherent recalls, based upon relatively secure reading comprehension of a culturally familiar text, are necessarily more highly cohesive than less coherent recalls, based upon less secure reading comprehension of culturally unfamiliar text. Steffensen's negative findings suggest that although there are differences in reading comprehension due to the interaction of readers' prior cultural familiarity, these are not necessarily revealed by tallying explicit cohesive ties in the surface structure of recall protocols. Explicit cohesion is not necessarily an indication of comprehension. Rather, Steffensen's findings suggest that other means of text analysis are called for in order to measure the "coherence" of reading comprehension as revealed in recall protocols.

The chapters by Cohen et al. and Alderson and Urquhart both present empirical investigations of the interactive nature of second language reading in the domain of English for special purposes (ESP), or more specifically, English for science and technology (EST). The Cohen et al. chapter reports a number of similarities across second language readers from different disciplines in relation to textual properties which cause difficulties in interactive reading. Thus, in terms of the interaction of reader with text, Cohen et al. reveals a number of specific text properties that apparently cause reading difficulties for readers from different disciplines. The Alderson and Urquhart chapter, on the other hand, explores the interaction between a reader's background knowledge of the discipline and the type of discipline-specific information demanded by the text. While incidentally questioning whether there are such things as "general purpose" texts that don't demand specialized information which readers may have in varying degrees, they find that discipline-specific information possessed by the second language reader dramatically interacts with the discipline-specific nature of the text to affect reading performance. Thus, these two chapters show the multifaceted nature of interactive second language reading in ESP/EST.

The chapter by Hudson empirically investigates Clarke's so-called short circuit hypothesis (Chapter 8) and demonstrates the interrelationship of language proficiency and background knowledge in second language reading. Hudson's results show that while proficiency in the second language may set limits on reading performance, relevant background knowledge possessed by the reader may interact with that language ability to facilitate reading comprehension.

Finally in this section, the chapter by Rigg applies Goodman's (Chapter 1) miscue analysis technique to empirical investigation of second language reading. Rigg not only shows how miscue analysis can reveal aspects of the interaction of reader and text, but she also touches on some important ways in which miscue analysis applied to second language reading differs from its application to first language reading. Rigg's discussion of the need to distinguish "dialect" miscues from "reading" miscues, and of the relationship between language proficiency and reading proficiency, is further development of the theme previously found in Chapters 6, 7, 8, and 13 (Eskey, Carrell, Clarke, and Hudson), on language proficiency versus reading proficiency.

In reading the chapters in this section, the reader may want to bear in mind the following questions: (1) What are some of the different ways a second language reader may conceptualize the reading process and how are these related to reading behavior? (2) What are the specific properties of certain types of texts, for example, scientific texts, that affect the interaction of a second language reader with such texts? (3) How does discipline expertise affect second language reading? (4) How may background knowledge and second language proficiency interact to offset limited second language skills? (5) What does the evidence from oral miscue analysis indicate about second language reading?

9 A case study of two readers: models of reading and reading performance

Joanne Devine

The current assumption underlying much of the work in ESL reading is that research in second language reading as well as instructional materials should be based on a clearly articulated and consistently applied model of the reading process (see, for example, Rigg 1977, reprinted as Chapter 14 in this volume, and 1981; Clarke and Silberstein 1977; Hudelson 1981; Renault 1981). A "model" might best be understood as a set of assumptions about what happens when a reader approaches a text, that is, the ways a reader derives meaning from printed material. For the individual reader, a model of reading can be regarded as the guiding principles by which that reader will process available textual information. As Harste and Burke (1977) explain, a model of reading is a "system of assumptions through which experiences [in this case, the experience of confronting printed material] are organized and acted upon ... [they are] schemata which govern behavior" (1977:32).

Studies of children learning to read in English have demonstrated the importance of readers' internalized models of the reading process (Harste and Burke 1977; Rhodes 1979). This research has identified at least three distinct theoretical orientations (or models) that readers hold; these models have been termed sound-, word-, and meaning-centered to indicate the language unit or focus that a reader considers important to good/effective reading. (See Figure 1.) When the models of reading that young readers held were later compared to samples of their oral reading, it was found that theoretical orientations affect both the ways reading is approached and to some extent the success of a reader in the recall and comprehension of that text (Rhodes 1979). The results of this study and others of young, native English readers (see Ogle 1974; Delawater 1975 and Dank 1976) provide convincing evidence that readers do indeed have internalized models of the reading process that they bring to bear when they read. The results also suggest questions about second language readers: How do L2 learners conceive of the reading process? How might their internalized models influence reading behavior?

My own recent research (Devine 1984) has focused on these questions. In a study of twenty low-intermediate ESL readers from a variety of language backgrounds, the subjects were given an oral reading interview

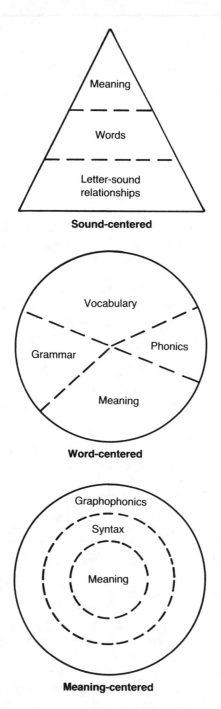

Figure 1   Three models of the reading process (from Harste and Burke 1977: 32, 37, 38; reprinted with permission of The National Reading Conference)

consisting of questions designed to uncover general attitudes about reading and notions about what constitutes good/effective reading. (Appendix A at the end of this chapter contains sample questions from the reading interview.) On the basis of their answers to these questions, subjects were classified as sound-, word-, or meaning-centered. Their responses in the reading interview were then compared with samples of the subjects' oral reading and with evaluations of their recall and comprehension of a text to determine what influence, if any, the readers' models had on reading performance. Nineteen of the twenty subjects were able to articulate their views about reading unambiguously enough for classification into one of the three model groups mentioned earlier. A close analysis of the oral reading errors (miscue analysis) showed a significant difference ($p<.001$) in the ways that readers with the three internalized models processed the information available in a printed text. For example, sound-centered readers focused their attention on the graphic information in the text; as a result, their oral reading errors had a very high graphic and phonemic correspondence with text words. It should be noted, however, that these readers did not necessarily preserve the sense or meaning of the reading selection, since they produced a high percentage of nonword substitutions. Evaluations of unaided retellings of the reading selections also suggested that the internalized models of reading held by the subjects affected recall and comprehension. Those readers who in their interviews indicated that they considered understanding what the author wanted to say as the measure of successful reading (that is, meaning-centered readers) not surprisingly demonstrated good to excellent recall and comprehension of the text. On the other hand, and again not surprisingly, readers who equated good reading with sound identification or good pronunciation usually failed to understand or recall what they had read.

To summarize, the study of internalized models of reading of beginning/low intermediate ESL subjects and the impact of those models on reading performance suggested the following conclusions: first, ESL readers do appear to have theoretical orientations toward reading which they bring with them to the reading classroom. Second, a significant ($p<.001$) correspondence exists between the model that the reading subjects hold and the type of information (graphic/sound, syntactic, or semantic) that the readers focus on in oral reading. Finally, a further relationship can be found between the internalized model of reading and the success of the reader in comprehending text material.

The research described in this chapter focuses on two of the subjects studied in Devine (1984). The chapter begins with a close examination of the readers' attitudes about reading, as seen through the reading interview. On the basis of these interviews, one of the subjects, Stanislav, was identified as a sound-centered reader, while the other, Isabella, was classified as a meaning-centered reader. A close examination of the reading behavior of these two subjects with clearly different notions about what constitutes good/effective reading illustrates very specifically the interaction of notions about reading and reading performance, as demonstrated in a more general way in the earlier study. In addition, the study demonstrates the importance of these models by suggesting, first, that a reader's theoretical orientations toward reading may determine, to some extent, the degree to which low proficiency in the language restricts second language reading ability and, second, that the models that readers hold may be of critical importance in allowing them to strike a successful balance between bottom-up (or data-driven) and top-down (or conceptually driven) processing necessary for the interpretation of a text.

As with any investigation involving the study of complex cognitive activities like reading, the results must be interpreted with caution. It is often difficult for readers (and language users more generally) to articulate models of mental processes; these mental operations may simply not be available for introspection. For L2 readers, such as those in this study, the difficulty may be compounded by lack of fluency in the second language. In addition, as is often noted, complex cognitive processes very probably involve a number of interacting strategies. Readers, for example, may employ one strategy for reading a novel, another for reading scientific or technical material, and a combination of strategies for reading a newspaper. To posit a single model, however intricate, may be to overlook this complexity.

The study

Subjects

As previously mentioned, this research focuses on two of the subjects from the earlier research (Devine, 1984). Both were recent arrivals to the United States and were studying in a community-based ESL program in East Lansing, Michigan, attending classes for three hours a day, five days a week. They were beginning/low intermediate students (level two in a program with four proficiency levels) as determined by the University of Michigan Placement Test. Entrance test scores appear in Table 1. The first subject, Stanislav, was a 40-year-old Polish male who had studied English in high school and college. He held a Ph.D. in chemistry and before coming to the United States had worked as a research chemist. The second subject, Isabella, was a 54-year-old Spanish female high school graduate, who had studied English while in high school. She listed her occupation as "housewife."

TABLE I. PLACEMENT SCORES — UNIVERSITY OF MICHIGAN PLACEMENT TEST

	Listening	*Grammar*	*Vocabulary*
Stanislav	5 (of 20)	12 (of 30)	13 (of 30)
Isabella	5	13	15

Data collection and analysis

Three sets of data were gathered on these readers after they had been attending classes for three weeks: an oral reading interview, a sample of oral reading, and a retelling (summary) of the oral reading.

As discussed earlier, the reading interview provides information about the readers' theoretical orientations toward reading – that is, the type of model the readers held. In order to examine the interaction of the readers' models of reading and their reading behavior, a detailed analysis of the oral reading samples was performed using miscue analysis. Profiles of the readers' use of the various cues available in the text – sound/letter, grammatical, and meaning cues – and of their production of nonword substitutions were then compared with their models to determine the nature and extent of the influence of notions about reading on actual reading performance. The retelling or summaries of the oral reading were transcribed and evaluated on a very broad six-point scale ranging from very poor to excellent, depending on the amount and accuracy of the information the subject could provide about the characters, events, and implied meaning of the text. In the examination of the interaction of models of reading and reading behavior, these retellings were treated as the measure of reader success in understanding the material. All data were evaluated and checked by at least two researchers (details in Devine 1984).

Oral reading interview

When asked what he thought made a good reader, Stanislav neatly summarized a sound-centered approach: "I think that a good reader must speak slowly and look for the text and for the good pronunciation of the words." When he had problems with a text he looked to the dictionary for help, but indicated that this resource was not always useful since he still could not pronounce the words in the text. In the following exchange with the interviewer, Stanislav very clearly illustrates the concerns of a reader whose attention is focused on graphic and phonemic information while reading.

I: When you are reading English, what would you like to do better?
S: For me reading is very difficult. Spelling is different from Polish.

I: Do you think that if the spelling system were more regular it would be easier to read in English?

S: Maybe, yes. The irregularity makes it difficult to pronounce.

On the basis of his responses to the interview questions, Stanislav was classified as a sound-centered reader. Readers of this type typically believe that the written language should be broken down and approached on the level of sound – witness Stanislav's distress over irregularities in sound/spelling correspondences. Once the sounds of the language have been correctly identified, the reader may then build words (Stanislav did mention the importance of vocabulary recognition) and eventually meaning from the information in the text; however, as this reader makes quite clear, it is the sounds, not the words or the meaning, that are most important to him.

Isabella's responses to the reading interview questions indicate that her ideas about what constitutes good/effective reading are quite different from Stanislav's. When asked what she does when she comes to something that she doesn't understand in reading, she replied, "Well, I make a guess...I still keep reading." A good reader, for Isabella, is someone who "knows the interpretation of the author." A final indication of her ideas about reading came in Isabella's response to the question of what she would like to do better as a reader:

I guess I would like to read more...the more you read, the better you get, like with writing, no? The more you write, the better the ideas get in your mind. With reading too, the ideas get better in your mind if you read more.

The ideas about reading voiced by this reader – her concern for "the interpretation of the author," "getting the ideas inside her head," as well as her willingness to "make a guess" and to "read more" – echo those expressed by other readers identified as meaning-centered. Readers possessing this theoretical orientation regard the ability to understand the meaning of a text as the measure of success in reading. Meaning-centered readers reject the notion that meaning can be found in the sounds and words in the text; as Isabella explained: "I just try and read and if I can't, I guess the meaning. If I don't know a word, I just write the word on the paper. I don't want to use the dictionary." Like other meaning-centered readers, Isabella often guesses at the meaning of what she is reading, using the sounds, words, and grammar of the text to help her formulate her guesses. (For a sample of the questions used in the Oral Reading Interview, see Appendix A.)

Oral reading analysis and retelling

It is quite obvious from their responses to the reading interview questions that Stanislav and Isabella hold very different attitudes about what is

TABLE 2. RETELLING EVALUATION AND MISCUE PROFILE

	Retelling evaluation	% of high graphic similarity	% of high phonemic similarity	% of SYN ACCEP	% of SEM ACCEP	% of nonwords
Stanislav	Very poor	55	65	69	35	26
Isabella	Very good	33	22	53	55	7

important in reading. How do these ideas (or internalized models of the reading process) affect their reading behavior? Samples of oral reading and retellings of those readings were compared to the subjects' models of reading to examine what influence, if any, these models have on reading behavior. Table 2 summarizes the miscue and retelling information for these two readers. These data suggest that as with their views on reading, the reading behavior of Stanislav is very different from that of Isabella. In both cases their reading behavior closely matches the reading behavior projected for readers with these theoretical orientations; that is, for Stanislav and for Isabella, a close correspondence exists between the model of reading and the degree to which they focus on the various cueing systems available in the text and the extent to which each is successful in understanding what has been read.

As a sound-centered reader, Stanislav would be expected to demonstrate primary concern in his oral reading with preserving the sound/print features found in the text. This indeed appears to be the case. In his slow, laborious decoding of the reading selection, he made relatively few miscues, only 23 in a more than 600-word story, and these miscues match the graphic features of text words in 55% of the cases and the phonemic (or sound) features 65% of the time. Stanislav's faithful rendering of the text material might superficially appear to be fluent reading and may suggest that this reader comprehends well. However, the semantic acceptability of Stanislav's miscues (only 35%) and his retelling of the story indicate otherwise. Rather than building meaning through his close attention to "good pronunciation," he appears to sacrifice understanding because of his overreliance on print information. As Stanislav explained at the conclusion of his oral reading: "I don't understand very well. When I read, I want to read well; it's therefore hard to pay attention to meaning." Stanislav's use of grammar cues in the text was fairly good, as evidenced by the syntactic acceptability of his miscues (69%). This score is consistent with findings in other miscue studies which show that readers at all proficiency levels tend to produce a fairly high percentage of syntactically acceptable miscues; it might well be the case, however, that the high percentage of syntactically acceptable miscues reflects more a careful attempt to reproduce the text words exactly than the successful use of grammatical information in the text as a way of understanding meaning. Like other sound-centered readers, Stanislav produced a relatively high percentage of nonword substitutions in his oral reading (26%). These nonwords closely match the letters and sounds of the text words, Stanislav's main concern in his reading.

By his own admission, Stanislav understood very little of what he had read of the selection "A Dangerous Act" (see Appendix B for a story summary.) The following illustrates Stanislav's initial, unaided retelling.

Mr. Purcell, problems, from his life and this . . . Excuse me, but I don't understand this problem. And this man about 60 feet high . . . this is the problem. Maybe if I can read this more slowly . . .

It is important to note that he has just read the story very slowly and carefully. Persistent questioning yielded little other information from Stanislav. This reader has, of course, set himself an impossible task – that of attending to the exact details of the print as a way of arriving at meaning. And he is quite right in concluding that it's hard to pay attention to the meaning while reading – if reading is defined as faithful reproduction of a text.

The second reader, Isabella, produces a surprisingly high number of miscues in her oral reading (80) compared to Stanislav's 23, yet her comprehension of the text is quite good, suggesting that it is the quality of the miscues, rather than the quantity, that determines a reader's effectiveness in understanding the meaning of a text. As a meaning-centered reader, Isabella would be expected to demonstrate central concern with deriving meaning from what she is reading; this concern may result in less reliance on the graphophonic cueing system as a way of comprehending a text. Isabella's miscues do show a rather low correspondence with the print and sound features of the text (33% high graphic similarity with text words and 22% high phonemic similarity compared to Stanislav's 55% and 65% respectively). Despite the high overall frequency of miscues, and their relative lack of correspondence with graphic and phonemic text features, the degree of semantic acceptability of Isabella's miscues (55%) and the low occurrence of nonword substitutions (7% – only 5 of the 80 miscues were nonwords) illustrate this reader's concern for preserving sense and meaning in her reading. A further illustration of this concern, and a clear example of Isabella's active engagement in what she is reading, and her willingness to make predictions (her guesses) based on her sense of the meaning, comes near the end of her oral reading. At this point in the story, the young stranger has completed his "dangerous act" – his dive – and has turned down Mr. Purcell's repeated offers of money to join the circus. When the man says no to $150 a week, Isabella pauses in her reading and says, "I guess he wants more money...I don't read this but I imagine."

Isabella's retelling included mention of the three characters (Purcell, his wife, and the stranger) and a clear, if slightly rambling, recapitulation of the events of the story. In addition, she offered the following observation:

In the circus, you know some people like to see the other people being more dangerous, maybe get killed; the more danger, the more they like...if the circus does not have the dangers, the people don't like...so I think that Mr. Purcell will have to close the circus because the stranger man will not come and so the people won't come to the circus...

While much of this information is implied in the story, at no point are these specific statements made. Isabella is able to both reconstruct the narrative line of the story and indeed to move beyond that line to an understanding of the author's meaning. She can do this because, unlike Stanislav, she is not tied in an exact rendering of the words of the text. In fact, by minimizing her reliance on details of the text (graphic and sound features), she is free to use other types of information in her efforts to understand the meaning. Some of this "other information" is suggested by the text through syntactic and meaning cues, but as Isabella recognizes, some of this information she brings with her to the reading of the text – hence her willingness to "guess" or "imagine" the motivation of the stranger in refusing Purcell's offer of money to join the circus. The fact that Isabella was wrong, that is, that the stranger had other reasons for not joining the circus, is beside the point. In her willingness to go beyond explicitly stated text information, she reveals how her conceptions about the reading process affect her reading behavior.

Examination of Stanislav's and Isabella's attitudes about reading and subsequent comparisons of their reading behavior to those attitudes illustrate the keen interaction between ESL readers' theoretical orientations toward reading and the ways in which those readers approach a text and their comprehension of that text. Understanding of this interaction underscores the importance of the recognition that ESL readers, even those at low proficiency levels, bring to the reading task a set of assumptions or operating principles concerning what is important in reading. Both Stanislav and Isabella demonstrate the importance of these operating principles in determining the language unit focused on reading and the ability of the reader to derive meaning from a text. The following brief discussion focuses on two other related ways that readers' internalized models of the reading process may affect reading performance.

The first concerns the relationship of general language proficiency and reading ability. Studies of the transfer of effective first language reading strategies into a second language have led researchers to conclude that limited proficiency in a second language may severely restrict the ability to read in that language (see Cziko 1978; Clarke 1980, reprinted as Chapter 8 in this volume; and Hudson 1982, reprinted as Chapter 13 in this volume) by causing a "short circuit" in a reader's ability to apply reading skills from the native language. Both Stanislav and Isabella have relatively low proficiency in English; in fact, their scores on the placement test (Table 1) are almost identical. If this low proficiency places a limit on the ability to transfer effective reading strategies from L1, it is reasonable to assume that the ceiling would operate equally for these readers. However, this is not the case. Stanislav, who claims to be a skilled reader in German, Russian, and his native Polish (recall that he holds a Ph.D. in chemistry), does indeed appear to be hampered in his reading by low English proficiency. Isabella, on the other hand, despite the same proficiency level, is far more successful in her efforts to read in English.

A possible explanation for this discrepancy (I am currently doing research on this issue) is that readers' theoretical orientations toward reading may determine the extent to which low second language proficiency restricts reading ability in the second language. Specifically, a sound-centered approach to reading, such as Stanislav holds, when combined with low proficiency results in severely restricted transfer of effective reading skills to the second language, whereas a meaning-centered approach to reading, such as Isabella holds, may mitigate the effects of low general language proficiency, thus allowing the reader to successfully transfer good first language reading strategies to the second language. More research is needed on this interaction.

A second way that a reader's theoretical orientation may affect reading behavior is in regard to that reader's ability to effectively combine "bottom-up" and "top-down" processing, as researchers into schema theory have clearly demonstrated they must do for successful reading. Carrell (Chapter 7 in this volume) discusses research which suggests that misconceptions about reading may restrict the ability of children reading in their native language to apply conceptually based schemata while reading. These readers appear to suffer from the misconception that all "meaning is in the text" and hence fail to use any top-down processing in their reading. In a related observation, Hudson (1982) suggests that the inability to apply existing knowledge-based schemata is one reason for a breakdown in ESL reading. Perhaps it is a reader's theoretical orientation (the model) of reading that permits or prohibits top-down processing, or the application of knowledge-based schemata. Specifically, a sound-centered model of reading could be regarded as a serious misconception about the role of knowledge-based schemata in successful reading. Sound-centered readers, such as Stanislav, might be characterized as "data-driven" in the extreme; it is not surprising then that their recall and understanding of what is read is so severely limited. On the other hand, meaning-centered readers can be seen as striking a successful balance between text-based and knowledge-based processing; recall Isabella's willingness to make use of extra-textual information.

This section has focused on the relationship between readers' theoretical orientations toward reading and (1) the impact of general language proficiency on successful second language reading and (2) the reader's ability to effectively combine data-based and knowledge-based processing in second language reading tasks. These two areas – language proficiency ceiling and schemata activation – were discussed as though they were totally separate. But perhaps there is an important interaction between the two. As Hudson (1982) has demonstrated, induced schemata may override the effects of low language proficiency. The results of the current study present a tantalizing possibility: Hudson's idea might be taken a step further to suggest that it is a meaning-centered internalized model of reading that allows even very low proficiency ESL readers to use knowledge-based schemata, which in turn may mitigate the effects of that low proficiency on L2 reading ability.

Appendix A.   Reading Interview

Sample questions from Reading Interview (see Burke 1978)

1. When you are reading and you come to something you don't understand, what do you do? Do you ever do anything else?
2. Who is a good reader that you know? What makes _____ a good reader?
3. If you knew someone who was having difficulty with reading, how would you help that person?
4. What would you like to do better as a reader?

Appendix B.   Summary of "A Dangerous Act"

Circus owners Mr. and Mrs. Purcell are worried that they will have to close their circus because not enough people are coming. A variety of promotional activities has failed to interest the public. Mrs. Purcell suggests that they need a dangerous act to attract crowds since their last dangerous act was successful, especially after someone was killed. They advertise for an act, and finally after several weeks, just when they are about to close the circus, a stranger inquires about the job. He says that he can dive into a small tank of water from a 60-foot-high pole and agrees to demonstrate his act. The owners are excited about the prospect. The stranger climbs to the top of the pole, pauses, and successfully dives into the tank. The Purcells are overjoyed because they think they have found a dangerous act that will save their circus. Mr. Purcell offers the man hot2$100 a week. The stranger refuses. Mr. Purcell offers $125, $150, and finally

$200. The stranger still firmly refuses. Mr. Purcell has no more money to offer. The dejected owner asks the man why he refused the job. The stranger replies that he had never done the dive before and having now tried it, he knew that he didn't like it.

References

Burke, C. 1978. The reading interview. Unpublished guide. The Reading Program, Indiana University.

Clarke, M. A. 1980. The short circuit hypothesis of ESL reading – or when language competence interferes with reading performance. *Modern Language Journal* 64(2): 203–209. [Reprinted as Chapter 8 in this volume.]

Clarke, M. A., and S. Silberstein. 1977. Toward a realization of psycholinguistic principles in the ESL classroom. *Language Learning* 27(1): 135–154.

Cziko, G. A. 1978. Differences in first and second language reading: the use of syntactic, semantic and discourse constraints. *Canadian Modern Language Review* 34: 473–489.

Dank, M. E. 1976. A study of the relationship of miscues to the model of formal reading instruction received by selected second graders. Ph.D. diss., University of Massachusetts.

Delawater, J. A. 1975. The relationship of beginning reading instruction and miscue patterns. In *Help for the reading teacher*, W. D. Page (Ed.). Urbana, Ill.: National Council of Teachers of English.

Devine, J. 1984. ESL readers' internalized models of the reading process. In *On TESOL' 83*, J. Handscombe, R. A. Orem, and B. P. Taylor (Eds.), 95–108. Washington, D.C.: TESOL.

Harste, J. C., and C. L. Burke. 1977. A new hypothesis for reading teacher research: both *teaching* and *learning* of reading are theoretically based. In *Reading: theory, research and practice*, P.D. Person (Ed.), 32–40. 26th Yearbook of the National Reading Conference. Clemson, S.C.: National Reading Conference.

Hudelson, S. (Ed.). 1981. *Learning to read in different languages*. Washington, D.C.: Center for Applied Linguistics.

Hudson, T. 1982. The effects of induced schemata on the "short circuit" in L2 reading: non-decoding factors in L2 reading and performance. *Language Learning* 32(1): 3–31. [Reprinted as Chapter 13 in this volume.]

Ogle, D. M. 1974. A study of the relationship of instructional methods to the oral reading errors made by first grade readers. Ph.D. diss., Oklahoma State University.

Renault, L. 1981. Theoretically based second language reading strategies. In *Reading English as a second language: moving from theory*, C. W. Twyford, W. Diehl, and K. Feathers (Eds.), 64–80. Bloomington: Indiana University School of Education.

Rhodes, L. 1979. Comprehension and predictability: an analysis of beginning reading materials. In *New perspectives on comprehension*, J. C. Harste and R. F. Crey (Eds.). Bloomington: Indiana University School of Education.

Rigg, P. 1977. The miscue-ESL project. In *On TESOL '77* J. D. Brown, C. A. Yorio, and R. H. Crymes (Eds.), 106–118. Washington, D.C.: TESOL. [Reprinted as Chapter 14 in this volume.]

1981. Beginning to read in English the LEA way. In *Reading English as a second language: moving from theory*, C. W. Twyford, W. Diehl, and K. Feathers (Eds.), 81–90. Bloomington: Indiana University School of Education.

10 Changes in cohesion in the recall of native and foreign texts

Margaret S. Steffensen

In the field of reading, there is a great deal of interest in cohesion (Halliday and Hasan 1976), in terms of both the theoretical insights it provides and its pedagogical implications. Cohesion is a system of analysis that describes the coherence of a text as a function of semantic relations realized in surface-level features. Thus, according to Halliday and Hasan (1976:14), the textual structure in a passage such as

"Did the gardener water my hydrangeas?"
"He said so."

is created by the cohesive ties between "he" (reference) and "the gardener," and "so" (substitution) and the proposition in the first sentence.

The proposal that the source of textual coherence is contained in surface features is an attractive one for those involved in reading, since it suggests a straightforward way to improve comprehension: teach students to attend to the cohesive devices, and their understanding of the meaning of a passage will greatly increase. There appears to be some experimental support for such a position. In the development of native language reading proficiency, Chapman (1979) found that children who were reading fluently were able to complete anaphoric relations in a cloze test, and he concluded that mastery of textual features, including cohesive ties, is a central factor in fluent reading and comprehension. A study by Cohen and his colleagues (1979, reprinted as Chapter 11 in this volume) showed that foreign readers of English in the sciences and economics did not pick up on conjunctive words in their specialized texts. The researchers proposed that nonnative speakers read more locally than do native speakers and, because they do not attend to the conjunctive ties, they have trouble synthesizing the information at the intra- and intersentential level as well as across paragraphs.

Teaching methods are being developed to remedy such deficiencies. For example, Williams (1983) provides a system of symbols and strategies for teaching foreign readers how to use cohesive signals in order to increase their comprehension of texts.

However, a number of researchers have objected to Halliday and

Hasan's basic premise that coherence is created by cohesion. Morgan and Sellner (1980) argue that the concept of cohesion is an attempt to locate coherence in the text and ignores the contribution of the reader in constructing textual meaning. In their view, it is textual coherence that effects cohesion, not the reverse, and cohesion is the result of a coherent rendering of content. While they reject a strong statement of cohesion, that it creates coherence, they appear to accept a weak position, that cohesion is related to coherence. Carrell (1982) also adopts an interactive view of reading, in which the meaning of the text is created by the reader, who taps the relevant schemata to reconstruct the meaning intended by the author. Widdowson (1978) points out that cohesion is less important than coherence for meaning.

In an empirical study, Tierney and Mosenthal (1981) analyzed cohesion as a measure of coherence. They found that cohesion is not causally related to coherence and that while there was patterning of ties across text types, familiarity was not a factor in the frequency of cohesive ties, although it was in coherence.

It should be noted that this study used a between-subject, not a within-subject, design. If there is individual variation in the use of cohesive devices, with some individuals using more of them across the board than others, then a within-subject design might provide a more rigorous test of the hypothesis that cohesion and coherence are related. Furthermore, subjects worked from outlines supplied by the experimenters. Free recall might have yielded differences since the writing would have been less constrained. It might also be argued that subjects would have given less attention to surface aspects of their writing if they had had to generate the entire content from memory, and greater variation would thus have been produced. Finally, the familiarity condition was created by having subjects view a filmstrip about the topic. Long-term cultural knowledge might have resulted in different linguistic realizations.

The study

Predictions and rationale

The study was directed to the question of what changes occur in text structure when a reader recalls a native and a foreign text. From research conducted within the framework of schema theory, there is considerable evidence that readers will understand and recall significantly more information if texts involve a familiar topic for which they possess the relevant background knowledge (Anderson et al. 1977; Rumelhart 1977; Anderson, Spiro, and Anderson 1978; Steffensen, Joag-dev, and Anderson 1979). The information content of a text is conceptualized as a potential that readers may or may not realize as they construct the meaning of the text.

Similarly, it can be argued that the cohesive devices are also a potential (see Steffensen 1986). If readers possess the generalized framework for the text being read, more of the cohesive ties that are present in the original should occur in the recall because they will be anticipated, understood, stored, and recalled under the direction of the relevant schema. It was therefore predicted that an analysis of the cohesive ties (reference, repetition, substitution, ellipsis, and conjunction) in the recalls of foreign and native texts would show a higher rate of occurrence in the native text.

It was also expected that this would result in greater sentence length in the native recall protocols. Conjunction and ellipsis are cohesive devices that counterbalance each other: The former produces longer sentences while the latter produces shorter ones. If both forms are used at the same rate, a highly cohesive paper would have approximately the same average sentence length as a paper with a low level of cohesion. However, this was not expected to be the case. Intuitively, ellipsis seems to be a less frequently used device than conjunction. Given a high use of conjunction, longer sentences would result.

These predictions were based on the weak view of cohesion, which correlates cohesion and coherence but does not claim that cohesion causes coherence. If a logical relationship between ideas, actions, and concepts is perceived, or if the activities and sequences of a particular social transaction are familiar, then it might be expected that a reader (or observer) would focus on the principal sequences, actors, and actions involved. Recall would reflect this structuring with high rates of repetition, reference, substitution, and ellipsis. Similarly, a high frequency of conjunctive devices would be used to convey the perceived relationships. Such distributions would result from the greater coherence of the episode for the informed reader/viewer. For the uninformed or naïve viewer, on the other hand, the recall would be expected to be fragmentary and episodic, with a lower level of cohesive ties, reflecting a perception of the event that lacked focus and structuring.

There were several reasons why it was predicted that there would be more cohesive ties in the recall protocols of the native than those of the foreign text. In the earlier study (Steffensen et al. 1979) the result clearly showed that subjects understood more of the text based on their own cultures. This understanding should be reflected in greater use of certain categories of cohesion. For example, if a reader understands that a real world event X causes a real world event Y, it might be expected that such information would be conveyed using the conjunctive tie *because*.

Second, an examination of the recall protocols showed more dysfunctional paragraphs in the foreign protocols. For example, an American "recalled" the following from the Indian text:

They went to Nagpur. The groom is called Shiva.

Here, disparate facts were pulled from two paragraphs that described different events in the marriage ceremony. The information about the couple going to Nagpur, accompanied by the groom's immediate family, is not related to the detail about the groom's name, which is taken from a description of the naming ceremony.

The reader will recognize that in the following recall of the American text by an Indian subject ideas are concatenated in a way that suggests that no schema was operating:

Everything was old-fashioned except for the cake.
The priest was an old family friend.
There were a bride and groom on the cake but when the cake was cut, there
    was devil's food.

There appears to be no underlying conceptual framework guiding the process of recall or dictating which concepts belong together, nor any reflection of the organization of events in the real world: the information about the priest (the original term, incidentally, was *minister*) is misplaced and should not have been sandwiched in the middle of the wedding cake description. The possibility of cohesive ties occurring is greatly reduced in such a passage.

Third, there were major problems in the ordering of events in the foreign protocols even when the details in each of these episodes were more or less correct. Blocks of information that were internally consistent, such as those describing the main events occurring the days preceding the actual Indian wedding ceremony, were in scrambled order in American protocols. Again, this reflects the absence of background knowledge undergirding the foreign text. When Indians read the passage, there was a great deal of information they were able to bring to bear on its processing; in fact, they "came equipped" with a knowledge of the sequence of events. They did not have to learn this structure of social events from the text as they were reading it; rather they simply had to "plug in" or instantiate the details from the passage into their own existing schema. It was expected that coherence at this level would also affect the proportion of cohesive ties.

Materials for analysis

Twenty recall protocols from an earlier study of reading and recall (Steffensen et al. 1979) were the materials analyzed. Twenty East Indians and twenty Americans matched for age, sex, education, area of academic specialization, and marital status participated in that experiment. (One Indian subject was subsequently dropped because she had not understood the directions.) Briefly, subjects were asked to read two texts about weddings in each of the cultures, presented in a counterbalanced order. After they had read the text and completed a task to inhibit short-term memory, they were asked to recall the text as completely as they could, to maintain the original order of events, and to use the same wording or to paraphrase as closely as possible if they could not remember the exact wording.

The recall protocols were analyzed for amount of information recalled on the basis of idea units; for elaborations, in which information was intruded from the appropriate schema; for distortions, in which the competing schema was a factor; and for other overt errors. Because it had been shown that background knowledge was a highly significant factor in reading comprehension, with these subjects recalling and elaborating more of the native passage and distorting and making errors at a higher rate with the foreign passages (Steffensen et al. 1979), these protocols seemed to be ideal texts to analyze for cohesion. They would provide a fairer test of the cohesion hypothesis because the materials were based on long-term, semantic information rather than knowledge acquired in an experimental setting, as in the case of the Tierney and Mosenthal study (1981).

Analysis of recall protocols

Cohesion exists both between sentences and within sentences (Halliday and Hasan 1976). It is intersentential cohesion that is important for textual cohesion; intrasentential cohesion is related to grammaticality. However, for this study, both inter- and intrasentential cohesive ties were analyzed. This makes the results more comparable with those of other studies, in which both types have been included (e.g., Williams 1983). More important, it was predicted that the sentences in the native recall protocols would be longer than those in the foreign. If only intersentential cohesion were analyzed, the results would be biased against the longer sentences anticipated in the native recall and an incorrect picture of cohesion would result.

Five categories of cohesion – reference, repetition, substitution, ellipsis, and conjunction – were analyzed. According to Halliday and Hasan (1976:31), unlike most lexical items which are "interpreted semantically in their own right," items of reference "make reference to something else for their interpretation." The pronouns in the following excerpt from one of the subjects' protocols are understood through their relationship with the nouns in the preceding sentence:

You should have seen the *ring* given to Pam by *George*. *It* must have cost *him* a fortune.

The reader understands the meaning of "it" through reference to "ring" and "him" through reference to "George." Demonstratives also function cohesively, with "there" referring to "wedding":

It was not very good that you were not present at Prema's *wedding*. We had all been *there*.

Repetition, reiteration of a lexical item, may occur in contexts similar to those for reference and may signal the same referent:

Prema's husband had to wear *a dhoti* during the ritual to which he was not accustomed and they teased him that *it* was going to come off during *marriage*. But *the dhoti* did not come off during *marriage* nor the day after.

Cohesive repetition often includes an article change from indefinite to definite, with "a dhoti" becoming "the dhoti," the article being a case of reference. This passage also includes the form of cohesion more commonly used in such a case, reference, with the pronoun ("it") immediately following the noun ("dhoti"). Only after the use of reference does the writer use repetition. In the repetition of "marriage," the absence of articles shows the interference of the writer's first language.

Reiterated words do not have to have the same referent to function cohesively:

Rest of the brides [undecipherable] girls wore the light blue *dresses* which were made to match the brides *dress*. Pam's maid of honor wore a bright blue *dress*.

These three occurrences of "dress" make reference to different things in the real world. Nevertheless, textual cohesion is created through the repetition of the lexical item (Halliday and Hasan 1976:282).

Substitution is a textual relation in which "a sort of counter . . . is used in place of the repetition of a particular item" (Halliday and Hasan, 1976:89). Types include nominal, clausal, and verbal:

Prema's parents didn't want to *allow her* but after all they *did*.
Prema's parents were afraid that they might *ask for scooter before* but they *didn't*.

"Did" is a verbal substitution for "allow her" in the first example and "ask for scooter before" in the second.

In the following example, "same" is a nominal substitute for "dress":

Pam's mother wore this *dress* at her wedding and she insisted that Pam also wear the *same*.

Ellipsis is described as "substitution by zero" (Halliday and Hasan 1976:142). This involves those cases in which there is a structural gap that must be completed by reference to a related structure in the immediate text, usually preceding:

George's ring *was* of gold and that of Pam's _____ platinum to match her engagement ring.
George was wearing gold ring and Pam _____ the platinum _____.

Ellipsis may involve nominals or verbals, shown above, as well as clausals.

Unlike the other forms of cohesion already discussed, conjunctions create cohesion through their meanings rather than by specific reference to other items in the text (Halliday and Hasan 1976:226). In effect, a conjunction tells the reader to relate two chunks of text in the way it specifies. These fall into the four categories of additive, adversative, causal, and temporal. There were numerous examples of conjunction in subjects' protocols:

A chain was with beads and a pendent (*and* it was very beautiful). [additive]
All his friends and sisters were teasing that that might fall of anyway it didn't neither that day *nor* the next day in the wedding. [additive]
Prema's mother insisted on some old rituals and *hence* they were done. [causal]
Prema could not come to the in-laws the day before *so* we, her close friends and relatives went over to this place. [causal]
Though he is their only son they didn't give much trouble. [adversative]
Prema's parents were worried that the in-laws might ask for a scooter, *but* that did not happen. They had not taken any dowry *though* he was their only son. [adversative]
Pam's niece was the flower girl and was doing her job well *untill* she saw her mother when she stopped and gave her a number of flowers. [temporal]
Finally there was a wedding cake with a couple at top, but when it was cut it was a devil's cake. [temporal]

Results

The main results of this study are summarized in Table 1. Contrary to predictions, there was a higher proportion of cohesive ties in the foreign recall protocols (mean proportion = .233) than the native (mean proportion = .228). A *t*-test showed this difference to be nonsignificant (SD = .0446, $t(19) = 1.189$, nonsignificant at $p < .05$).

Because the analysis of sentence length did not meet the assumptions for a parametric test, a nonparametric test was performed. Mean sentence length was 13.73 for the native and 12.65 for the foreign recall protocols. Of the 20 observations, 15 were higher for the native passage. A two-sided sign test showed this distribution to be significant at the $p < .05$ level.

TABLE I. MEAN PROPORTION OF COHESIVE DEVICES IN RECALL PROTOCOLS

	Native text	Foreign text
Reference, repetition, ellipsis, substitution[a]	.178	.187
Conjunction[a]	.049	.043
Total[a]	.228	.233
Mean sentence length (words)[b]	13.73	12.65

[a]Nonsignificant
[b]$p < .05$

A post hoc analysis was done of the category of conjunctions contrasted with the other four types of cohesion – reference, repetition, substitution, and ellipsis – on the assumption that the longer length of native recall sentences may in part have reflected a higher level of conjunction. While the analysis suggested that different types of cohesion occurred differentially in the two recall protocols and were in the expected directions, the differences were not significant. The mean proportions for conjunctive devices was .049 for the native and .043 for the foreign (SD = .0228, $t(19) = 1.2436$, nonsignificant at $p<.05$). For the category of reference, repetition, substitution, and ellipsis, the mean proportions were .178 for the native and .187 for the foreign (SD = .0444, $t(19) = 1.102$, nonsignificant at $p<.05$).

Discussion

This research was based on the expectation that while cohesion does not create coherence, it is positively related to coherence. Thus a more coherent recall protocol, which reflected greater understanding of the events involved, would have a proportionally greater number of cohesive ties. However, this premise was not supported. The analysis of conjunctive devices was in the expected direction, though nonsignificant. An examination of native recall protocols showed that as predicted, there was some tendency for subjects to make relationships explicit that were only inferred in the original. For example, the Indian text read:

The wedding reception was a combination of old and new styles. They had retained some of the traditional rituals, but not all. It seems that Prema's mother-in-law wanted it that way.

An Indian subject recalled:

Her wedding was celebrated with old and new styles of rituals because her mother-in-law wanted it that way.

No one would want to claim that this was not a strong invited inference. However, for this passage, Americans typically remembered only one proposition, that the wedding was composed of old and new styles. The information that the mother-in-law was making such major decisions dropped out, probably under the pressure of the schema for American weddings, in which the role of the groom's mother is generally a trivial one.

It was also anticipated that conjunctive ties would occur at a lower frequency in the foreign recalls either because they were not processed during reading and thus were not in memory, or they were not recalled. This also tended to occur. Here is the original description of the American wedding cake:

The only thing that really broke tradition was the wedding cake. It looked like the usual type, with several tiers and a bride and groom on top, but when George and Pam cut the first piece, everyone was amazed to see that it was devil's food...

This was reduced to a series of short, staccato sentences by an Indian subject:

Then they (had) their marriage cake cutting ceremony. It was not special. It was an ordinary cake, was made on several tiers. There was a bride and groom on the top of the cake. When they cut it was angel food cake. Everyone was happy.

However, there were also cases in which subjects produced more cohesive renderings of the passage:

But there are some surprises for them. The wedding cake was unusual, with tiers, and even the car in which they go to the airport was strangely decked. Thus there wedding wasn't too traditional, i.e., all the way.

It will of course be noted that this example is far less coherent than the original, incorporating details about the couple's "getaway" car which occurred much later in the text. This highlights a major problem in attempting to use cohesion as a measure of textual coherence: Cohesive devices may be used at a high frequency, relating items that should not be. In such cases, the cohesive devices show explicitly that the original passage has not been understood. The following recall is highly cohesive due to the use of reference, repetition, and conjunctions, but it shows a high level of cultural distortion:

Pam wore her grandmother's traditional dress, which was made of lace on a satin cloth. She looked all right except the dress was too old and out of fashion.

Here the well-accepted tradition of wearing an heirloom dress has been misunderstood and balanced to Indian customs, which do not include such an alternative to having a new, expensive sari for the marriage ceremony.

Conversely, cohesion may be greatly eroded while a coherent rendering is still maintained through an appropriate inferencing by the informed reader. For example, the following text would still be coherent, in spite of the omission of the cohesive conjunction "but" of the original:

It looked like the usual type, with several tiers and a bride and groom on top. When George and Pam cut the first piece, everyone was amazed to see that it was devil's food.

The effect of inferencing may have been a significant factor in the present results. It may be that when a subject is able to rely on background knowledge, less is spelled out than would otherwise be the case. The fact that the experimental passage was an informal letter that assumes shared knowledge may have increased such an effect. For an Indian reading the following passage, the fact that the bride's parents were worried about a possible demand for a scooter *because* there was no dowry would be so obvious that it would not have to be specifically encoded.

Since they did not ask for any dowry, Prema's parents were a little worried about their asking for a scooter before the wedding, but they didn't ask for one.

More than that, the Indian reader/recaller might not even be aware that she or he was *not* making the relationship of the two concepts explicit. On the other hand, when a reader is learning about a new system of beliefs or a new social structure, there may be a tendency to build in an unnecessary level of redundancy, which inflates the cohesive count, as in the following recall of the Indian text by an American:

It's too bad you couldn't attend Prema's wedding. They had met only a couple of times before the ceremony. Prema's financé had asked to see her before the wedding. Prema's parents did not know what to say...

Many of the details in the original text were dropped and the time phrase is repeated, perhaps to clarify in the reader's own mind exactly the sequence of events.

There was some evidence that vocabulary was reduced in range and the variety that was present in the original was lost. For example, an American subject used "traditional" several times in her recall, which inflated the count for repetition:

It was a mix of traditional and new.
The wedding was traditional in the exchange of gifts.
The bride received the traditional pendant necklace with black beads.
Anyway, he was wearing the traditional wedding dress...

While all of these sentences were correct, the diversity of wording, which may reflect the richness of conceptualization underlying the original, was lost. Only the wedding necklace was described as traditional in the original:

The wedding was a combination of old and new styles.

There was a verbal agreement about the gifts to be given to the in-laws, and what they asked for sounded reasonable.

Her wedding necklace is the traditional gold pendant and black beads on gold chain...

Prema's husband had to wear a dhoti for that ceremony and for the wedding the next day, and he was not use to it.

The fact that vocabulary is restricted in recall is worth further investigation.

In summary, this study provides evidence that when cohesion in recall protocols is analyzed and is restricted to the categories of reference, repetition, ellipsis, substitution, and conjunction, the mean proportion of ties for foreign and native materials is not significantly different. Thus no support is provided for either the strong claim regarding cohesion, that it creates coherence, or for the weak claim, that it is correlated with coherence. The slightly higher level of cohesion in the foreign protocols may be a reflection of psycholinguistic responses to the task, such as using a high level of repetition to consolidate the information one is learning or a restriction of vocabulary usage (not knowledge of lexical items) as one focuses on understanding the content rather than the nuances of communication. Another possibility is that the demands of this particular task biased the results. It may be that if the text had not been an informal one, a personal letter in which shared knowledge is assumed, the results would have been different.

Given these results, it seems that a bit of caution is called for in using instruction in cohesion as a methodology for overcoming the problems involved in reading a foreign language. No one would want to argue that the cohesive devices should be ignored in the foreign language classroom because mastering them is important for achieving competence in the target language. However, in terms of reading, a variety of strategies must be used, including vocabulary development, training in the use of advance organizers and styles of reading, practice in developing topical questions before reading and in reviewing material that has been read, and enrichment of background knowledge. Only with much greater insight into how cohesive ties function in the reading process should a methodology using cohesion extensively be introduced into the foreign reading classroom.

References

Anderson, R. C., R. E. Reynolds, D. L. Schallert, and E. Goetz. 1977. Frameworks for comprehending discourse. *American Educational Research Journal* 14: 367–382.

Anderson, R. C., R. J. Spiro, and M. C. Anderson. 1978. Schemata as scaffolding for the representation of information in connected discourse. *American Educational Research Journal* 15:433–440.

Carrell, P. L. 1982. Cohesion is not coherence. *TESOL Quarterly* 16:479–488.

Chapman, L. J. 1979. The perception of language cohesion during fluent reading. In *Processing visible language*, Vol. 1, P. Kolers, M. Wrolstad, and H. Bouma (Eds.), 403–411. New York: Plenum.

Cohen, A., H. Glasman, P. R. Rosenbaum-Cohen, J. Ferrara, and J. Fine. 1979. Reading English for specialized purposes: discourse analysis and the use of student informants. *TESOL Quarterly* 13: 551–564. [Reprinted as Chapter 11 in this volume.]

Halliday, M. A. K., and R. Hasan. 1976. *Cohesion in English*. London: Longman.

Morgan, J., and M. Sellner. 1980. Discourse and linguistic theory. In *Theoretical issues in reading comprehension*, R. Spiro, B. Bruce, and W. Brewer (Eds.). New York: Erlbaum.

Rumelhart D. E. 1977. Toward an interactive model of reading. In *Attention and performance VI*, S. Dornic (Ed.). Hillsdale, N.J.: Erlbaum.

Steffensen, M. S. 1986. Register, cohesion and cross-cultural reading comprehension. *Applied Linguistics* 7: 71–85.

Steffensen, M. S., C. Joag-dev, and R. C. Anderson. 1979. A cross-cultural perspective on reading comprehension. *Reading Research Quarterly* 15: 10–29.

Tierney, R. J., and J. Mosenthal. 1981. *The cohesion concept's relationship to the coherence of text*. Technical Report No. 221. Urbana: University of Illinois, Center for the Study of Reading.

Widdowson, H. G. 1978. *Teaching language as communication*. London: Oxford.

Williams, R. 1983. Teaching the recognition of cohesive ties in reading a foreign language. *Reading in Foreign Language* 1: 35–53.

11 Reading English for specialized purposes: discourse analysis and the use of student informants

Andrew Cohen, Hilary Glasman,
Phyllis R. Rosenbaum-Cohen,
Jonathan Ferrara, and Jonathan Fine

Nonnative speakers of English around the world frequently need to read specialized English language material as part of their university course work. A traditional view held by the instructors in such specialized courses is that a knowledge of the technical terms, via a glossary, will provide the nonnative reader with what he needs, particularly in scientific texts. Experience has shown, however, that even students with mastery over the technical terms become so frustrated in reading technical English that they seek native-language summaries of the English texts, or native-language books covering roughly the same material, or do not read the material at all, but concentrate rather on taking verbatim lecture notes. This approach tends to produce a passive learning attitude rather than the active, exploring approach so necessary if students are to develop sufficient competence in English to read their subject matter freely.

As researchers have begun to investigate the reading problems of nonnatives, it has become clear that the difficulties extend beyond technical vocabulary. Fortunately, volumes are beginning to appear which document numerous ways in which subject matter written in English may be problematic for nonnative readers from one or various language backgrounds (see, for example, Todd-Trimble, Trimble, and Drobnic 1978). Several empirical studies in particular influenced the research reported in this article. Selinker and Trimble (1974: 81–82), for example, reported on their detailed research into the use of articles and verb tense in English for Specialized Purposes (ESP), because it seemed most crucial to the needs of engineering students. Generally, they found that student

From "Reading for specialized purposes: Discourse analysis and the use of student informants" by A. Cohen et al., 1979, *TESOL Quarterly*, *13*(4), pp. 551–64. Copyright 1979 by Teachers of English to Speakers of Other Languages.

This is a revised version of a paper presented at the 12th Annual TESOL Convention, Mexico City, 1978.

We would like to acknowledge the following EFL teachers who took part in the research effort: Ruth Rigby, Trudy Zuckerman, Victor Kagan, David Goldberg, Marilyn Landes, and Judy Greenbaum. We wish to thank Chris Candlin for his critical comments regarding our work and we also wish to thank Larry Selinker and Eddie Levenston for their comments and encouragement.

difficulties in ESP were not merely a result of technical vocabulary. In fact, they found that nontechnical words in technical writing would sometimes give students more difficulty than technical ones – e.g., adverbial phrases, conjunctions, or words used in anaphoric reference. They attributed much of the difficulty in reading comprehension to the structure of the writing.

They also found that use of articles and verb tenses in ESP texts reflected rhetorical or organizational decisions made by the author about the piece of prose. In other words, the choice of definite or indefinite article might reflect the amount of generalization the author wished to presuppose, and the choice of tenses would be based on rhetorical discourse rules. These devices were often not apparent as such to the nonnative reader. Conventional EFL training, however, might not provide the students with the appropriate set of rules and guidelines for interpreting such article or tense use. The same investigators also showed how nonexplicit definitions and classification schemes could cause problems for nonnative readers (Selinker, Todd-Trimble, and Trimble 1976). "Causing problems for the nonnative" often means simply the lack of information or awareness of the function of the rhetorical devices.

The studies which we undertook were an outgrowth of a graduate seminar that Larry Selinker conducted at the Hebrew University of Jerusalem, 1975–76. The research questions that the seminar investigated were: 1) what is the EFL teacher's understanding of specialized texts? and 2) what can the native English speaker, who is a specialist in the field, add to the EFL teacher's understanding of such material? (Selinker 1979). A question that remained to be investigated, among others, was: What is problematic for nonnative readers when reading material in English in a specialized field?

A series of four studies was implemented in an effort to arrive at empirical answers to this question. In some ways, the studies can be viewed as developmental; the methodology was refined with each subsequent investigation. Although the studies span three different specialized fields, certain problems emerged which were shared by students reading material in all of these diverse fields. These studies were conducted at a time when other investigators were beginning to document how learners go about solving problems in reading—both in the native language (see Aighes et al. 1977) and in a second language (see Hosenfeld 1977, 1979).

First, we will describe the subjects, texts, and research procedures for each of the four studies, and then discuss findings from all four studies relating to the following ESP areas:

a. *Heavy noun phrase subjects or objects*: The use of the term *heavy* with respect to noun phrase subjects or objects is borrowed from Berman (1979) and is intended to suggest that such constructions, although they may not in fact appear very lengthy or complex, are difficult to process.

b. *Syntactic markers of cohesion*: This refers to conjunctive words (Halliday and Hasan 1976) – i.e., words which grammatically signal the interconnection of sentences with a text (e.g., *however, thus, also,* and *finally*).

c. *The role of nontechnical vocabulary in technical texts*: By nontechnical vocabulary in technical texts, we are referring to nontechnical words which may: 1) take on a technical meaning in a particular field (Cowan 1974, referred to these as *subtechnical vocabulary*), 2) appear as contextual paraphrases for other words or phrases, or 3) form part of a specialized nontechnical lexis (e.g., vocabulary items indicating time sequence, measurement, or truth validity).

Informants

There was one informant in the first study (hereafter referred to as the genetic study), a second-year chemistry and bio-chemistry student at Hebrew University and a native Hebrew speaker with a high school matriculation score of 8 (out of 10) in English (see Table 1). The second study (the biology study) had two informants, a male and a female, both first-year biology students at Hebrew University; both were native Hebrew speakers with high school matriculation scores of 6 or 7 in English. These two students were, at the time of the study, enrolled in the intermediate EFL course (4 hours per week). The third study (the political science study) had one informant, a first-year international relations and economics major at Hebrew University who was a native speaker of Hebrew, with a matriculation score of 7 in English. He was enrolled in the two-hour advanced EFL course. The fourth study (the history study) had 8 informants: four (3 males and a female) were first-year East Asian history majors at Hebrew University, all native Hebrew speakers, and four (all males) were English-speaking American students in Israel for a year, taking college-level classes in Jewish Studies. The female East Asian history student had lived in the United States from age 8 until a year before the study, so she was considered an English speaker for the purpose of the study (although a native Hebrew speaker). Of the remaining three East Asian history students, two had an 8 on the matriculation exam and one had not taken the exam. All the students were in their twenties except for the East Asian history student who had not taken the matriculation exam; he was in his forties.

All the students volunteered to act as informants for the study. They were told that the purpose of the research was to better understand student problems in the reading of texts so as to improve the service course in EFL at the University. It is important to note that the nonnative subjects participating in these studies would be considered fairly good

TABLE I. SUMMARY CHARACTERISTICS OF INFORMANTS

	First study: Genetics	Second Study: Biology	Third Study: Pol. Science	Fourth Study: History
No. of informants	1	2	1	8
Sex	F	M, F	M	7M, 1F
Major	Chemistry & bio-chem.	Biology	Economics & international relations	East Asian hist. (4), Jew. studies (4)
Year at university	2nd	1st	1st	1st
Dominant language	Hebrew	Hebrew	Hebrew	Hebrew (3) English (5)
H.S. matriculation score[a]	8	6, 7	7	8 (2 students), not taken (1 stud.)
Status re EFL classes	Exempt	Intermediate (4 hr.) class	Advanced (2 hr.) class	Exempt (1) Intensive summer course (1) Advanced (2-hr.) class (1)

[a]Science – 8, 9, 10 exempt; social science & humanities – 9, 10 exempt.

readers in English. Thus, if anything, the results of these studies speak to what is problematic for more advanced nonnative readers when reading in specialized English, and not to the problem of the weakest students. That would be a separate study in and of itself.

Texts

The text for the genetics study was P. C. Hanawalt's "Repair of Genetic Material in Living Cells," (1972: 83–87). This is a survey article, typical of material assigned to first-year genetics students at Hebrew University. It was selected by an English-speaking professor in the field and the same text was used in Selinker's seminar to investigate what knowledge the expert brings to such a text in order to understand it (Selinker 1979). The student informant had not read the article previously. In the presence of the interviewer, she read the first 160 lines of text, which took her 1 3/4 hours.

The text for the biology study was selected by the informants and comprised a section from a chapter entitled, "Genetic Basis of Cell Diversity," in A. B. Novikoff and E. Holtzman, (1976: 332–338). The students had been assigned the chapter in biology class and had also discussed parts of it in their ongoing EFL class. They reported that the material took about 1–2 hours to read.

The text for the political science study was selected by the informants from a collection of articles for a first-year political science course. It was R. Rose and R. Mossiwir's "Voting and Elections: A Functional Analysis," (1967: 173–201). The student had not yet been assigned the article in class. He read the first 300 lines (to page 182), which reportedly took him 4 hours.

The text for the history study was selected by the East Asian Studies department head as representative of a basic introductory reading in that department. It was the introduction to E. O. Reischauer and J. K. Fairbank's *East Asia: The Great Tradition* (1960: 3–19). The text took the nonnatives between 1–2 hours to read. The natives completed it in about 20 minutes. In the interview, the students were asked questions about two passages (23 lines and 38 lines, respectively). The students had not yet been assigned the text in class.

Procedures

In the first three studies (genetics, biology, and political science), the student informants were instructed to underline all vocabulary and structures that they found difficult to understand. In the biology and political science studies, the informants underlined the problem areas before the interview sessions. In the political science study, the informant also made note of which words he looked up in the dictionary. Despite these different procedures, we will see that the four studies elicited a surprising amount of similar data.

For all four studies, the researchers prepared sets of points to investigate. For the genetics study, the investigator (Glasman) prepared questions based on a series of lexical and grammatical categories that she predicted would be problematic for her informant. For the biology and political science studies, the researchers (Cohen, Rosenbaum-Cohen, and Ferrara) analyzed the texts in consort with a group of some six or so other EFL teachers,[1] and developed a series of questions on the basis of a checklist of features in reading technical English. The checklist encompassed the following broad categories: graphic organization, rhetorical principles or devices, grammar, and vocabulary. In these first three studies, the focus of the researchers' questions was overtly on problematic areas – i.e., asking whether some word or structure was a problem In the biology and the political science studies, after students indicated whether a word or structure was problematic, they were also asked whether, in retrospect, this word or structure interfered with comprehension of the sentence, section, or passage overall. In the fourth, the history study, the focus was different: it was not overtly on problematic areas but rather on comprehension. The researchers (Cohen and Fine) asked both *macro* questions, or questions which required some integration or generalization from specific sentences in order to answer, and *micro* questions, questions which were focused directly on specific sentences or parts of sentences.[2]

Interview sessions were generally conducted in Hebrew. Questions were occasionally asked in English, particularly if the investigator felt more comfortable, but answers were usually not solicited in English unless the purpose was to obtain a target language paraphrase of a sentence or phrase. The more usual form of checking for meaning among nonnative students was to ask for a translation into the native language (Hebrew).

In the genetics and political science studies, and in sessions with native English speakers in the history study, the informants were interviewed individually by one or more interviewers. The two subjects in the biology study and the three nonnatives in the history study were interviewed in a group. Sessions in the biology, political science, and history studies

1 Except for Cohen and Fine, all the investigators were by design either EFL teachers or teachers-in-training, in order to promote the involvement of teachers in this line of investigation.
2 This fourth study has appeared elsewhere in its entirety (Cohen and Fine 1978).

were tape-recorded. These recordings were played back several times in the data analysis phase.

As can be seen a variety of methodological procedures were used, not so much out of design as out of a lack of one. But although methodological approaches varied, it will be seen that findings from the different studies converged.

Findings

The description of results will focus on a few of the problematic areas that cut across the disciplines, despite differences in both procedures and types of texts.[3] As noted above, these areas were: heavy noun phrase subjects and objects, syntactic markers of cohesion, and the role of nontechnical vocabulary in technical texts.

Heavy noun phrase subjects and objects

Heavy noun phrases, in various syntactic functions (e.g., subject of the main clause, subject of a subordinate clause, object of the preposition), not only caused difficulties for informants across all four studies, but were among the few structures that were predictably problematic for students. In the genetics study, for example, all but one of the seven sentences that the informant identified as being problematic had heavy noun phrases in them. The following is one example:

Thus, it was conjectured that such treatments as holding cells in buffer after irradiation before placing them on nutrient agar plates might function by inhibiting normal growth processes while repair systems completed their task. (Hanawalt 1972: 84)

In the above sentence, a 16-word clause functions as the subject of the subordinate sentence introduced by "that."

In the biology study, the text produced troublesome sentences like the following:

In many unicellular organisms and in some lower plants, nuclei contributing to the zygote are transferred between two cells without the formation of obviously specialized gametes by processes such as partial and temporary fusion (*conjugation*) of ciliated protozoans. (Novikoff and Holzmann, p. 332)

In this sentence, the relatively short noun phrase subject, "nuclei contributing to the zygote" was troublesome because it was not perceived

---

3 Some other problematic areas that we found to cut across disciplines, but which are not discussed in this paper, include: the interpretation of modals, the significance of punctuation or the lack of it, and various problems relating to long, complex sentences.

as one unit.[4] In the political science study, the informant missed the purpose of the paper because of the fact that the purpose was stated as the noun phrase object of a preposition:

The purpose of this paper is to try to redress the resulting imbalance by concentrating detailed attention upon the multiple functions, i.e., observable consequences, of voting for individuals and of elections for political systems in contemporary societies. (Rose and Mossawir, pp. 173–174)

In the history study, we did not ask about structures directly, but rather assessed their difficulty indirectly through comprehension questions. For example, the students were asked to focus on the following paragraph:

The gap between East and West has also been widened by a growing discrepancy in material standards of living. Nowhere is the contrast sharper than between Americans and the peoples of Asia. In part because of accidents of history and geography, we enjoy a far more favorable balance between population and natural resources than do they. As a result we live on an economic plane that appears unattainable by them under existing conditions. This economic gap perpetuates and sometimes heightens the difference between our respective attitudes and ways of life. (Reischauer and Fairbank 1960: 6)

Then the students were asked as a micro question, "Which people have the better balance between population and natural resources?" They answered correctly, "The West." The informants were then asked, "Why?" a question which was meant to probe whether or not they correctly interpreted the adverbial modifier with its noun phrase object: "In part because of accidents of history and geography." The natives gave the correct answer right away. One nonnative answered, "Because they understand the existing conditions" and another mentioned "economic plane."

Thus, we found that across texts and across specialized fields, long groups of words performing a single grammatical function, (noun phrase) were difficult for nonnative readers to perceive as such. The investigator in the genetics study (Glasman) constructed an experimental teaching exercise where the student marked the point at which each noun or verb began and ended and then had to make a one-word noun or verb substitution, whichever was appropriate. Apparently this exercise helped the student to recognize such structures. Once aware of their existence, the nonnative reader can then analyze and understand such rankshifted structures when they appear in a text. The native appears to make such an analysis with far greater ease than the nonnative – and in many cases does so automatically.

Perhaps the methodological approach in the last study (the history

4 The rest of the sentence also created serious problems of grammatical interpretation.

study) is the most crucial – namely, inquiring as to what the student interpreted the passage containing the heavy noun phrase to mean. Candlin (1979) and others would first of all argue that syntactic complexity need not make for difficulty in construing the meaning of the text. Second, they would suggest that it is dangerous to group together structures of the same type, such as heavy noun phrase subjects and objects, in that the meaning they convey may vary greatly depending on the nature of the discourse. For this reason, they would warn teachers against preoccupation with the teaching of lower-order syntactic skills. Thus, the issue is not only that of deciding what structures to teach, but also of determining how much time to devote to teaching them.

Syntactic markers of cohesion

All four of the studies revealed that learners were not picking up on the conjunctive words signaling cohesion, not even the more basic ones like *however* and *thus*. The informant in the genetics study, for example, noted that she had never known the meaning of *thus*, and had simply thought it marked off sentences.

Perhaps the most striking example of difficulty in processing markers of cohesion comes from the history study, specifically with respect to the sequential correlative "also" and "finally." The students were asked the macro question, "Why do the authors favor the historical approach?" in reference to the following passage:

The Approach to East Asia Through Its History. The historical approach seems to us the best for a number of reasons. One is that the peoples of East Asia, more than those of the rest of the world, see themselves in historical perspective. They are strongly aware of their heritage from the past and also conscious of the historical judgment of the future. To approach them through their history is to look at them as they see themselves, which is the first requisite for understanding.

The historical approach is ALSO necessary for a clear understanding of the major aspects of our subject. We are interested first in the distinctive aesthetic, intellectual and institutional achievements of the peoples of East Asia during their long period of semi-isolation from the rest of the world. These cultural achievements can best be studied genetically as they evolved. They should be looked at separately from the rapidly changing, hybrid cultures of the contemporary East Asian countries.

A clear understanding of the traditional cultures of those countries, FINALLY is essential to any comprehension of what is happening in East Asia today. The past is the unseen hand that molds the present; it would be futile to describe a situation of flux in static terms. Only as we look at the long flow of East Asian history can we understand what is happening there now and perceive the direction of motion, which is often more important than the momentary situation itself.

The essence of the present turmoil in East Asia is the interaction between new forces, many of which were derived from the West, and traditional habits and modes of thinking. Our story divides naturally into two major phases: the evolution of traditional East Asian civilization in relative isolation over three thousand years, and the upheavals and modernization of that civilization in recent times under the impact of the modern Western world. This is the reason for dividing the history into two volumes under separate titles.[5]

The rationale for the question was to see if students could perceive the cross-paragraph structure, particularly as signaled by these conjunctive elements (indicated by small caps in the text above). The investigators thought that there were three reasons why the authors favored the historical approach: 1) the peoples of East Asia see themselves in historical perspective, 2) cultural achievements are best studied historically, and 3) one can understand the present *only* in terms of the past. The natives got these three reasons and two of the natives also reanalyzed the first reason into three separate reasons, which included "seeing selves in historical perspective," "heritage," and "seeing future judgment in historical terms." The nonnative did not mention reasons 2) and 3) above at all. One spoke of "heritage" and another mentioned "consciousness of historical judgment." The nonnatives, unlike the natives, thus did not organize the material that they had read when that organization stretched across different paragraphs, although cross-paragraph markers of cohesion were provided in the text.

Clearly, the task of finding the markers of cohesion is a part of good reading generally, even in the native language. But there is more to the task than basic native reading ability and speed. The nonnatives were not attuned to recognizing the conjunctive words, whereas the natives' responses would suggest that these words played a significant role in their understanding of the passage. Upon closer scrutiny of the text, we note that "also" and "finally" are not conspicuously placed: rather, they are buried in their respective sentences. In fact, "finally" appears after a long (10-word) noun phrase subject. Such conjunctive words may have particularly little functional value if, in fact, the nonnative reads more locally than the native – in other words, if s/he has more trouble linking up parts of sentences, linking sentences with other sentences, and linking paragraphs with other paragraphs.

Instances in the history study in which the natives did not answer a question correctly but the nonnatives did, generally were a result of the nonnatives' more "local" reading. The natives tended to pass over specific details which they mistakenly considered unimportant. The nonnatives assigned all material equal value, which in these cases produced

---

5 From: East Asia: The great tradition, by Edwin A. Reishauer and John K. Fairbank (pp. 7–8). Copyright © 1958 and 1960 by Edwin O. Reishauer and John K. Fairbank. Reprinted with the permission of Houghton-Mifflin Company, Boston, Mass., U.S.A.

the correct answer, since the questions concerned detail. For example, with respect to the question, "Why is the study divided into two volumes?" (expected answer, "To separate off the period of isolation of the East from the period of contact with the West," cf. last paragraph of the text above), the natives either did not know or gave too general an answer. Regarding another question, "What do the authors think should be studied historically?" (expected answer, "Aesthetic, intellectual, and institutional achievements," cf. second sentence, second paragraph of above text), the natives again gave too general an answer.

It is important to keep these findings in perspective. First, there may be cases of conjunctive cohesion which are not signaled by conjunctive words. Urquhart (1977) found that native readers, for example, had only slightly more difficulty processing texts that were not marked for intersentential relationship than they did processing texts that were so marked. His finding was that the marking of statements with connectors did not usually affect recall. He concluded that implicit relationships holding between sentences (i.e., relationships not signaled by a conjunctive marker) were important to consider – examples like the following: "The woodpecker is an unusual bird. It bores holes in trees." The point here is that students may attend too much to overt markers, if they are so trained, and may not be ready for texts that do not use them. Furthermore, the same marker may be used somewhat differently in a new text and so be misinterpreted (Candlin 1979).

Furthermore, *cohesion* has been identified as a lower-level element in the obtaining of meaning from a text than is *coherence*, which refers to how the sentences in the text function to produce discourse (Widdowson 1978; Candlin et al. 1978). In other words, a student may see the way two sentences are linked cohesively and yet miss the fact that together they function as an hypothesis or as a refutation. Thus, a teacher may wish to check both for a student's perception of cohesion and of coherence.

The role of nontechnical vocabulary in technical texts

The series of studies underscored for us the reality that knowing the technical terms (i.e., terms that have a specialized meaning in a particular field and are used consistently in that field) is not a sufficient condition for successful reading of specialized material. It was, in fact, the nontechnical terms which created more of a problem. We found that the informants did not give an accurate translation or target-language paraphrase of a surprisingly large number of nontechnical words in context. In the genetics study, these were words like: *essential, giant, diversity, enhance, efficient, maintain, required, emphasis, supplied*, and *determined*: in the biology study: *pattern, distinctive, contributing, resemble*, *however, predict, adequately,* and *invariable;* in the political science study: *decades, assertion, ambiguities,* and *devices;* and in the history study: *discrepancy, futile,* and *perceive.* And this list is merely representative.

To put this in numerical perspective – in the biology study, only 9 out of 32 technical words investigated were indicated by the students as being problematic (e.g., *chiasma, recombinant, episomal*), whereas 45 out of 53 nontechnical words were found to be problematic. In the political science study, the student reported looking up in the dictionary 10 words which we would classify as technical (e.g., *balloting, nomination,* and *duopolistic*) and 34 nontechnical words. In this study, 23% of the terms which the reader considered difficult were technical, a higher percentage than in the biology study. We attributed this difference to two factors: First, biology receives more emphasis in high school than does political science; second, in biology many, if not most, of the technical terms are part of the international scientific vocabulary (I.S.V.), which is transcribed into Hebrew – and this is not the case with the terminology in political science.

In attempting to classify vocabulary as technical or nontechnical, we came to the realization that nontechnical words can be difficult for a variety of reasons, only three of which will be discussed here. The first area of difficulty arises because nontechnical terms may take on a technical meaning in a particular field; and the nonnative reader may only be aware of one of these meanings (either the technical or the nontechnical one). An example from the genetics text was the term *recognition,* which in context appeared to suggest that a particular damage referred to had to be recognized or noticed in some way by the scientist. Checking with the specialist in the field (Selinker 1979), we learned that the term had a technical meaning here, i.e., that there is some biological system present in the organism that becomes aware that a damage has occurred. Another example from the same text was the term *specific,* which was being used in reference to the genetic notion of *specificity,* which is a characteristic of enzymes.

A second area of difficulty with respect to all vocabulary items concerned whether or not they were being used in contextual paraphrase, that is, whether or not the author was using two (or more) words, or phrases, to refer to the same concept. In the political science study, for example, the student did not perceive that *balloting* was used interchangeably for *voting,* and that *assertions* were *statements.* In the genetics study, the issue was more complex. *Repair processes* appeared 10 times in the text, *repair mechanism* 4 times, *repair mode* 3 times, and *repair scheme* 3 times. According to the specialist in the field, *repair processes* and *repair mechanism* were contextual paraphrases, as were *repair mode* and *repair scheme,* but the former pair were more technically specific than the latter. So here we found problems of lexical cohesion not only at the level of synonymy, but across two different levels of specificity. The lexical repetition of the word *repair* seemed to be adding to the difficulty, by suggesting synonymy even when there was no synonymy.

Although we were not able to establish empirically what information the nonnative is missing by not interpreting these contextual paraphrases correctly, it would at least seem that the reading load (i.e., storage and retrieval of information) is greater if he is storing a number of lexical items separately, without realizing that they are to be equated in meaning.

A third area of difficulty that emerged was that of specialized non-technical lexis. We will give one example, that of vocabulary items which indicate time sequence or frequency. In the genetics study, for example, it was found that of 17 words in this category, the student knew only 5: *initial, final, following, gradually,* and *later.* She did not know: *eventual, perpetual, succeeding, ensuing, preceding, progressively, simultaneously, alternately, consecutively, intermittently, subsequent,* and *successive.*

It would appear that useful work can be done in teaching students different categories of nontechnical vocabulary – for it is often these words which are carrying much of the meaning of the text, particularly with regard to scientific writing. But just as there is a question as to how to teach syntactic structures, there are problems in trying to teach lexical meaning. If terms take on meaning as part of the dynamic process of interpreting a text and if the meaning of such lexical items will differ from text to text, how can such terms be taught as if constants? Perhaps it would be necessary to discuss different categories of nontechnical vocabulary and to indicate that the meaning of individual entries may vary according to the nature of the text.

Conclusion

In conclusion, we see that working with student informants from different fields, reading different types of texts (e.g., a survey article, textbook material, and a theoretical analysis), and using different methodological approaches, it is nonetheless possible to derive similar conclusions about certain problematic areas in specialized texts.

Teachers have been preparing texts for many years. If something new is being introduced here in the approach to specialized texts, it is the rigorous analysis of texts in terms of potentially confusing grammatical patterns such as heavy noun phrase subjects and objects, forms signaling grammatical cohesion, and problematic nontechnical vocabulary.

Methodologically, it would appear that the fourth study was the most refined, in that heavy noun phrases and markers of grammatical cohesion were investigated in a way paralleling, as much as possible, the natural task students are faced with in reading technical material – namely, understanding what the passage is about. It is true that students may not come up with appropriate answers under pressure. Although attempts were made to have the subjects prepare the passages ahead of time, there is no question that the interview situation created a certain amount of anxiety and thus deviated from the usual circumstances under which a student would read such text. Another, perhaps more natural approach would be to sit next to and observe individual students while they take part in reading and discussion activities in class (perhaps with videotape backup, if possible – in order to aid in getting student verification afterwards). Then, during the breaks, the observer asks a series of questions about the process that the student used in his reading, and about the meaning that he derived from the material.

Asking students questions about the meaning of a passage without asking about particular structures is intended to discover whether the meaning is perceived regardless of given structures. All the same, finding out whether the meaning was obtained with or without knowledge of the way forms functioned in that segment of the text can still be valuable, particularly when the student does not arrive at an appropriate interpretation of the meaning; for example, what structures may be responsible (if any)? The current line of research is intended to help provide the teacher with research-based insights into what specific elements in the text may be causing inappropriate interpretations.

Perhaps a compromise between asking overtly whether students have difficulty with certain structures and having them give free-response answers to questions would be to have the informants discuss their answers to carefully worded multiple-choice items. The informants would be asked to choose the best answer and explain why it is the best, as well as to explain why each of the distractors is unacceptable (based on Munby 1978). Such a format would impose greater structure on the research activity and would enable us to tap the informants' comprehension strategies.

It may well be that the question posed in this study. "What is problematic in reading texts in a foreign language?" is ultimately less fruitful for curriculum writers and teachers than the question, "How do learners go about solving problems in reading?" The former yields findings as to forms to teach, and the latter yields insights into cognitive strategies to teach. If, in fact, forms may vary in the meaning that is attached to them depending on the text (Candlin 1978, 1979), then the best the teacher can hope to do is alert the reader to strategies that will help him derive meaning despite the shifting function of specific forms.

There is even a further question: Is there only one meaning for a given text? In that the text itself only has "meaning potential" (Halliday 1973, ch. 4), and it is the reader who creates meaning for the text (Candlin 1979), then it may be misleading just to suggest that syntactic structures and lexical items may have different meanings in different text. Rather, it may be important to add that such syntactic structures and lexical items may also be interpreted differently by different readers within the same text – and that the instructor's interpretation of the meaning may only be one of several possible interpretations.

References

Aighes, B., et al. 1977. *Progress report on the BBN group*. Report No. 3720, prepared for NIE. University of Illinois at Urbana/Champaign & Bolt Beranek and Newman, 50 Moulton St., Cambridge, Mass. 02138.

Candlin, C. N. 1978. Discoursal patterning and the equalizing of interpretive opportunity. Lancaster, England: Institute for English Language Education, University of Lancaster.

1979. Discourse analysis: interpretive strategies and the process of reading. Presentation at a Regional University Teachers of English in Israel (UTELI) Meeting, Jerusalem, Israel, January 10, 1979.

Candlin, C. N., J. M. Kirkwood and H. M. Moore. 1978. Study skills in English: theoretical issues and practical problems. In *English for Specific Purposes*, R. Mackay and A. Mountford (Eds.), 190–219. London: Longman.

Cohen, A. D., and J. Fine. 1978. Reading history in English: discourse analysis and the experiences of native and non-native readers. *Working Papers on Bilingualism*, 55–74.

Cowan, J. R. 1974. Lexical and syntactic research for the design of EFL reading materials. *TESOL Quarterly* 8(4): 389–399.

Halliday, M. A. K. 1973. Explorations in the functions of language. London: Edward Arnold.

Halliday, M. A. K., and R. Hasan. 1976. *Cohesion in English*. London: Longman.

Hanawalt, P. C. 1972. Repair of genetic material in living cells. *Endeavor*.

Hosenfeld, C. 1977. A preliminary investigation of the reading strategies of successful and nonsuccessful second language learners. *System* 5(2): 110–223.

1979. Cindy, a learner in today's foreign language classroom. In *The learner in today's environment*, W. C. Born, (Ed.). Montpelier, Vt.: Capital City Press.

Munby, J. 1978. A problem-solving approach to the development of reading comprehension skills. Presentation at the University Teachers of English in Israel (UTELI) Regional Meeting, Jerusalem, January 25.

Novikoff, V., and E. Holtzman. 1976. *Cells and organelles*, 2nd ed. New York: Holt, Rinehart and Winston.

Reischauer, E. O., and J. K. Fairbank. 1960. *East Asia: the great tradition*. New York: Houghton Mifflin.

Rose, R., and R. Mossiwir. 1967. Voting and election: a functional analysis. *Political Studies* 15.

Selinker, L. 1979. On the use of informants in discourse analysis and language for specialized purposes. *International Review of Applied Linguistics in Language Teaching* 17: 189–215.

Selinker, L. and Louis Trimble. 1974. Formal written communication and ESL. *Journal of Technical Writing and Communication* 4: 81–90.

Selinker, L., R. M. Todd-Trimble and L. Trimble. 1976. Presuppositional rhetorical information in EST discourse. *TESOL Quarterly* 10: 281–290.

Todd-Trimble, M., L. Trimble and K. Drobnic (Eds.). 1978. *English for specific purposes: science and technology.* Corvallis, Or.: English Language Institute, Oregon State University.

Urquhart, A. H. 1977. The effect of rhetorical organization on the readability of study texts. Unpublished doctoral diss., University of Edinburgh.

Widdowson, H. G. 1978. *Teaching language as communication.* London: Oxford University Press.

12 This test is unfair: I'm not an economist

J. Charles Alderson *and* A. H. Urquhart

The studies reported in this chapter were designed to test the hypothesis that an English foreign language (EFL) student's background discipline – that is, his knowledge of a particular academic field – would affect his performance on tests of reading comprehension. In other words, we hypothesized that a student of, for example, engineering, would perform better on an engineering text than would a student of economics, even though the general level of EFL proficiency of the two students was equivalent.

In what might be considered the traditional position towards the selection of texts for testing purposes, the aim is to select texts which are sufficiently "general" so as to avoid favouring any particular group of students. It can be seen that underlying this position is a belief that certain texts will favour particular groups, presumably because of the background knowledge available to these groups. To this extent, the traditional position is in line with the hypothesis being investigated here. Where we differ is in our view of the possibility and desirability of using general texts.

The traditional view depends crucially on the following assumptions:

1. that it is possible to find truly "general" texts, that is, texts which are so neutral in content and cultural assumptions that they will not in any significant way favour any particular group.
2. that in English for Academic Purposes (EAP), at least, performance on such texts can be used as predictive of students' performance on texts in their academic field; that, for example, the performance of a would-be post-graduate student of dentistry on a text about piracy in the seventeenth-century Caribbean can be used to predict his or her ability to read research material in dentistry. Both the above assumptions are open to doubt....

If readers bring their background knowledge to the comprehension process, and this knowledge is bound to vary from reader to reader,

From "This test is unfair: I'm not an economist" by J. Charles Alderson and A. H. Urquhart, in P. Hauptman, R. LeBlanc, and M. Bingham Wesche (Eds.), *Second language performance testing/L'Evaluation de la "performance" en langue seconde* (University of Ottawa Press, 1985). Reprinted by permission. A version of this paper was presented at TESOL in Toronto, March 1983.

then there can be no single text-bound comprehension, but rather a host of interpretations. This may not be a problem when all the readers, together with the tester, belong to the same cultural background and share a large number of cultural presuppositions. In EFL, at least at the tertiary level, this situation cannot be expected to occur often. Hence we may expect markedly different interpretations of the same text. Steffensen and Joag-dev (1984) have shown that comprehension can be radically affected by the reader's cultural background. In general, the increased recognition of the importance of background knowledge may lead us to doubt the existence of any text which is "neutral" across a wide range of readers. Certainly we may suspect the "generality" of themes popular with recent textbook writers – pollution, the women's movement etc. Paradoxically, in the EFL context, it is the more specialized texts to which we might expect a relatively homogeneous response. A popular magazine article may activate a wide range of differing schemata among a group of students; a physics text, on the other hand, will presumably be interpreted in similar ways by a group of physicists, regardless of their L1. Widdowson (1979) has argued that subject areas such as physics constitute sub-cultures of their own.

Thus the very existence of general texts can be doubted. Even if they existed, however, the second traditional assumption, that performance on such texts can be used to predict performance on more specialized texts, is very questionable. In part, this is because it seems to involve a belief in a very generalized reading ability, a belief that if one can read one English text, one can read them all. However, the skills involved in responding to a novel by Dickens are likely to be very different from those used in extracting information from an economics text. Still, the skilled reader may have a wide repertoire of skills, which testers may sample using general texts. Thus it is possible that success on general texts can be used to predict performance in other fields. Many L2 readers, however, whose use of English texts is much narrower, may have acquired a much more limited set of skills appropriate only for extracting particular kinds of information from a specialized range of texts. And these skills, successful in the contexts for which they were developed, may not be sufficient for dealing with general texts. Thus it may not be possible to use inability to perform successfully on texts to predict performance on texts more relevant to the student's field of interest. There is plenty of anecdotal evidence, for example English-speaking engineers able to read German texts related to their own speciality but not an article from a German newspaper, to suggest that such an extrapolation is likely to be invalid.

Doubts such as these, and associated fears that suitable students may be denied the possibility of studying in English-speaking countries because of their inadequate performance on traditional proficiency tests, have led to the development of English for Specific Purposes (ESP) tests, the best known of which in the U.K. is the British Council English Language Testing Service (ELTS) test. There is no doubt that such tests have a number of disadvantages compared to the traditional "general" test. They are inevitably more expensive and more difficult to administer. The number of specialist modules is very debatable: do we have a test for all engineers or one for chemical engineers, one for electronic engineers, etc? Then there is the problem of cross-disciplinary studies. If the ESP test contains at least three modules – law, economics, and technology – and a student wishes to study urban studies, with classes in law, economics and technology, which module should the student take? Problems like these are not, on the whole, encountered with general tests.

Should it be found, however, that general tests were discriminating against a major group, say engineers, or that they were having the effect of denying further study to students who were quite competent readers in their own academic area, then these practical advantages would not be enough to ensure the survival, in tertiary ESP, of general tests. The decision thus rests on empirical evidence. However, although we have presented above theoretical objections to the concept of general or neutral texts, together with opinions, based partly on anecdotal evidence, against using general comprehension tests to predict performance in specialized subject areas, it must be said that so far, hard empirical evidence in favour of either the general or the specific approach has been lacking. The two studies reported below were designed to gather such empirical data.

We hypothesized that students reading texts in a familiar content area, that is, related to their area of study, would perform better than students unfamiliar with that subject. The latter, it might be argued, would lack familiarity not only with the content of the subject area, but also with such aspects as genre effect, rhetorical organization, forms of argumentation, and linguistic and non-linguistic relations.

Design of study one[1]

Four groups of students from different academic disciplines were tested at Aston University at the end of a pre-sessional English and Study Skills (ESS) course. The groups were as follows:

1. Fifteen students about to do courses in either development administration or development finance. With one exception, they all had experience in administration or finance. Most had first degrees in economics.
2. Eleven engineers about to study in a variety of post-graduate engineering

---

1 An account of STUDY 1 has appeared in Hughes, A., and D. Porter (Eds.), *Current developments in language testing*. London: Academic Press, 1983.

TABLE 1. GROUP MEANS ON PLACEMENT TEST

Group	1	2	3	4
Score	48.2	48.8	46.0	57.4

fields, e.g., chemical, civil and electrical engineering. All had first degrees in engineering.
3. Six post-graduate students of mathematics and/or physics.
4. Five students of liberal arts, whose first degrees included education, psychology, and language and linguistics.

At the beginning of the ESS course, students had taken, for placement purposes, a 100-item pseudo-random cloze test, made up of nine short texts on various topics. Mean scores for the four groups, which may be taken as a rough guide to each group's linguistic proficiency, are presented in Table 1. It can be seen that, on this measure, the first three groups were virtually equal. Group 4, the Liberal Arts group, was somewhat more proficient.

Five texts were selected, each between 250 and 280 words long. Two were on engineering topics, of which one, dubbed *Electrolytes*, was from an academic monograph, (Gregory 1972), and the other, *Turbines*, was from an engineering periodical (Hulme 1981). Two more texts were related to economic development and finance: *Polanyi* and *Malaysia*, which were taken from the same university text-book (Lathan 1978). The fifth text, *Quixote*, designed to be the general text, was taken from the top level of the Science Research Associates 1963 (SRA) 3B Ratebuilder cards, intended, according to the publishers, for American junior-high and high-school students, and not infrequently used with L2 students. *Electrolytes* and *Malaysia* included a diagram and a table respectively.

As a very rough measure of linguistic complexity, the Fog Index (Gunning 1952) for each text was calculated. The indices were all very similar, ranging from 17.5 to 18.5. Thus in terms of sentence length and word length in syllables, all five texts were closely comparable.

From each text lexical items were deleted which, in the judgement of the authors of this study, were restorable from information in the text, i.e., their restoration was not intended to depend on students' knowledge of the subject area. Particular attention was paid to the selection of items whose restoration depended on understanding of the text as a whole, rather than short chunks of language. In the case of *Electrolytes* and *Malaysia*, some items required information from the diagram or table for successful restoration.

Example
In principle, the electrolyte is simply an ionically conducting layer which serves to prevent the two electrodes from coming into electronic contact, and

allows the passage of ions from one... where they are generated, to the... where they are discharged. This... takes place by diffusion, and does not involve physical movement of the ... itself. Indeed, fuel cells have been... using solid-phase electrolytes. (Extract from *Electrolytes*)

All texts were scored twice, once taking only exact word replacement as correct, then accepting any word which in the judgement of the investigators was suitable in the overall context.

Results

Mean percentage scores for all five texts, using both the exact and acceptable scoring methods, are presented in Table 2.

Comments

1. The Engineers as a group performed better on engineering texts than did Administration/Finance students:
   Exact Scoring: *Turbines*   35.9 vs 34.3
                        Electrolytes 32.7 vs 20.4
   Acceptable Scoring: *Turbines*   54.1 vs 44.0
                        Electrolytes 52.1 vs 34.2
2. Administration/Finance students performed better on administration/finance texts than did the Engineers:
   Exact Scoring: *Polanyi*   13.2 vs 8.7
                        Malaysia 29.4 vs 25.1
   Acceptable Scoring: *Polanyi*   42.7 vs 19.0
                        Malaysia 44.7 vs 34.2
3. It is noticeable from the above scores that the effect of acceptable scoring is to increase the differences between the groups.
4. The Liberal Arts group performed similarly on all texts to the Administration/Finance group. The Administration group (as expected) had a slight advantage on administration texts. The Liberal Arts group performed better than the Administration group on engineering texts. This may have been due to their superior linguistic proficiency.
5. The Science and Mathematics group behaved in a very similar fashion to the Engineering group, doing best on the two engineering texts, although (again as expected) their performance on those texts was somewhat inferior to the Engineering group.
6. There was a marked *text by method* effect. Thus on exact scoring, *Turbines* was the easiest text for all groups, and on aggregate, it was easiest on both scoring methods. The most difficult texts were *Quixote* and *Polanyi*. It should be remembered that *Quixote* was selected as being a general text, and was, moreover, the only text to be chosen from pedagogic English language material. On the basis of the results here, such texts appear to discriminate particularly against engineers and mathematics/physics students.

TABLE 2. MEAN PERCENTAGE SCORES BY TWO SCORING METHODS

| Group/Text | N | Economics | | | | Engineering | | | | General | |
| | | Polanyi | | Malaysia | | Turbines | | Electrolytes | | Quixote | |
		Ex[a]	Acc	Ex	Acc	Ex	Acc	Ex	Acc	Ex	Acc
Development Administration/Finance	15	13.2	42.7	29.4	44.7	34.3	44.0	20.4	34.2	12.2	33.3
Engineering	11	8.7	19.0	25.1	34.2	35.9	54.1	32.7	52.1	7.0	22.5
Science & Mathematics	6	6.1	21.2	23.5	33.3	30.8	40.0	26.7	42.2	14.7	22.5
Liberal Arts	5	15.5	38.2	28.2	34.1	38.0	49.0	26.7	36.0	14.1	30.6
All groups	37	10.9	30.3	26.6	36.6	34.8	46.8	26.6	41.1	12.0	27.2

[a]Ex = exact; Acc = Acceptable

Conclusions: Study 1

The hypothesis was supported that students from a particular discipline would perform better on tests based on texts taken from their own subject discipline than would students from other disciplines. That is, students appear to be advantaged by taking a test on a text in a familiar content area.

For the Engineering and Mathematics/Physics groups in particular, tests in familiar content areas were easier than tests in unfamiliar areas. It will be noticed that on *Quixote*, the administration students performed at least as well as the Liberal Arts group, even though one would be inclined to place it in the academic area of the second group.

It is interesting that, with minor differences, engineering and mathematics/physics students can perhaps be regarded as forming two closely related groups. Similarly, there are close resemblances between the Administration/Finance group and the Liberal Arts group. Should this be confirmed by wider testing, it would seem to be relevant to the problem of how specialized tests should be.

Design of Study 2

Study 1 was intended as a pilot experiment. The numbers of students involved were very small, particularly in the cases of the Liberal Arts and Mathematics/Physics groups. Thus we decided the following year to replicate and extend only minimally the first experiment.

The second study was in two parts. The first was an attempt to replicate exactly the study of the previous year, i.e., the same tests on the same texts were given to a highly comparable group of students on the same pre-sessional course at Aston University one year later. Many of the students would later be studying the same courses as the previous year's students. To these subjects were added a number of comparable students studying on the University of Lancaster's pre-sessional course.

The second part was an attempt to extend the first study by changing the nature of the *test task* – from gap-filling to short answers. However, where possible, the same range of supposed skills and language abilities were covered – the ability to interpret tables, diagrams and associated texts and relate them to each other, the ability to interpret anaphoric reference, to process cohesive items, to identify main ideas, etc.

At Aston, students fell into very similar groups as in the previous year, namely:

1. Development Administration and Finance. To this group were added a number of Economics students (DAFE).

TABLE 3. GROUP MEAN SCORES ON PLACEMENT TEST

Group	1	2	3	4
Score	46.0	41.3	43.3	57.8

TABLE 4. GROUP MEAN SCORES ON ELBA

Group	1	2	3	4
Score	57.8	48.25	42.3	64.6

2. Engineering.
3. Science and Mathematics. This was a broader group than the previous Mathematics/Physics group.
4. Liberal Arts.

For these students, the same measure of linguistic proficiency was available, the 100-item Placement Test. Scores are presented in Table 3. It can be seen that these scores are quite similar to the group scores of the previous year.

At Lancaster, the groups were very similar, namely:

1. Economics
2. Engineering
3. Science and Mathematics
4. Liberal Arts

For these groups English Language Battery (ELBA) scores were available, and they are presented in Table 4.[2] It can be seen that, as at Aston, the Liberal Arts group were the most linguistically proficient. Unlike Aston, the Economics group was markedly superior in proficiency to both the Engineering group and the Science and Mathematics group.

At this point it seems appropriate to comment on the difficulties encountered when placing a student in a particular group. For example, how does one place a student who has a Masters degree in a liberal arts subject, is going to study librarianship, but works in her national institute for national planning, is concerned daily with reading texts on economics, and who, at the same time as the pre-sessional course, takes an optional course, *A Refresher Course in Economics*? More generally, there is the problem caused by the fact that many engineers enrol for management courses; thus one cannot conclude that because a student intends to study management, he is not an engineer. On the other hand, in our experience all students entering post-graduate courses in engi-

---

2 ELBA is a postgraduate admissions test for foreign students used until recently by the University of Edinburgh.

TABLE 5. NUMBER OF STUDENTS COMPLETING TEXTS BY EITHER OR BOTH
ANSWERING METHODS

	Gap-filling		Short answer		Both:	
	Aston	Lancaster	Aston	Lancaster	Aston/Lancaster	Total
DAFE[a]	18	8	24	9	16/8	24
Engineering	17	4	16	4	16/4	20
Science & Mathematics	32	6	28	6	24/6	30
Liberal Arts	13	9	10	16	10/9	19

[a]DAFE = Development Administration, Finance, Economics

neering have undergraduate degrees in the same subject. As mentioned
earlier, this is a general problem in ESP testing, and faces the tester with
the problem of whether students should be tested according to their
previous academic experience, or according to the course they are about
to enter. It is hoped that the present study and subsequent ones will
throw some light on this difficulty.

Students at both universities performed the gap-filling task first. The
short-answer test on the same texts was performed a week later. The
numbers of students involved in (a) the gap-filling test, (b) the short-
answer test, and (c) both tests are set out in Table 5.

Results

Gap-filling

Mean percentage scores for all the groups are presented in Table 6. On
this occasion, all tests were scored three times, taking (a) only exact
word restoration as correct, then (b) taking synonym replacement as
correct, and finally (c) taking any word considered acceptable in the
overall context.

Significant differences between mean scores are presented in Table 7.

COMMENTS

1. Students of Development Administration, Finance and Economics (DAFE)
   performed significantly better on *Polanyi* than did the Engineers or the Science and Mathematics group. They also performed better than the Engineers,
   though not the Science and Mathematics group, on *Malaysia*.
2. In contrast, the Engineers on this occasion did not perform better than the
   other groups on either of the engineering texts. However, the Science and
   Mathematics group performed better than the DAFE group on *Electrolytes*.

TABLE 6. GROUP MEANS AND STANDARD DEVIATIONS FOR EACH TEXT USING THE
GAP-FILLING TECHNIQUE SCORED BY 3 DIFFERENT METHODS

Group[a]		*Polanyi*			*Malaysia*			*Turbines*			*Electrolytes*			*Quixote*		
		a^b	*b*	*c*	*a*	*b*	*c*	*a*	*b*	*c*	*a*	*b*	*c*	*a*	*b*	*c*
DAFE[c]	M	9	31	43	17	33	39	33	47	56	19	34	40	10	28	33
	SD	9	23	22	8	16	22	14	20	21	12	18	16	9	18	20
Engi-	M	3	14	27	10	23	24	32	49	52	21	40	47	5	18	25
neering	SD	4	12	18	9	17	19	11	19	19	12	16	16	7	12	14
Science	M	6	17	27	20	31	33	30	42	47	28	47	54	7	20	22
& Math.	SD	6	13	17	7	11	14	15	21	20	11	13	15	6	11	14
Liberal	M	13	30	54	21	33	34	43	61	63	22	37	44	16	38	44
Arts	SD	12	19	24	14	23	21	13	17	23	16	21	21	11	20	21

[a]Variable *N*
[b]a = exact, b = synonym, c = acceptable
[c]DAFE = Development Administration, Finance, Economics

3. The Liberal Arts did well on most texts, being much better than the Engineering and Science and mathematics groups on *Polanyi* and *Quixote* and better than the Science and Mathematics group on *Turbines*. Presumably this was due to their superior linguistic proficiency, although even this did not enable them to perform better than the Engineers on the two engineering texts.

Short answers

Mean scores are presented in Table 8. Significant differences between groups are set out in Table 9.

COMMENTS

1. The DAFE group did better than the Engineers on both the (DAFE) texts. They did not, however, outperform the Science and Mathematics group.
2. On the other hand, there was no significant difference in means between the DAFE group and either the Engineers or the Science and Mathematics group on the two engineering texts.
3. The Liberal Arts group did well on *Polanyi*, outperforming the Engineers and the Science and Mathematics group, though not the DAFE group, and, as expected, outperformed all groups on *Quixote*.

Discussion

On the whole, the results support the hypothesis. On both test methods, the DAFE group performed significantly better on DAFE texts than did

TABLE 7. SIGNIFICANT DIFFERENCES BETWEEN MEAN SCORES FOR EACH TEXT ACCORDING TO SCORING METHOD

Text	Group	Engineering a[a]	b	c	Science & Mathematics a	b	c	Liberal Arts a	b	c
Polanyi	DAFE[b]	NS	$p \leq .05$	$p \leq .05$	NS	$p \leq .05$	$p \leq .01$			
	Engineering							$p \leq .05$	$p \leq .05$	$p \leq .05$
	Science & Mathematics							$p \leq .05$	$p \leq .05$	$p \leq .001$
Malaysia	Engineering				$p \leq .01$	NS	NS	$p \leq .05$	NS	NS
Turbines	Science & Mathematics							$p \leq .05$	$p \leq .05$	$p \leq .05$
Electrolytes	DAFE				NS	$p \leq .05$	$p \leq .01$			
Quixote	DAFE				NS	NS	.05			
	Engineering							$p \leq .01$	$p \leq .01$	$p \leq .01$
	Science & Mathematics							$p \leq .01$	$p \leq .01$	$p \leq .001$

Note: Only the results yielding significant differences have been reported.

[a] a = exact; b = synonym; c = acceptable

[b] DAFE = Development Administration, Finance, Economics

TABLE 8. GROUP MEANS AND STANDARD DEVIATIONS FOR EACH TEXT USING
THE SHORT-ANSWER TECHNIQUE

Group		Polanyi	Malaysia	Turbines	Electrolytes	Quixote
DAFE[a]	M	47.1	56.1	53.8	42.0	55.4
	SD	25.1	22.3	17.1	28.7	22.0
Engineering	M	24.5	42.3	58.1	45.1	48.5
	SD	22.7	23.7	24.1	25.9	21.9
Science &	M	34.9	46.1	58.0	47.5	40.8
Mathematics	SD	22.3	20.8	16.4	18.6	21.3
Liberal	M	55.7	54.4	60.3	46.6	70.8
Arts	SD	22.8	20.0	20.2	19.4	14.3

[a]DAFE = Development Administration, Finance, Economics

TABLE 9. SIGNIFICANT DIFFERENCES BETWEEN GROUP MEANS (T TEST) FOR
EACH TEXT

Text	Group	Engineers	Science & Mathematics	Liberal Arts
Polanyi	DAFE[a]	$p \leq .01$	NS	NS
	Engineering		NS	$p \leq .001$
	Science & Mathematics			$p \leq .01$
Malaysia	DAFE	$p \leq .05$	NS	NS
Quixote	DAFE	NS	$p \leq .05$	$p \leq .01$
	Engineering		NS	$p \leq .001$
	Science & Mathematics			$p \leq .001$

Note: Only texts yielding significant differences have been reported
[a]DAFE = Development Administration, Finance, Economics

the Engineers. The Liberal Arts group did best on the general text.
However, with one exception, the Engineers and Science and Mathematics groups did not outperform the other groups on the engineering
texts. Possible reasons for this will be discussed later; at the moment,
though, it looks as if these two groups would be disadvantaged by the
use of texts outside their own fields of study.

Before we return to a discussion of why some groups performed better
than others, it is worthwhile looking at some points of interest which
emerge from an examination of scores on both test methods.

1. There is evidence of a strong method effect. Although the overall
correlation between the gap-filling test and the short answer is fairly
high (.78) when results are summed across texts, correlations for individuals and groups vary widely. Moreover, the rank order of text dif-

ficulty does not remain stable across methods. On the gap-filling test, *Electrolytes* is ranked second in overall difficulty, that is, it is comparatively easy. *Quixote*, on the other hand, is ranked fourth, i.e., a difficult text. On short answers, however, the ranks are reversed, with *Quixote* ranked second and *Electrolytes* ranked fourth.

2. In spite of this, the text effect mentioned earlier remains reasonably constant. With both methods *Turbines* emerges as the easiest text and *Polanyi* the most difficult.

3. The suggestion made in Study 1 that we have, in effect, not four groups but two is supported by the results of Study 2. Taking both test methods into account, there are no significant differences between the Engineers and the Science and Mathematics group, and only one significant difference between DAFE students and the Liberal Arts group (short answers – *Quixote*). As said before, this result has relevance to the question of how many specialized tests are required.

Finally, we return to the problem of explaining the results. The "background knowledge" hypothesis was only partially confirmed: DAFE students did better on DAFE texts than did Engineers, but the converse was not the case.

Linguistic proficiency would clearly seem to be one factor involved. The fact that on both test methods the Liberal Arts group performed better than any other group on *Quixote* can be explained in terms of the hypothesis. The same explanation is not available when we try to account for the fact that the group also did best on *Polanyi* and *Turbines*. For the Lancaster students, scores on ELBA and ELTS were available, and correlations between the students' performance on these language tests and the present tests are presented in Table 10. As can be seen from the table, the highest correlations between the tests occur in the case of *Polanyi* and *Turbines*. This is, then, quite strong evidence that it was linguistic proficiency that enabled the Liberal Arts group to do well on these two texts.

We are left with the problem of why the Engineers did not do better than the DAFE group on the engineering texts. It may be that this is again a matter of linguistic proficiency – it will be remembered that the Lancaster economists were more proficient than the Engineering or Science and Mathematics groups. This does not explain, however, why the Engineers did at least as well as the DAFE group on the *Electrolytes* text (both methods) and on *Turbines* (short-answer method). What we need is an explanation which combines the effects of linguistic proficiency and of background knowledge so as to account for the totality of the results. An examination of the gap-filling scores might lead one to the following explanation. *Turbines* and *Electrolytes* are overall the easiest texts, ranking first and second respectively. That is, the two engineering texts are, on average, the easiest texts. It might be possible

TABLE 10. TEST CORRELATIONS WITH ELBA AND ELTS

	ELBA			ELTS		
	1	2	Total	G1	G2	M1
Short answer[a]						
Malaysia	.45	.38	.43	.45	NS	.38
Polanyi	.52	.52	.56	.68	.63	.69
Turbines	.42	.50	.50	.55	.41	.49
Electrolytes	NS	NS	NS	.44	NS	NS
Quixote	NS	.45	.40	.61	NS	.49
Gap-filling (acceptable scoring method)[b]						
Malaysia	NS	.34	NS	.55	NS	.54
Polanyi	.53	.61	.63	.67	.51	.71
Turbines	.57	.66	.66	.73	NS	NS
Electrolytes	NS	NS	NS	NS	NS	NS
Quixote	.50	.46	.51	NS	NS	NS

Note: ELBA: 1 = Listening Skills, 2 = Reading Skills. ELTS: G1 = Reading Skills, G2 = Listening Skills, M1 = Study Skills.
[a]ELBA: $N = 35$; ELTS: $N = 20$.
[b]ELBA: $N = 21/25$; ELTS: $N = 11/13$.

to claim that below a certain level of text difficulty (of necessity undefined), a certain score could be arrived at by means of (a) linguistic proficiency and (b) general knowledge of the world. Thus on an easy text, all groups could be expected to get roughly the same score, with the possible exception of Liberal Arts, who might score higher. And Table 6 seems to bear this out: for example, on *Turbines*, exact scoring, the groups scored as follows: DAFE 33, Engineering 32, Science and Mathematics 30, and Liberal Arts 43.

Beyond a certain level of linguistic difficulty, the argument continues, more specialized background knowledge would become more important, being used to "top up" linguistic proficiency scores. Thus on the two economics texts, which on gap-filling are ranked overall third and fifth, the DAFE group were able to use their background knowledge to gain an advantage over the Engineers.

Such an explanation has a certain superficial attraction. Admittedly the idea of a "pure" linguistic proficiency base, added to by means of background knowledge, is probably the antithesis of the schema-based view of comprehension. However, gap-filling is not a "natural" comprehension task, and it might be argued that in the context, such an explanation might be appropriate.

The explanation does not, however, stand up to further data analysis. In the gap-filling test, *Electrolytes* was a comparatively easy text; in the short answer test, however, it was a difficult text, yet this did not prevent the DAFE group from doing as well on it as the Engineers.

Secondly, if on the gap-filling test, *Electrolytes* was a genuinely easy text linguistically, then one would have expected the Liberal Arts students to do well on it. However, if one compares their performance with that of the other groups, it can be seen that this was not the case.

Thirdly, if *Electrolytes* was a linguistically easy text, one would expect a high correlation between performance on it and scores on language tests. However, examination of Table 10 shows that this was not the case: there was virtually no correlation between *Electrolytes* and the two language tests.

This explanation having apparently failed, we can at present see no obvious alternative explanation. Probably the best way forward would be to replicate the study using a wider range of texts, in order to get rid of what may be the idiosyncratic effects of particular texts.

Conclusions

The studies described in this paper have shown that academic background can have an effect on reading comprehension. They are thus a contribution to research into the nature of comprehension in general. They have also shown that particular groups of students may be disadvantaged by being tested on areas outside their academic field. If these findings are supported by further studies, then they will represent important evidence in support of the need for ESP proficiency tests.

References

Gregory, D. 1972. *Fuel cells.* London: Mills and Boon.

Gunning, R. 1952. *The technique of clear writing.* New York: McGraw-Hill.

Hulme, B. 1981. Development of off-shore turbine packages for power generation and mechanical drive. *General Electric Company Journal of Science and Technology* 47.

Latham, A. 1978. *The international economy and the under-developed world, 1864–1914.* London: Croom Helm.

Steffensen, M. S., and C. Joag-dev. 1984. Cultural knowledge and reading. In *Reading in a foreign language,* J. C. Alderson and A. H. Urquhart (Eds.). London: Longman.

Widdowson, H. 1979. *Explorations in applied linguistics.* Oxford: Oxford University Press.

13 The effects of induced schemata on the "short circuit" in L2 reading: non-decoding factors in L2 reading performance

Thom Hudson

First component effects on L2

Second language research in the past few years has attempted to determine the extent to which the psycholinguistic perspective of L1 reading can explain L2 reading. Goodman (1971) hypothesizes that the reading process, a process in which proficient readers make generally successful predictions, will be much the same for all languages. Data-based research has supported this psycholinguistic concept of reading universals for L2 reading, and has indicated that one's first language does not determine one's reading proficiency in L2 (Rigg 1977a, and 1977b [reprinted as Chapter 14 in this volume]). However, Clarke (1979) found that a language ceiling in L2 effectively prohibits the complete transfer of L1 reading skills to L2 reading. The results of his study suggest that although the psycholinguistic assumptions of universals may be justified, the role of language proficiency in L2 may be greater than has previously been assumed by L2 researchers interested in the psycholinguistic perspective of reading. Thus, a "short circuit" in the good reader's system is caused by a limited control over the language. Cziko (1978) suggests that syntactic, semantic, and discourse constraints serve as important sources of information for the fluent L1 reader and that much of the difficulty in L2 reading may be due to an inability to make full use of those constraints because of low language proficiency. The conclusions drawn imply that an increasing emphasis in L2 reading problem remediation should lie in the first component rather than in the second component. In terms of

Reprinted by permission from "The effects of induced schemata on the 'short circuit' in L2 reading: non-decoding factors in L2 reading performance" by Thom Hudson, *Language Learning* 32(1), pp. 3–31. (The first page and a half of the original article have been deleted here.)

This is a revised version of a study done while the author was a graduate student at the University of California, Los Angeles. The data reported were collected as part of a larger project (see Hudson 1978). I would like to thank Frances Hinofotis and John Schumann for their insights and help. Further thanks go to Richard Schreck and James Melia for their comments on an earlier draft of this paper.

L2 reading then, there is a renewed emphasis on the traditional or decoding view of reading as parasitic on language.

An additional implication for L2 reading relates to the short circuit and its causes across levels of language proficiency. Cziko indicated that the reading behaviors of advanced proficiency L2 readers paralleled native speaker reading behaviors, while those of intermediate and low level L2 readers did not. While all three proficiency levels read anomalous texts more rapidly than random texts, indicating the use of syntactic constraints, only the native speakers and the advanced L2 readers read meaningful texts significantly faster than anomalous texts, indicating the use of both syntactic and semantic constraints. Further, the native speakers and the advanced L2 readers were aided by the discourse constraints available in normal prose over 5th and 25th order approximations of normal prose (see Oller 1975, for description), as measured by cloze passage exact response. Intermediate L2 readers were not aided and no data were collected for beginning level L2 readers. Clarke indicated that low level L2 readers who were good L1 readers showed a reduced ability to utilize the good reader strategy of relying more heavily on semantic than on syntactic cues when reading in L2, and thus indicated a reduced measured superiority over poor L1 readers when both read L2 materials. Despite this reduced ability to transfer L1 skills, however, the good readers were still significantly better L2 readers than the poor readers at the same level of language proficiency. Thus, while the results from Cziko and Clarke would indicate that basic language competence is involved in reading comprehension, the fact that the good L1 readers maintained an advantage over poor L1 readers at their proficiency level when both were reading L2 indicates that some nonlanguage skill operates. That is, it seems likely that reading skills per se, second component factors, affect the degree to which the proficiency ceiling restricts comprehension, just as the proficiency ceiling may restrict the degree to which good reading skills are applied. In this symbiosis, either component can affect the degree to which the other affects comprehension.

Second component factors in the short circuit

While language competence is obviously a major factor in L2 reading, a question arises as to whether the results of the research indicate a need to place the cause(s) of the "short circuit" in the first component or whether some alternate factor in the second component, a factor not indicated through cloze passages or syntactic to semantic comparison, may require attention. Results of the research discussed above have indicated a breakdown in the first component processes by L2 readers, but there is a need to consider the part played by nonsyntactic, nonsemantic, and nondiscourse elements in L2 reading, and to consider whether, and how, the role played by these elements changes across levels of language proficiency. It is necessary to look at what second component factors are involved in the nontransference of good reading behaviors and how these interact with differing levels of a first component linguistic ceiling to form, in effect, a combined linguistic and psycholinguistic ceiling.

Research by cognitive psychologists into the influences on L1 reading comprehension of "schemata," that is, knowledge structures which the reader brings to the text, provides two important insights into the non-visual information processing problems the L2 reader may confront (Anderson and McGaw 1973; Anderson and Ortony 1975; Anderson et al. 1976; Anderson et al. 1977; Frederiksen 1975; Schallert 1976). First, the research provides insight into the effects of extratextual background knowledge on processing. Second, it indicates how during the process of "schemata" reconciliation, the process of fitting new input to existing knowledge structures, good reader strategies may cause a breakdown in comprehension.

First, while decoding based theories of reading hold that difficulties in reading comprehension can be traced to failures of skill, Anderson et al. (1977) conclude that "schemata" which the reader brings to the text are far more important than structures and patterns which are in some sense "in" the text. Further, applicable to L2 reading, Anderson et al. conclude that "the schemata by which people attempt to assimilate text will surely vary according to age, subculture, experience, education, interests and belief systems" (1977:378). From the perspective of schemata theory, the principal determinant of the knowledge a person can acquire from reading is the knowledge he or she already possesses. In their experiment, Anderson et al. (1977) produced two passages of about 145 words each. Each passage could be given at least two distinct interpretations. One passage could be interpreted as being about either a convict planning his escape or a wrestler trying to break the hold of an opponent. The other passage could be interpreted as being about friends coming together to play cards or about a rehearsal session of a woodwind ensemble. The passages were given to subjects from the physical education department and to subjects from the music department. The results indicated that the interpretation which people give to a message is influenced by their backgrounds. Further, 62% of the subjects were unaware of any possible interpretation of the passage other than the one they gave. In discussing the implications of schemata theory, the researchers state:

It may turn out that many problems in reading comprehension are traceable to deficits in knowledge rather than deficits in linguistic skill narrowly conceived; that is, the young readers may not possess the schemata needed to comprehend passages. Or, they may possess relevant schemata but not know how to bring them to bear. Or, they may not be facile at changing schemata when the first one tried proves inadequate; they may, in other words, get stuck in assimilating text in inappropriate, incomplete, or inconsistent schemata. (Anderson et al. 1977:378)

Although this concept is directed toward the child native speaker, it may also be applicable to adult L2 readers. Any one, or combination, of the above three deficits may be active in the attempt to transfer L1 reading skills to the L2 condition.

The second implication of schemata theory for the L2 reading process is the indication that the process of attempting to utilize context to establish the meaning of a message which has been encoded in print inherently involves reading strategies which may themselves contribute to the short circuit. First, it must be borne in mind that reading is meaning oriented, and, in Smith's terms, the reader is not moving from words to meaning, but rather is moving from meaning to words (Smith 1971). In this, reading is similar to any other process of acquiring information, and the basic strategy is the reduction of uncertainty, with the reader "touching as few bases as necessary" to reduce the uncertainty. The significance for L2 reading research is the recognition that readers will apply meaning to a text regardless of the degree to which they successfully utilize syntactic, semantic, or discourse constraints. That is, while there may be a short circuit in the application of good reading skills as measured by an external instrument, there will not be a short circuit in the fact of meaning being applied. The application of meaning may prevent the reader from responding to linguistic cues. Here, the comprehended meaning of a message is fundamentally dependent upon a reader's knowledge of the world and analysis of context, in addition to his or her use of the local linguistic characteristics of the message. For the reader, the scope of context ranges from base linguistic constraints to his or her physical and social milieu, while meaning is seen as including the sense, reference, truth value, illocutionary force, perlocutionary effect, and significance of the message (Anderson et al. 1977). Only those local constraints which are necessary to fill out an internal representation will be attended to or determined to be salient. Here, syntactic constraints, semantic constraints, and basic comprehension are not static categories, and the production of semantically correct responses is relative to whatever internal representation has been generated by the reader in terms of the particular textual constraints he or she has determined to be salient. The fact of "touching as few bases as necessary," a good reader strategy, thus may itself restrict the use of local cues. That is, the reader may internally establish comprehension by using good strategies and ignore local constraints which militate against his or her "comprehension." Thus, this process of utilizing context to match meaning involves basic strategies which when transferred from L1 to L2 may place a ceiling on the utilization of linguistic, semantic, and textual cues.

Schemata instantiation

The process whereby schemata and factors of personal history influence comprehension is seen in terms of how schemata are "instantiated" (Anderson et al. 1976). Instantiation refers to the particularized representation of the general abstract and stereotypical schemata which the reader brings to task. The schemata are abstract in the sense that they contain a slot or place holder for each constituent element in a knowledge structure. They are stereotyped in that they indicate typical relationships among the elements. The reader is involved in a process of constructing a correspondence between the relevant schemata and the givens or knowns of a message. The ingredients needed to fill the slots will not always be found in the message itself, but may be reader supplied. As the correspondence is constructed, the reader gains a sense that the message in the input has been and is being comprehended. When the slots of the schemata are filled with enough particular cases, a schema is said to be instantiated. It is not known until the schema is instantiated that the representation in the message makes sense and is consistent. In other words, comprehension of a message entails drawing information from both the message and the internal schemata until sets are reconciled as a single schema or message in which the constraints of both the graphic message and the internal schemata are satisfied (Anderson et al. 1976). What is semantically complete will depend upon the amount of completeness needed to reconcile the schemata as defined by the reader.

As an example of this process, consider the following three sentences:

He picked up his axe. He held it softly for a moment and blew sharp notes through its bell. The crowd listened and cheered him; they loved his saxophone playing.

When the first sentence is read, it is interpreted and a schemata is produced. However, when followed by the second sentence, the constraints of *axe*, *blew*, *sharp notes*, and *bell* are not reconciled. At this point the reader may either dismiss the initial schemata or become confused and continue to attempt reconciliation of the two sentences. Yet, when the third sentence is added, the reader may reconcile the schemata in reinterpreting and instantiating the definitions of axe as a jazz instrument, namely a saxophone. Alternatively, the reader can retain the schemata from the first sentence and impose a reconciliation from his or her background knowledge, a reconciliation which is not correct. Anderson and Ortony (1975) have indicated that the mental representation of the to-be-comprehended sentences is generally more elaborate and detailed than the words in the utterance might appear to entail. Thus, the first image may be so full and so strong that it will not be reinterpreted. This is not a first component problem or the result of a linguistic ceiling. Only enough slots need to be filled to provide the meaning which leads to reconciliation and recognition. The image may be reconciled and no incoming information allowed to fill slots and contradict the instantiated schema.

Schemata instantiation and associated meaning

The process of instantiation is further important to an understanding of L2 reading problems with regard to the semantic associations which the reader has available when instantiating a schema. Here, the robustness of the associations and networks of relations among the constituents of the schemata which the reader employs to produce a complete image will determine whether the reader is able to reconcile information correctly. That is, the reader is required to reevaluate which associated meanings, or distinctive features of relations, are being emphasized in the message. Consequently, according to Anderson and Ortony, it would follow that our knowledge is not a static knowledge, but rather is a continuously reorganized construct, reorganized during the cognitive processing of information into available schemata. For instance, different associations are called for in the following sentences:

1. Pianos are pleasant to listen to.
2. Pianos are heavy to move.

Notice the different associations with piano and the need for different available slots in the schemata. In the first sentence, the musical aspect of pianos is important and it is immaterial whether they are heavy or not. The reverse is true in the second sentence (Anderson and Ortony 1975:169). Thus, our knowledge of both attributes is important, and the schemata we construct around the piano in making sense of the message is continually reorganized. Both aspects must be available to us in processing meaning. Without knowledge as to one or both aspects of pianos, the corresponding sentence would be difficult to process.

Thus, people's internal representations for messages contain elements which could not be derived directly or solely from the constituent words. Anderson and Ortony insist that models of human memory will have to allow for an interaction between incoming information and existing knowledge if they are to cope with the elaboration and particularization of images. They specifically claim that the comprehension and memory of input involve the construction of representations within the schemata which cannot be adequately predicted from mere dictionary knowledge of the words which are read. Rather, the representation of the image is generally more detailed than that which would arise from considering simply the words themselves. The store of knowledge about the world and the analysis of context are heavily involved in the process of fitting meaning to schemata.

It should be noted here that the reading problems of the L2 reader are not due to an absence of attempts at fitting and providing specific schemata, since the projection and fitting of schemata is inherent in the model of information processing. Rather, the problem lies in projecting appropriate schemata. The high level dominant schemata which L2 readers bring with them from their culture and background are givens. Just as with L1 readers, dominant schemata are often imposed on a text, even when, according to some third person, some distortion and damage is done to the information contained in the text (Anderson et al. 1977). Frequently, intrusions appear and ambiguous material is distorted in order to place the message and the schemata in correspondence. Distortions and intrusions will appear when there is a lack of correspondence between the schemata contained in the text and the schemata by which the reader assimilates the text (Anderson et al. 1977). Additionally, it will happen when the initial representation is strong enough to prevent consideration of alternates.

Thus, if schemata theory is applicable to L2 reading, it may explain the part played in the reader's short circuit by second component factors. It may further help to explain why the good readers in Clarke's research lost an advantage over poor readers, and why the lower level readers in Cziko's study did not appear to be aided by the use of discourse cues. Basically, the issue here is whether the non-use of semantic and discourse constraints by L2 readers is a symptom of low L2 proficiency, or whether it is a symptom of false schemata production and reconciliation in conjunction with low language proficiency.

The study

The purpose of the present study is to examine the role played by schemata in L2 reading by adult ESL students who are proficient readers in their native language. Specifically, this study examined the effects of three types of reading treatments to determine the following:

1. Can schemata theory explain the L2 short circuit of good reading strategies by proficient L1 readers as a second component factor?
2. If readers are induced to produce consistent initial schemata, can this override the effects of an L2 linguistic ceiling?

3. Is the inducement to produce consistent schemata equally effective across levels of L2 language proficiency?

Confirmation of the schemata theory was to be recognized if comparison indicated that subjects utilized induced schemata in comprehending a text. That is, schemata theory would predict that subjects would utilize induced schemata to reconcile the incoming information, and would be better able to select relevant textual information than when they did not have induced schemata. If this obtains (i.e., if scores indicate superiority of induced schemata within or across levels of proficiency), then there is support for the view that the nontransference of good reading skills is partially due to second component factors.

Method

Three methods of intervention which allowed three types of schemata reconciliation were designed to provide Ss with text. The three methods are termed Pre-Reading (PRE), Vocabulary (VOC), and Read-Test/Read-Test (RT). The PRE method was designed to explicitly induce schemata prior to reading and to indicate the effects of systematic schemata exercises. The VOC and RT methods served as controls for self-reconciliation through the text. The VOC method was designed to provide vocabulary items which might be unknown but were essential for comprehension of the text. This indicates the effectiveness of lexical knowledge in schemata reconciliation. The RT method was designed to allow self-reconciliation through exposure to text. That is, it tested the effectiveness of utilizing local context to reinterpret an instantiated, or partially instantiated, schema.

Subjects

The subjects for the study were 93 students studying ESL at an intensive language institute. The majority of the subjects were planning to attend universities in the United States, and most intended to study in scientific or technical fields. The subjects comprised the school population of beginning, intermediate, and advanced level readers as defined by their reading class level. The group was heterogeneous in terms of language background. A profile of the Ss is shown in Figure 1.

Materials

Nine graded reading passages from Science Research Associates Reading Lab IIIa (1973) and Lab 3a (1964) were selected. Three of the selected passages fell into each of the proficiency levels which matched Ss' reading

Language background:	Farsi	43
	Japanese	16
	Spanish	12
	Arabic	14
	Chinese	5
	Turkish	1
	Portuguese	1
	Indonesian	1
Sex:	Male	71
	Female	22
Age range:	18 to 30 years	

Figure 1 Background information on Ss

levels. The proficiency levels were defined as: Beginning $= 3.0–4.5$ (SRA), Intermediate $= 6.0–7.5$ (SRA), Advanced $= 9.0–12.0$ (SRA). For each of these reading passages, pre-reading activities were developed. These activities involved a set of visuals about the general topic of the passage, and a set of questions about the visuals. Second, a vocabulary list for each passage was developed which included essential lexical items. Third, a ten-item, four-distractor multiple choice reading comprehension test was developed for each passage.

Design and procedure

The basic design of the study is a split-plot (repeated measures) design in which the within-subjects treatment, type of reading intervention, has three levels: PRE, VOC, and RT. The between-subjects portion of the design consists of subjects nested within classes which are nested within order (of within-subject treatment) which are crossed with levels of proficiency. The researcher performed all instruction during the regularly scheduled reading workshop hour. The instructional sequence was counterbalanced to account for possible maturation or sequence effect. See Figure 2 for sequence of instruction by level.

Each reading passage was taught using each of the three treatments. In the PRE condition, Ss were given the set of cue pictures and instructed to briefly look through the set. They were then asked the set of focus questions which accompanied each set of cue pictures. During the last two minutes of the cue picture discussion, each subject silently wrote self-generated predictions of what he or she expected to find in the reading passage. These predictions were written on the page following the set of cue pictures (see Appendix for sample instrument). Ss then had fifteen minutes in which to read the passage. After fifteen minutes, the passage and pictures were collected and the reading comprehension

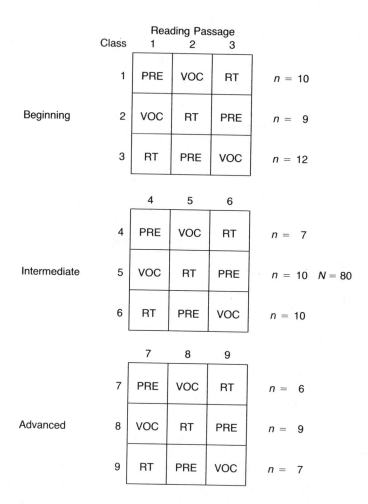

Figure 2   Sequence of instruction by level, counterbalanced for maturation and order effects. N = all Ss for whom no data were missing.

test was distributed. Ten minutes were allowed for completion of this test.

In the VOC condition, Ss were given a list of vocabulary items which would appear in the reading passage. They were allowed time to read the list silently. It was then gone over aloud item by item, and definitions were given for all items. Following the vocabulary list presentation, the post-prediction sequence of the PRE condition was followed.

In the RT condition, Ss were given the reading passage and instructed to read silently for fifteen minutes. The reading selection was then collected and the ten-minute comprehension test was distributed. The test was col-

Time in minutes

	0 5 10 15 20 25 30 35 40		
Prereading (PRE)	Visual presentation & questions	Silent reading	Comprehension test
Vocabulary (VOC)	Vocabulary list discussion	Silent reading	Comprehension test
Read-test (RT)	Silent reading	Compre-hension test	Silent reading Comprehension test

Figure 3 Definition of treatments and temporal relationships of three treatments

lected at the end of ten minutes, and the Ss received the identical reading passage. They were allowed ten minutes for this reading. At the end of this time, passages were collected and a comprehension test identical to the first was distributed. Ss were allowed five minutes for this test. See Figure 3 for a definition of treatments and the temporal relationships.

Data analysis

A 3×3 analysis of variance (BMDP2V) with one trial factor (3 levels), types of treatment, and two grouping factors, order and level, was used to determine overall effect on scores due to type of treatment or sequence of treatments. Subsequently, a comparison for differences among means in the comprehension scores for the three treatments (Kirk 1968) was carried out on the scores for level, treatment, and treatment order. The first test in the RT (RT1) is not considered in the analysis, being assumed to have served as the preparation exercise analogous to PRE and VOC presentations, and is thus part of the treatment. However, RT1 scores are indicated in the descriptive data (Figure 4) presentation for discussion purposes.

Results

In considering the data results, the descriptive statistics in Figure 4 and Figure 5 point out the significant interactions indicated in ANOVA Table 1, and in the Table 2 comparisons for differences among means. The treatment across levels is shown in Figure 4 and the mean scores for treatment by level are shown in Figure 5. Of the origianl 93 Ss, complete data for the ANOVA were available for only 80 Ss at the conclusion of the study. Descriptive data include the data available on all 93 Ss.

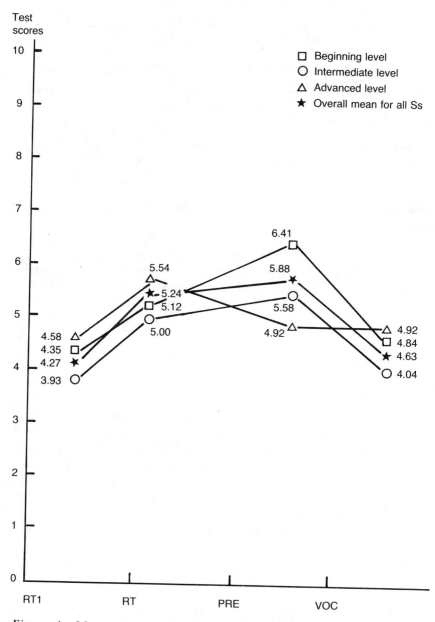

Figure 4   Mean scores for treatment across level

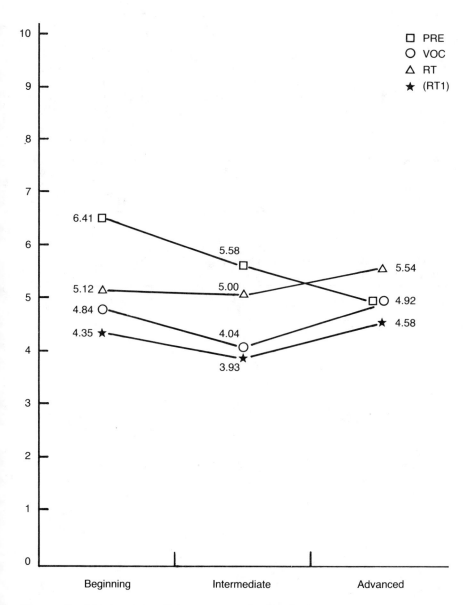

Figure 5   Mean scores for treatment by level

TABLE I. SOURCE TABLE FOR THE ANOVA: PRE TO VOC TO RT

Source of variation	Sum of squares	df	Mean square	$f_{observed}$
Mean	6352.48828	1	6352.48828	1225.83
Level	11.91064	2	5.95532	1.15
Order	9.20923	2	4.60461	0.89
Level + order	38.03540	4	9.50885	1.83
Error	367.93530	71	5.18219	
Treatment	47.64087	2	23.82043	*12.27
Treatment + level	25.93237	4	6.48309	*3.34
Treatment + order	26.60229	4	6.65057	*3.43
Treatment + level + order	49.12280	8	6.14035	*3.16
Error	275.70093	142	1.94156	

*$p < .05$

TABLE 2. COMPARISONS FOR DIFFERENCES AMONG MEANS ON ANOVA TABLE I

	A priori t ratio	Post hoc Tukey's HSD
Overall treatment		
PRE vs. VOC	*1.8093	
VOC vs. RT	.9262	
PRE vs. RT		2.8014
Beginning		
PRE vs. VOC	*4.5580	
VOC vs. RT	1.0100	
PRE vs. RT		*4.8895
Intermediate		
PRE vs. VOC	*1.8590	
VOC vs. RT	*2.4600	
PRE vs. RT		2.6299
Advanced		
PRE vs. VOC	1.0220	
VOC vs. RT	.4715	
PRE vs. RT		1.4463

*$p < .05$

From these figures, it may be seen at the beginning and intermediate levels, PRE scores were higher than either VOC or RT. Table 1 shows the ANOVA Source Table for the test results. The ANOVA indicates significant effects for treatment, treatment by order, and further indicates a significant treatment by level by order interaction. In examining the results of PRE, VOC, and RT several conclusions may be made. The mean scores in Figure 4 and 5 indicate an interaction between the particular treatment and level. The results of the ANOVA show no significant overall effect for level or order and no significant interaction level by order. This is to be expected in that reading difficulty was adjusted for level, and since order was adjusted solely to counterbalance for maturation or sequence effect in the treatments.

The most striking factor in the data is the indication of different types of intervention being effective at different levels of proficiency although the levels of difficulty of the passages were adjusted. Comparisons using a *t* ratio for a priori and Tukey's HSD test for the post hoc comparisons are summarized in Table 2. These comparisons indicate significant differences in overall treatment between PRE and VOC. They further indicate that type of treatment has a greater effect at the beginning and intermediate levels than at the advanced level. A breakdown of treatment by level indicates that PRE is significantly more effective at the beginning level than is VOC or RT ($p < .05$). The intermediate level indicates a significant difference between both PRE and VOC to RT, and the descriptive data show a superiority of PRE over RT, though not at a statistically significant level ($q_{crit.}$ at 3.40). The advanced level data show no statistically significant main effects although the descriptive data in Figures 4 and 5 indicate RT possibly being more effective than either of the two other methods at the advanced proficiency level. Descriptive data further indicate an inversion of the relative effectiveness of PRE in relation to VOC and RT observed at beginning and intermediate levels.

Summary

The results of the study indicate that advanced level L2 readers in English apparently do have more facile or robust networks for fitting meaning than do the lower level readers. While the VOC and RT treatments were less effective than the PRE treatment at the beginning and intermediate levels, they were as or more effective at the advanced level. Thus, there appear to be differences in the abilities to form schemata from printed input between levels of proficiency. Advanced level Ss have less trouble processing visual information and altering schemata than lower level Ss and are able to bring more nonvisual "behind the eyeball" information to bear on the reading process than the beginning or intermediate level Ss.

Discussion and conclusions

While the present study has attempted to examine L2 reading factors, its conclusions must be seen as limited and suggestive. Its limitations should be borne in mind. First, there is always a question as to whether the type of instruments used are responsible for the findings. Relevant to this concern would be the degree to which RT scores are due to a testing effect and memory at the advanced level. Further, the results of the study may reflect a third component factor of purpose in reading and hence be limited to settings in which a teacher or reading monitor is present. The results may only approximate a true and natural reading setting. Third, multiple-choice recall instruments themselves may not elicit exact representations. It is possible for a reader to be given some type of recall protocol, score well and yet still have an incorrectly reconciled schema. While the reader may read a passage concerning ants, and answer questions with a high degree of accuracy, the reader's schema may actually contain a representation of termites, crickets, or cockroaches. There is a need, therefore, to examine the effects of induced schemata on other instruments, such as cloze passages, oral miscue analysis procedures, and approximations of prose. With this stated, however, the results of this study are clearly suggestive in their general implications for L2 reading processes, particularly as to the role second component factors may play relative to the linguistic ceiling in the short circuit.

The results of this study indicate that much of the research into the L1 effects of schemata and context is applicable to L2 reading. The answer to the research questions would be "partially," "yes," and "no." First, schemata theory can partially explain as a second component factor the L2 short circuit of good reading strategies by proficient L1 readers. The results would indicate that a breakdown in second component processing can cause disruption in first component processing. This is tied to the answer to the second research question of whether if readers are induced to produce consistent schemata, this can override the effects of an L2 linguistic ceiling. The induced schemata in this study apparently allowed access to language decoding which was otherwise not available. The significance of this finding is that the linguistic ceiling is only one determinant of reading comprehension. The fact that it can be overridden indicates that it is not a fixed or static proficiency, but is rather a relative proficiency. However, this is modified by the answer to the question of whether the inducement to produce consistent schemata is equally effective across levels of L2 language proficiency. The advanced level readers found self-reconciliation through the text more effective than externally induced schemata. This finding indicates that advanced level readers are in some way applying skills differently from the lower level readers, or rather, that the strategies which are chosen themselves change across levels of reading and language proficiency. It may be that the process of learning to read in L2 is partially a matter of first experiencing skills and strategies as usable, and then abstracting principles for successful reading. Thus, the motivational factors of having experienced, for example, finding invariants of patterns and order, and inducing rules successfully in L2 may lead the advanced level reader to utilize skills and strategies which the lower level reader has not yet experienced as usable. This is also indicated by the finding that for the beginning and intermediate level readers in the study, the VOC and RT treatments were not significantly different and thus equally unusable because of second component interference. Further research is needed to determine whether this is due to the particular type of schemata examined here or whether advanced level readers are just more flexible at changing schemata when the first one tried proves inadequate.

Appendix: Sample instrument* (advanced level)

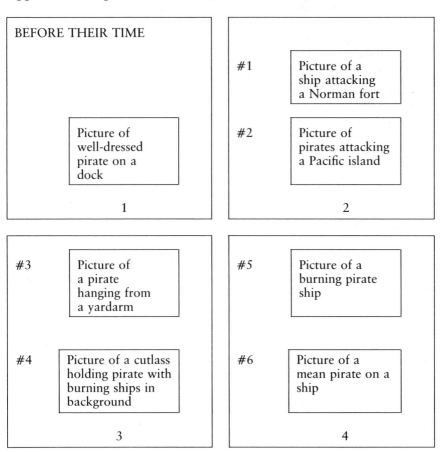

*For complete sample instruments, see Hudson (1978).

Pre-reading activities: "Before Their Time"

1. Take a moment and look at the title of the article. Look at the pictures. Do not read, just look.

2. ORAL QUESTIONS

    Does the title tell you anything about the reading?

    What is picture #1?
    Where is it?
    What is it doing?
    Why?

    What is picture #2?
    Where do you think it is?
    What are they doing?
    Why?

    What is in picture #3?
    Who do you think he is?
    Why is he hanging?

    What is in picture #4?
    Who is he?

    What is in picture #5?
    What are they doing?
    Why?

    Who is in picture #6?
    How does he look?

    What do you think the title means?
    Do you know anything about pirates?
    Did you have them in your country?
    How did they live?

3. What do you think this article will be about? Write a list before you read the article.

    1. _____
    2. _____
    3. _____
    4. _____
    5. _____

"Before Their Time": Do you know these words?

sea rover	cruise
pirate	capture
republic	sailor
abolition	sentiment
slavery	expedition
volunteer	outlaws

man-o'-war	be able
quarterdeck	native
sloop	marooned
ship	bloodthirsty
freedom	propound
booty	

"Before Their Time" * *by Hamilton Cochran*

From the beginning of recorded history there have been men who would rather steal from others than earn an honest living. Ashore they were called thieves, robbers, or highwaymen; on the high seas they were called pirates. The sea rovers' greatest period of prosperity and domination of the seas spanned the century from 1650 to 1750.

Although the vast majority of pirates were cruel, ignorant, and bloodthirsty, there were a few exceptions: the most remarkable was the trio of Misson, Caraccioli, and Tew. Each was individualistic, courageous, and intelligent, and together they founded a pirate republic, propounded and practiced advanced ideas on the abolition of slavery, and prohibited the death penalty for crime.

Captain Misson was born in France of an ancient, honorable, and wealthy family, but having a great number of brothers and sisters, he felt his future depended on the fortune he could carve out with his sword. He was enthralled with the carefree, roving life of the privateer, and so he told his father he wished to follow the sea. His first berth was aboard the *Victoire*, a French man-o'-war, and he immediately fell in love with the life of a seaman.

While the *Victoire* was docked at Naples during that first voyage, Misson received permission to visit Rome; it was there he met a young priest, Signor Caraccioli, who was also fascinated by the sea. It took little to persuade Caraccioli to leave the priesthood and volunteer for service aboard the *Victoire*.

Misson and Caraccioli were engaged in numerous battles while aboard the man-o'-war, but their fortunes did not improve. When an opportunity presented itself, however, they were quick to take advantage. While cruising in the Carribean off the island of Martinique, the *Victoire* met the *Winchelsea*, an English man-o'-war of forty guns. Neither vessel hesitated to attack the other, and a very smart engagement followed, during which the *Victoire*'s captain, second captain, and three lieutenants were killed. Rather than allow the *Victoire*'s colors to be struck and the ship surrendered, Misson assumed command, appointed Caraccioli to act as his lieutenant, and contrived to destroy the *Winchelsea* with all hands.

Deciding to take permanent command, Misson called the crew to the quarterdeck, told them that he would devote himself to a life of liberty, offered freedom to all those who did not choose to follow him, and promised to share equally all booty and to use his power for the collective good of

*Adapted with permission of Macmillan Publishing Company from *Freebooters of the Red Sea* by Hamilton Cochran. Copyright © 1965 by Hamilton Cochran. Adaptation copyright © 1973 by Science Research Associates, SRA Green Lab IIIa #8, reprinted by permission.

those who stayed. His proposal was accepted with cheers, and the crew elected Caraccioli and a schoolteacher to be second and third in command.

Misson was indeed a remarkable fellow. Although now a pirate, he had a highly developed sense of justice and mercy and was an ardent advocate of liberty and the concept of equality for all. Like Caraccioli, he was dedicated to the freedom of the individual and independence of thought in every area, including religion. The flag he chose, a white ensign with "Liberty" and the motto "For God and Liberty" painted on it, symbolized his uprightness and resolution.

After cruising the Caribbean for several months, Misson decided to head for the coast of Guinea, where he and his men might reasonably expect to run athwart East Indian vessels loaded with money and other rich cargo. One of the captures they made was the *Nieuwstadt* of Amsterdam; aboard were seventeen slaves and gold dust to the value of approximately £2,000. It was with regard to the slaves that Misson's remarkable attitude became apparent. Misson declared to the crew that no man had the power of liberty over any other and that the slaves were thenceforth to be treated as free men – the very name of slavery was to be banned. He divided the slaves into two groups, mixing them with the others so that they could learn French and become useful sailors. It is worth noting that Misson voiced and acted upon antislavery sentiments more than 150 years before Abraham Lincoln, one of the United States' most illustrious presidents, declared that slaves in the United States should be freed.

Within a short time Misson and his men had collected such a vast amount of gold and silver that they decided to settle down permanently in the Far East. They selected the island of Johanna, raised a fort on each side of its natural harbor, mounted forty guns taken out of a captured Portuguese ship, and began to build homes and magazines for storing their weapons. But Misson felt he needed more men to settle his pirate colony, which he had named Libertatia, and so he set out on another expedition; it was on this voyage that he met Captain Tew, a native of Bermuda and, like himself, a sea rover. Misson intrigued Tew with his description of the pleasant life at Libertatia. Persuaded that Misson's colony would be an ideal haven, Tew returned to his own ship and convinced his crew that they too should become citizens of Misson's republic. Apparently Tew fell under the spell of Misson and Caraccioli and approved of their behavior toward prisoners and slaves, for later, after capturing an English slaver with 240 black men, women, and boys aboard, Tew knocked off their chains and invited them to join Libertatia.

This was the beginning of an unusual republican government, which united a crowd of seagoing outlaws who had the whole world for enemies. Eventually Misson, Caraccioli, and Tew asked the men to form into companies of ten, with each company choosing a representative to set up a form of government; they also proposed that the treasure and cattle be divided equally and that any land an individual enclosed with a fence should in future be considered his property.

The representatives assembled to consider a proposal by Caraccioli that one man be elected to enforce the laws they chose to establish. He further proposed that this power be awarded for a period of only three years to ensure that the ablest man would always be head of state. Misson was elected unanimously as the first Lord Conservator and from then on was addressed with the title of Supreme Excellence.

Apparently the pirates did not feel there were any pressing matters to be resolved, for they decided to meet only annually, unless the conservator and his council called more frequent gatherings. During the first session, which lasted for ten days, Tew was appointed admiral and Caraccioli secretary of state, and a council of the ablest was selected to supervise the division of booty and cattle.

The next few years were peaceful and prosperous. Eventually, however, an unexpected outside force destroyed this unique democracy. Two bands of Johanna's natives attacked the colony one night, killing Caraccioli and slaughtering most of Libertatia's startled inhabitants. Fighting a courageous rearguard action, Misson managed to get forty-five of his men aboard two sloops and also to salvage a small portion of the rough diamonds and gold bars in the colony's treasury.

In the meantime, Tew had been marooned on an isolated part of Madagascar while out hunting for treasure ships and was unaware of the fate of Libertatia. By great good fortune, Misson's two sloops approached Madagascar four months later and sighted fires Tew had built to attract attention.

It was a sad reunion, for the two men realized they had lost most of their treasure along with their cherished friend Caraccioli and that there was little hope of reestablishing Libertatia. But even then Misson did not discard his democratic ideals: he divided what was left of Tew's crew between his two sloops, distributed the salvaged fortune among them, and gave Tew one of the sloops with its crew.

The sloops headed westward, bound for the American colonies where both Misson and Tew planned to settle. But off Cape Infantes a great storm overtook the tiny vessels, and Misson's was lost, carrying him to his death. Thanks to good luck and good seamanship, Tew survived the storm and eventually landed in New York, where he lived luxuriously for a number of years. But he too was destined to die at sea. Members of his crew, who had squandered their shares of the booty and were hungry for more, finally persuaded him to captain another voyage. This time Tew's luck deserted him: he met an East Indian ship in the Red Sea, and in the battle that followed he was fatally wounded. Libertatia, the noble experiment, died with him.

Comprehension questions

NAME _____

Answer the following questions according to the article whether you agree or not. *Circle* the correct answer.

1. Misson, Caraccioli, and Tew were exceptional pirates because they

    A. came from wealthy families
    B. were idealistic and intelligent
    C. respected the rights of the natives on their island
    D. refused to use violence

2. The *Victoire*'s new flag was significant in that it

    A. reflected Misson's concept of freedom
    B. proclaimed the pirate's patriotism
    C. showed the pirate's view of mercy
    D. symbolized Caraccioli's religious views

3. Tew finally returned to the sea because

    A. his former crew convinced him to
    B. he had squandered all of his money
    C. he grew tired of the peaceful life on land
    D. the citizens of the American colony were against him

4. The first proof of Misson's belief in the equality of men was his

    A. appointment of Caraccioli as lieutenant
    B. statement to the *Victoire*'s crew
    C. treatment of the *Nieuwstadt*'s slaves
    D. election as Lord Conservator of Libertatia

5. Tew was invited to join Libertatia because Misson

    A. defeated him in battle
    B. liked sea rovers like Tew
    C. decided more settlers were needed
    D. convinced Tew's crew it would be worthwhile

6. Companies of ten men were formed so that

    A. discipline could be stringently enforced
    B. a representative government could be formed
    C. booty could be divided more equally and quickly
    D. land could be distributed to the groups

7. Libertatia could be called a democratic republic because

    A. private property was not allowed
    B. the Lord Conservator could serve only three years
    C. the treasure was divided equally
    D. the head of the government was elected by the men

8. Libertatia's collapse was caused by

    A. Misson's fleeing with the treasure
    B. Johanna's natives attacking
    C. Tew's being marooned and unable to return
    D. the council did not meet often enough

9. The author probably wrote this article because he wanted to

    A. discuss the value of democratic republics in history
    B. discuss an unusual historical phenomenon
    C. prove Libertatia was the first democracy

D. argue against slavery in favor of racial integration

10. Misson first assumed command of the *Victoire* because
   A. he caused a mutiny against his cruel commanders
   B. he believed in democracy
   C. his commanders were killed in battle
   D. he managed to destroy the *Winchelsea*

References

Anderson, R. C., and B. McGaw. 1973. On the representation of the meanings of general terms. *Journal of Experimental Psychology* 101:301–306.

Anderson, R. C., J. W. Prichert, E. T. Goetz, D. L. Schallert, K. V. Stevens, and S. R. Trollip. 1976. Instantiation of general terms. *Journal of Verbal Learning and Verbal Behavior* 15:667–679.

Anderson, R. C., and A. Ortony. 1975. On putting apples into bottles: a problem in polysemy. *Cognitive Psychology* 7:167–180.

Anderson, R. C., R. E. Reynolds, D. L. Schallert, and T. E. Goetz. 1977. Frameworks for comprehending discourse. *American Educational Research Journal* 14:367–381.

Clarke, M. A. 1979. Reading in Spanish and English: evidence from adult ESL students. *Language Learning* 29:121–150.

Cziko, G. A. 1978. Differences in first- and second-language reading: the use of syntactic, semantic, and discourse constraints. *Canadian Modern Language Review* 34:473–489.

Frederiksen, C. H. 1975. Effects of context-induced processing operations on semantic information acquired from discourse. *Cognitive Psychology* 7:139–166.

Goodman, K. S. 1971. Psycholinguistic universals in the reading process. In *The psychology of second language learning*, P. Pimsleur and T. Quinn (Eds.), 135–142. Cambridge: Cambridge University Press.

Hudson, T. D. 1978. The effects of pre-reading activities on reading comprehension and student attitude. Unpublished master's thesis, UCLA.

Kirk, R. E. 1968. *Experimental design: procedures for the behavioral sciences.* Belmont, Calif.: Brooks/Cole.

Oller, J. W. 1975. Cloze, discourse and approximations to English. In *On TESOL '75*, M. K. Burt and J. C. Dulay (Eds.), 345–355. Washington, D.C.: TESOL.

Rigg, P. 1977a. Reading in ESL. In *On TESOL '76*, J. Fanselow and R. Crymes (Eds.), 203–210. Washington, D.C.: TESOL.

   1977b. The miscue-ESL project. In *On TESOL '77*, H. D. Brown, C. A. Yorio, and R. Crymes (Eds.), 106–118. Washington, D.C.: TESOL. [Reprinted as Chapter 14 in this volume.]

Schallert, D. L. 1976. Improving memory for prose: the relationship between depth of processing and context. *Journal of Verbal Learning and Verbal Behavior* 15:621–632.

Smith, F. 1971. *Understanding reading: a psycholinguistic analysis of reading and learning to read.* New York: Holt, Rinehart and Winston.

14 *The Miscue-ESL Project*

Pat Rigg

The Miscue-ESL Project was a lengthy, in-depth study of the ESL reading of four language groups. The project began in 1973 at the Reading Miscue Research Center, Wayne State University, under the direction of Kenneth S. Goodman; this chapter is a report of some of the early major findings. The Miscue-ESL Project was prompted by the results of an earlier study (Goodman and Burke 1973) in which the miscues of children from 2nd, 4th, 6th, 8th, and 10th grades were analyzed.

One of the major points of that report was that the reading process was the same for all subjects, regardless of race, age, or reading proficiency. That is, all the subjects clearly used three cuing systems – graphophonic, syntactic, semantic – and clearly followed the basic process of sampling from these systems, predicting and confirming. There was wide discrepancy among individuals as to how effectively and how efficiently this process was carried out, but the process itself did not differ from individual to individual. The result prompted the question, "Are there universals in the reading process?"

As a first step, the question was restricted to English, and rephrased as "Are there universals in the reading process when the reading is in English?" Four groups of subjects, children in 2nd, 4th, and 6th grades whose languages were not English, were selected. The groups spoke, respectively, Arabic, Navajo, Samoan, and Spanish as their first language. The Arabic speakers were recent immigrants, primarily from Lebanon, to an urban suburb of Detroit. The area in which many of the Arab immigrants live is under the shadow (and the smoke) of one of the world's largest industrial plants. About half of the children at the school from which our subjects were drawn spoke Arabic, according to the school principal. At the time the data were collected, only one teacher spoke Arabic; he taught a small ESL class. Many of the stores and restaurants in the area offer Arabic specialities, and many of the signs

"The Miscue Project"by Pat Rigg from *On TESOL '77: Teaching and Learning ESL: Trends in Research and Practice* (pp. 106–18) by H. D. Brown, C. A. Yorio, and R. Crymes (Eds.), 1977, Washington, D.C.: TESOL. Copyright 1977 by Teachers of English to Speakers of Other Languages. Reprinted by permission.

outside and within these places are written in Arabic. This area is some-what bilingual in the sense that two languages are used by many of the residents daily.

The Navajo-speaking subjects were residents of a boarding school run by the Bureau of Indian Affairs in the Arizona desert. None of the teachers spoke Navajo, although some of the teacher-aides did. The school was physically isolated from both Navajo- and English-speaking communities. There was no bilingual program, and the only ESL program was a cursory one in 1st grade. The children were members of two monolingual communities – Navajo in the summer, English in the school year.

The Samoan-speaking subjects were recent immigrants from American Samoa to an urban, polyglot community – Honolulu, Hawaii. They were acquiring a dialect of ESL, Hawaiian-Creole, when the data were collected. They lived in a housing project close to their school; the school had no bilingual program and a very small ESL program.

The Spanish-speakers were born in the small ranching community (population about 2,000) in east Texas, where the data were collected. About a third of the school and the community are native Spanish-speakers. There are a few Spanish signs on grocery items, menus, and store windows. The community is partly bilingual in the sense that two languages are commonly used by many of the people, though with vary-ing degrees of fluency. The school these subjects attended had no ESL classes, and at the time of data collection, the school was just beginning a bilingual program in the first grade. None of the subjects in this study had had a bilingual program; few had had formal ESL training.

With the exception of some older Arabic-speakers, who had attended school in their native land, and were literate in their language, all of the subjects in this study received all reading instruction in English. English was the sole medium of instruction in all the selected schools.

The four groups were chosen for their diversity. They were all ESL-speakers, but they were drawn from urban and rural communities, bilingual and monolingual communities, native American and immigrant groups, Indo-European and non-Indo-European language backgrounds, from groups who had a long history of written literature and those who had none. If the study showed that the reading process was basically the same for each group, despite the wide differences, then the suggestion that there are universals in reading, at least in English, would be supported.

Ten students from each grade, 2nd, 4th, and 6th, from each group were chosen, but not through statistical sampling. At each school, teachers were asked to choose the "most average" readers from their classes, that is, the students they considered the most average for their class in that school. It became apparent immediately that the teachers were selecting their best readers, and so the instructions to the teachers were changed. They were asked to list their ten best readers and their ten worst readers; ten subjects were then drawn from those not listed in either group. Each subject read two stories, one on one day, the second a day or two later. (A list of stories each group read is included as Appendix A.) The students were instructed to read the story without any assistance, and when they had finished the story, to tell the researcher everything they could remember about the story. The reading, done orally, and the retelling were both tape-recorded. All data were collected by researchers trained by Dr. Goodman at the Reading Miscue Research Center, and all data were sent there for analysis. Four subjects from each subgroup of ten were selected for analysis, primarily on the basis of clarity of the tape-recording, to a lesser extent on the basis of other factors, such as gender or further information about the subject. For example, one subject who could not be used had been characterized by his teacher as a recent immigrant from Lebanon who spoke Arabic at home, but actually the boy had been born in Modesto, California, of a Brazilian mother and Lebanese father, and they spoke Portuguese at home.

The reading and retelling of these 48 children, on two stories each, was analyzed using the Goodman Taxonomy. The Taxonomy is described and explained in detail in Allen and Watson's *Findings of Research in Miscue Analysis* (1976) and will not be explained at length here. Basically, the Taxonomy asks fifteen questions of each deviation from the text, each miscue. The answers to these questions are coded in Fortran, and then subjected to various computer programs.

I think the most important thing this study shows is that these children are better readers than they are usually given credit for. First, they are generally accurate readers: on an average they made miscues on less than 20% of the text, reading the other 80% just as it was printed. The measure of quantity of miscues that the Goodman Taxonomy uses is Miscues Per Hundred Words (MPHW). MPHW is arrived at by taking the number of different deviations from the text, dividing by the number of words in the text, and multiplying by 100. Identical repeated miscues, such as the repeated substitution of *Keeko* for *Keoki*, are counted as one miscue. The range of MPHW for the ESL subjects was seven to twenty; their mean MPHW was about ten. The average, then, of what was read accurately, was 90% for all three grades, all four groups.

Second, when the children do deviate from the text, they often produce miscues which make sense in that text. They substitute names, for example, calling Tupa the shark *Tabu*, calling Mr. Barnaby *Mr. Barnberry*. Sometimes they read contractions as two words, saying *I am* for *I'm*. The Goodman Taxonomy codes these sorts of miscues, i.e. miscues which make sense in the text, as semantically acceptable. Table 1 shows

TABLE I. PERCENTAGE OF SEMANTICALLY ACCEPTABLE MISCUES BY GROUPS

Group	Mean (%)	Range (%)
Arabic	36	18–53
Navajo	41	20–48
Samoan	36	16–66
Spanish	41	20–69

the means and ranges of percent of non-dialect miscues that were coded semantically acceptable for each group: this includes all three grades and both stories.

Clearly, there is a great deal more variation within each group than between groups, but the means suggest that, generally, at least a third of the miscues, before correction, make sense.

Third, when their miscues do not make sense, these children often regress and try again. When a child regresses and succeeds in producing the text item(s) accurately, the Goodman Taxonomy codes regression as *correction*. The measure of quality used by the Taxonomy is a percentage of the miscues which were semantically acceptable or were corrected. This figure is called the Comprehending Score. The next two examples would both be included in this score. The first is semantically acceptable:

Reader: Henry did not have a pet.
Text: Henry didn't have a pet.

The next example is semantically unacceptable, but is corrected, so it too would be included in the comprehending score:

Reader: ©
              didn't not
Text: Henry didn't   have a pet.

                    (Aaron et al. 1971: 1)

The mean Comprehending Scores for all grades on both stories are: Spanish – 60%, Navajo – 51%, Arabic – 49%, and Samoan – 47%. On the average, then, about half of these children's miscues either made sense or were corrected. Again, differences between individuals within groups were greater than differences between groups.

The fourth indicator of these ESL-speakers' ability to read unfamiliar and difficult text is their percentage of syntactically acceptable miscues. The average for each group is 55% or higher, and this is before correction. The range within groups and within grades is high – 30% to 66% for Navajo second graders, for example: this is another indication of the greater variation within groups than between them.

The early results of this study, then, do not distinguish any one of the language groups involved as being better or worse readers of ESL. These results do show that on the average, these ESL-speakers read accurately; they produce meaningful miscues; they can correct when their miscues lose meaning; they are handling English syntax. The ESL-speakers in this study do not differ greatly from the native English speakers in the Detroit study (Goodman and Burke, 1973) in any of these aspects, except that their Comprehending Scores tend to be slightly lower. The number and types of nondialect miscues the ESL-readers make are much more similar to those made by subjects in the Detroit study than they are different. To the question, "Are there universals in the reading process when the language is English?" we can say, "It looks like there are." The focus of this chapter, however, is not on what this study tells us about the reading process, but on what it tells us about the reading of ESL-speakers.

All the children made miscues which were obviously due to the fact that Standard English was not their first language or dialect. These miscues were phonological, grammatical, and lexical. The phonological miscues were not coded. That is, the pronunciation of *teacher* as *teasher* by a Spanish-speaker was noted on the transcript of the story, but was not analyzed. There are two reasons for this. First, control over the phonological system of English generally seems to follow control over the syntactic system, for both native and ESL-speakers, so that, although we expected the 6th grade Arabic speakers, for example, to read this sentence in the passive, we didn't expect them to distinguish /p/ from /b/.

Reader: At last the carbet was finished.
Text: At last the carpet was finished.

(Larson 1966: 12)

Second, coding phonological deviations from an idealized Standard English pronunciation would not have told us anything about their actual reading. How much can one learn about a person's reading by noting how he pronounces *tomato* or *rodeo*?

Grammatical and lexical miscues caused by English being their second language were coded in the category called *dialect*. All dialect miscues are coded as grammatically and semantically acceptable, because the Taxonomy defines "acceptability" as acceptable within the reader's dialect. Most of the grammatical dialect miscues these children made are just what ESL teachers would expect: inflectional suffixes such as past tense *-ed*, plural *-s*, possessive *-'s* were not pronounced. A few of the children indicated that they had been instructed to "sound out the endings," because they produced supercorrect dialect miscues: *walkeded*, *slumpeded*, *lookeded*. Since some children produced more dialect miscues than others, and since we wanted to code an equal number of

TABLE 2. MEASURES OF QUALITY AND QUANTITY OF MISCUES ON
"FREDDIE MILLER"

Group	MPHW	Comprehending score (%)	ResMPHW
Spanish	7.3	58	2.48
Arabic	10.6	52	4.7
Samoan	12.2	44	5.78
Navajo	18.9	40	9.06

miscues for each subject, the dialect miscues were not counted in arriving at the total of the first fifty miscues. That is, each child had his/her first fifty non-dialect miscues coded; with dialect miscues included, one child had 52 total miscues coded, another 64.

The number of dialect miscues (ESL-miscues) varied widely from child to child. The Spanish-speaking group had a slight tendency to produce fewer dialect miscues than the other three: the average number of their dialect miscues per hundred words was one; the other groups' averages ranged from one and a half to two. These differences between groups are not significant. The types of ESL-miscues were similar for each subject and for each group: the large majority of these miscues (about 80%) were the substitution of a null-form for an inflectional suffix; some were the substitution of the base form of a verb for an irregular past or participle.

Taking means across grades and across stories lumps together ages and stories, and perhaps obliterates important differences. A clearer comparison can be made by looking at one grade reading the same story. All the 4th graders read "Freddie Miller, Scientist" (Betts and Welch 1963). Table 2 lists three measures of quantity and quality for this grade on this story. The Comprehending Score, the Taxonomy's measure of quality, does not indicate quantity of miscues, as MPHW does. A measure that combines quality and quantity is the Residual Miscues Per Hundred Words (ResMPHW); this is the number of semantically unacceptable miscues which were not corrected per hundred scores. It is inversely related to the Comprehending Score. An ideal Comprehending Score is 100%; an ideal ResMPHW is 0.0. What could account for the very wide differences between the Spanish and Navajo readers on this story? The Spanish-speakers do not have much higher percentages of syntactic or semantic acceptability, indicating that their miscues are not better quality than those of the Navajos; that is, both groups are making the same *types* of miscues [Table 3]. A comparison of their correction percentages strongly suggests that at least part of the answer lies in their ability and willingness to regress and correct. The Navajos corrected only 7% of their miscues, and only 2% of the semantically unacceptable

TABLE 3. MEANS AND RANGES OF SYNTACTIC AND SEMANTIC ACCEPTABILITY

	Navajo	*Spanish*
Mean syntactic acceptability	58	57
Range	44–72	49–67
Mean semantic acceptability	35	35
Range	22–42	28–39

miscues were corrected; the Spanish-speakers corrected 30% of their miscues. Moreover, the Navajo 4th graders successfully corrected only 6% of their partial attempts; the Spanish 4th graders 25% of theirs. A partial attempt is less than a full word; the correction of a partial suggests that the reader has recognized that s/he was miscuing and was able to correct that miscue before it was completed.

Reader: Poor Free-
Text: Poor Freddie was in trouble again.

The much higher percentage of correction by the Spanish-speakers, of both full and partial miscues, together with the much lower number of MPHW made by the Spanish-speakers accounts for the large difference between their ResMPHW and the Navajos'. The Navajos miscued on almost one word in every five; the Texans made less than one-half that many MPHW. Of the Navajos' miscues, almost one in every ten words lost meaning and was not corrected. This is much higher than the Spanish-speakers' miscues; the number of uncorrected semantically unacceptable miscues for them was a little over one in every 50 words. That is, although both groups made the same type of miscues, the Navajos made many more, and corrected many less than the Spanish-speakers.

These figures, MPHW, correction percentages, and so on, do not identify the underlying causes of the disparity between these two groups. These underlying reasons perhaps have something to do with the story itself; perhaps with the general ESL proficiency of the readers; perhaps with the status and general use (or non-use) of the students' first language in their schools and communities.

"Freddie Miller, Scientist" is about a young boy who continually gets into trouble because of his mechanical and chemical experiments, but who finally makes his family proud of him by using his "scientific" knowledge to make a flashlight for his little sister, who is locked in a dark closet. It seems to me that the Navajo children at the boarding school are less likely than the Texas ranch children to be familiar with the idea of a boy having a chemistry set, his own workbench in the cellar, or his using a kitchen stepladder to drop a flashlight through a transom into a closet. Do hogans have transoms or kitchen stepladders or cellars or chemistry sets? Does the boarding school? I suggest that, for Navajo reservation children who have been at boarding school for four years and have not lived in town, reading this story about a "typical" American family from an old standard basal text is in many ways like our reading Chaucer's "Prioress's Tale." What the people in the story say and do, their whole way of life, is foreign. This foreignness makes it very hard to predict what will happen in the next paragraph or page. Prediction is also hindered in some spots by the syntax. This passage, for example, occurs when Freddie's sister is stuck in the hall-closet and Freddie is in the cellar.

... he heard his sister's voice calling, "Freddie! Freddie!"
"Where are you?" he shouted.
"In the hall closet!" came Elizabeth's tearful reply.
. . .
His sister's cries grew louder. "Don't leave me alone. It's dark in here."

The syntax of "came Elizabeth's tearful reply" forces readers to miscue. One predicts that "in the hall closet" will be followed by a dialog carrier like "said _____" or "_____ said," but there is no real dialog carrier in this sentence. Instead we have a clause with inverted order (verb-subject); the verb is an intransitive one; the heavily modified subject (reply) is not even an animate noun, much less a person's name. In addition, "tearful" usually modifies animate nouns; here it is metaphorically used to modify "reply." It's easy to see why so many readers, native English speakers as well as ESL speakers, produce: " 'In the hall closet,' s-, came Elizabeth (pause) tearfully replied."

"His sister's cries grew louder" is another stumbling block for most readers. It too is in the position of a dialog carrier, but is not one. One predicts, "His sister said" or "His sister cried" or even "His sister cries," and the graphophonic information certainly supports the last two predictions. Some readers produce "His sister cried louder"; others make a couple of attempts and then seem to give up: "His sister cried, cries, sister cried lo-, grew louder." One must be a very proficient speaker of ESL indeed to get to deep structure successfully through such syntactic mazes.

In addition to the unpredictability of the general setting and plot and of some syntactic structures, there is the unpredictability of lexical items. When reading teachers say a child "knows" a word, they usually mean either the child understands the concept behind the word, or the child says the word accurately when s/he sees it, or both. But in "Freddie Miller," as in most stories, one word may have more than one meaning. The word *allowance*, for example, occurs three times in "Freddie." Mrs. Miller tells Freddie, "I want you to save half your allowance"; three lines later the narrator says, "After the cut in his allowance, Freddie's chemistry experiments narrowed to those safely outlined in a library book." (There's another syntactic maze.) And on the last page of the story, Mrs. Miller tells her husband, "We must make some allowance for experiments that do not turn out so well." I wonder how many of the Navajo 4th graders know the concept of allowance as weekly pocket money; I wonder if any know what "make allowance for" means. It's true that lexical items are generally unpredictable, but when this unpredictability is accompanied by the reader's inability to translate the item into something meaningful, then the reader's prediction will be a very tentative guess, and s/he cannot test to confirm that guess. If readers don't know the meanings a word has in different contexts and if they don't get enough context to enable them to deduce the meanings, they cannot test by asking, "Does that make sense?" The readers are then forced to reply on very surface information, or graphophonic information, which slows down the reading and makes prediction even harder.

In order to read with any proficiency, one must be able to predict, to make a reasonable guess as to what's coming next. The basis for prediction is partly what's in the text, but much more what's in the head of the reader, what s/he knows about the language and the world that the author is presenting. When the reader knows little about the world being presented, and when the author's language differs greatly from the reader's, the reader is going to have a difficult time and probably will make many miscues, and be unable to correct them. The reader cannot correct unless s/he recognizes that a miscue doesn't make sense; if *nothing* s/he's reading makes sense, there's no way of knowing which oral responses to the text are OK and which aren't. While the world of "Freddie Miller" is not the world of east Texas Spanish-speaking ranch children, it is even less, I think, the world of reservation-boarding school Navajos. The language of "Freddie," although admittedly difficult in spots for any reader, is generally closer to the English controlled by the Spanish-speakers than to the English of the Navajos. Evidence for this comes mostly from the retellings: the Texas 4th graders volunteered lengthy paragraphs when asked to tell everything they could remember about the story; the Arizona 4th graders volunteered one or two sentences, sometimes only one or two words.

The Spanish-speakers were told before reading that they would retell the story in Spanish and in English; the Navajos only in English. What effect might this open acceptance of Spanish have had on the student's willingness to talk? The Spanish-speakers, like the Arabic speakers, live in a community where many of the people they know use two languages daily; the Navajo-speakers come from homes where Navajo is used almost exclusively, and live in a school where all the teachers, all Anglos, speak English exclusively. These differences in the use of two languages indicate two different attitudes toward the children's language, their culture, and themselves. What effect does this have on the children? On their reading? This study cannot answer those questions, because it did not investigate them. I hope others will.

What this study does answer, or at least begins to answer, are these questions: Can ESL readers, many of whom have not really mastered English yet, read with comprehension? Yes. Is ESL reading proficiency determined by one's first language? No. Are some aspects of the reading process universal? Tentatively, yes.

The Miscue-ESL Project has implications for both research and teaching. More research into the reading process and into second language involvement in the reading process is called for. The results of this study suggest that there are universals in reading English; are there universals in reading any language? Sarah Lopez's research (1977) with Spanish-speaking subjects reading in Spanish suggested that the reading process in Spanish does not differ from the process in English. Studies need to be carried out in languages which do not use the Roman alphabet, such as Arabic, and in non-alphabetic writing systems, such as Chinese. Studies focusing on second language effect on reading, similar to the Miscue-ESL Project, need to be carried out on different language populations. This research was a descriptive, in-depth study; others using statistical sampling techniques need to be done, for, although the results of this study suggest interesting insights, the results cannot be generalized. With growing interest in bilingual education and increasing fundings, bilingual educators and researchers could analyze the first- and second-language reading of a sample of students in a school committed to a bilingual program, and compare that to the first- and second-language reading of a sample in a school which has no bilingual program.

One of the major implications this study has for instruction is not in the results, it seems to me, but in the collection of data. One hundred twenty children were asked to read two complete stories each without any help and to talk about what they had read, and they did. A hundred and twenty children, 2nd, 4th, and 6th graders, from widely different language groups and cultural groups – every one of them read two complete, unfamiliar stories without help, and read them well enough to be able to talk about them. Even the poorest reader, one whose retelling score was very low and whose uncorrected miscues often destroyed both meaning and syntax, was able to finish his stories and to relate the major events. A few of the children said that this was the first time in their lives they had ever read a story all the way through at one sitting; they'd never been allowed to before, because someone was right there, stopping their reading whenever they hesitated or deviated from the text. The implication is clear, I think: our ESL students can read if we'll just let them. I remember the reaction I got from a TESOL Workshop when I showed the first page of a story as it was read by one of the Arabic-speaking subjects in this study: the Workshop participants were almost unanimous in condemning the story as too hard, and they were aghast when I told them I had allowed the student to finish the story, all fourteen pages. Most of them, they said, would have taken away the hard story and replaced it with something easier. But the student did read the whole story, and her retelling was excellent (Rigg 1977). We do our students no service when we interrupt their reading in order to correct them. We are not helping them become good readers by treating reading as an exact process requiring three people – author, reader, and teacher. It is easy to confuse reading with reading instruction, but the two are separate processes and should be treated so. Reading is what the student does alone, with the text. Reading instruction is what the teacher does with the students to help them when they read. Many teachers feel they aren't earning their pay if they're not talking, but actually it's harder work to remain silent when a student hesitates or makes an error than it is to jump in and read it for him. Allowing the reader to read without interfering strongly implies that s/he *can* read, and that the teacher recognizes that. It also lets the reader develop and use the strategies of prediction, confirmation, and correction, strategies which can be developed only through reading. In this respect, reading is like riding a bicycle; no amount of formal instruction can teach one as much as does that first wavering solo down the driveway.

A second aspect of the data collection that can be used in the classroom is the retelling. The students in this study were told before they began reading that they were expected to relate everything they could about the story after they had finished reading it. This instruction established comprehension as the purpose of the reading. It was tantamount to saying, "You'll have to think about what you're reading, because you'll be explaining it to me." The reader who knows s/he will retell must strive to understand the material well enough so it can be integrated into a coherent whole for presentation later. Just pronouncing the words won't do. Instructors who believe that good reading is a marvelous public performance, with every word pronounced exactly right, and with "beautiful expression," will want to train the students to be good performers, but instructors who think good reading is comprehension of the material will want to train for comprehension, not for performance. The two – comprehension and performance – are not automatically and mutually exclusive, but emphasizing perfect performance can reduce comprehension. "When you finish reading that to yourself, tell someone what you read." That is the kind of instruction that trains for comprehension.

Few, if any, teachers have time to listen to every student retell everything they read, but, of course, the retelling doesn't have to be to the teacher; it can be to a classmate. Students who have read the same story can share and compare their interpretations; those who have read different material can recommend what they have enjoyed.

A third implication from the Miscue-ESL Project for teachers is that they can use oral reading as a window on the reading process. Teachers can get a view of their students' strategies by listening to their students read unfamiliar texts and by asking themselves, "Do the student's miscues make sense in this story? Do the sentences sound like his/her English? Does the student self-correct everything, even those miscues which retain meaning?" I don't mean the teacher should call up a reading group and have each one read a sentence or two aloud; that doesn't tell the teacher very much and it's often horribly embarrassing for the students. I mean that once every week or two the teacher can sit quietly with a student for 10 minutes while s/he reads aloud (without help, remember). If the teacher can tape-record the reading and analyze each miscue later, perhaps using Y. Goodman and C. Burke's *Reading Miscue Inventory* (1972), so much the better. But even without equipment or extra time, it is possible to get a rough measure of the student's reading by counting all the sentences read, and noting what percent made sense as the student read them. (Y. Goodman, personal communication.)

Finally, I want to point out a basic strength of this study – its assumption that reading is a language-based process of communication. This research did not ask for recognition of isolated words, nor for "perfect pronunciation" (whatever that is) of letter combinations. It did not deal with hypothetical subjects or with contrived sentences demonstrating syllogistic reasoning. The Miscue-ESL Project studied real children reading real stories. The methods of collecting and of analyzing the data did not focus on exactness or on sets of skills, but on communication and on comprehension. A vital assumption underlying this research is that reading should make sense. The implication for teachers and for researchers is clear.

Appendix A

Author	Publication details	Book	Story
Emmet A. Betts C.M. Welch	N.Y.: American Book Co., 1963	*Around Green Hills*	The Big Surprise by M. Gartler, pp. 36–40
		Up the Street and Down	Two New Hats by E. McWebb, pp. 134–38
		Beyond Treasure Valley	Kitten Jones by R. G. Plowhead, pp. 60–66

		Adventures Here & There (Book V-3)	Freddie Miller, Scientist by Betts and Welch, pp. 61–68
		Adventures Here & There (Book VI)	My Brother is a Genius by W.D. Hayes, pp. 246–56
Ira E. Aaron, et al.	Glenview, Ill: Scott-Foresman, 1971	*Henry's Choice*	Henry's Choice, 16 pp.
Albert J. Harris, Sr., et al.	N.Y.: Macmillan, 1966	*The Magic Word* (Book IV)	Royal Race by R. Eskridge, pp. 356–67
Helen M. Robinson, et al.	Glenview, Ill: Scott-Foresman, 1967	*Open Highways* (Book VII)	Ghost of the Lagoon by A. Sperry, pp. 395–413
	Boston: Houghton-Mifflin, 1968	*Images* (Grade 5)	And Now Miguel by J. Krumgold, pp. 94–110
Scott O'Dell	N.Y.: Dell, 1973	*Sing Down the Moon*	Sing Down the Moon by S. O'Dell, 137 pp.
Mary Perrine	Boston: Houghton-Mifflin, 1968	*Salt Boy*	Salt Boy by M. Perrine, 31 pp.
Helen Rushmore	Champaign, Ill: Garrard Publ., 1972	*Sancho, The Homesick Steer*	Sancho by H. Rushmore, 63 pp.
	Lyons & Carnahan	*The Almost Ghost & Other Stories*	My Name is Miguel by Fay & Clifford, pp. 55–74
James Holding	N.Y.: Morrow, 1963	*Mr. Moonlight & Omar*	Mr. Moonlight & Omar by J. Holding, unpaged
Jean R. Larson	N.Y.: Scribner's, 1966	*Palace in Bagdad: Seven Tales from Arabia*	Fareedah's Carpet by J. Larson, pp. 46–59

References

Aaron, I., et al. 1971. *Henry's choice.* Glenview, Ill.: Scott-Foresman.
Allen, D. P., and D. Watson. 1976. *Findings of research in miscue analysis.* Champaign-Urbana: ERIC/NCTE.

Betts, E. A., and C. M. Welch. 1963. Freddie Miller, scientist. *Adventures here and there*; book 5. New York: American Book Co.

Goodman, K. S., and C. Burke. 1973. *Theoretically based studies of patterns of miscues in oral reading performance, final report*. Project No. 9–0375, Grant No. OEG-0-9-320375-4269, U.S. Office of Education.

Goodman, Y., and C. Burke. 1972. *Reading miscue inventory*. New York: Macmillan.

Larson, J. R. 1966. Fareedah's carpet. *Palace in Bagdad*. New York: Scribner's.

Lopez, S. 1977. Children's use of contextual cues. *The Reading Teacher* 30(7): 735–740.

Rigg. P. 1977. Reading in ESL. In *On TESOL '76*, J. Fanselow and R. Crymes (Eds.), 203–210. Washington, D.C.: TESOL.

PART IV:
IMPLICATIONS AND APPLICATIONS OF INTERACTIVE APPROACHES TO SECOND LANGUAGE READING – PEDAGOGY

The three chapters in this concluding section of the book identify for the classroom second language reading teacher a number of pedagogical implications and applications of the interactive approaches to second language reading. From the foregoing chapters that have presented and discussed interactive models of reading, from the chapters that have applied these models specifically to theoretical models of second language reading, and from the chapters that have reported empirical investigations of interactive second language reading, these three chapters identify the most salient and significant teaching implications and applications for the classroom reading teacher and teachers in training.

While discussing the general implications of interactive approaches to second language reading classrooms, both the Eskey and Grabe chapter and the Carrell chapter also identify specific classroom applications and make specific suggestions of what can and should go on in the classroom to try to bring about truly interactive second language reading. Both these chapters discuss these specific suggestions from the perspectives of making second language readers effective top-down processors as well as effective bottom-up processors of text.

The concluding chapter by Devine resumes the theme of the relationship between language proficiency and reading proficiency in the second language and discusses specific pedagogical implications and applications of this notion.

The chapters in this pedagogical section will no doubt provoke more questions than are addressed, much less satisfactorily answered. Some questions for which answers are attempted, and which the reader may want to read to answer, include: (1) What is the role of control of grammatical structures in second language reading and how can such control be facilitated in the classroom? (2) What is the role of control of vocabulary in second language reading and how can such control be facilitated in the classroom? (3) How can the second language reading teacher facilitate the building of relevant background knowledge where necessary? (4) How can the second language reading teacher teach students to activate appropriate background knowledge? (5) What do many successful extant pedagogical methods have in common? (6) What general as well as specific things can the second language reading teacher do to promote *interactive* second language reading? (7) How can the second language reading teacher positively affect both the language and reading skills of students?

15 Interactive models for second language reading: perspectives on instruction

David E. Eskey *and* William Grabe

The case for interactive models of reading

Anyone concerned with ESL reading cannot help but be struck by the dramatic improvements in ESL reading theory and practice during the past ten years or so. These improvements may be traced to multiple sources, including, for example, the general movement toward more communicative kinds of language teaching and a new concern for needs analyses in relation to particular populations of learners.[1] But clearly the major source of improvement has been the growing understanding and acceptance of psycholinguistic models of the reading process, especially as represented in the work of Kenneth Goodman and Frank Smith. Proceeding from the views of Goodman and Smith, such specialists as Eskey (1973), Clarke and Silberstein (1977), Coady (1979), Carrell and Eisterhold (1983; reprinted as Chapter 5 in this volume) and Carrell (1983) – and of course many others – have adapted this so-called top-down approach to *second* language reading, and have tried to relate it to the practical problems of curriculum design and teaching methods and materials.

Terms like *top-down* or the contrasting *bottom-up* (or, for that matter, *interactive*) are, of course, merely metaphors for the complex mental process of reading, *top* here referring to such "higher" order mental concepts as the knowledge and expectations of the reader, and *bottom* to the physical text on the page. Proponents of each of these approaches have argued that the former or the latter is the true starting point and thus the controlling factor in the process. Parry (1987) has summarized their differences concisely:

Some argue that reading is a "bottom-up" process: graphemes are perceived as forming words, words as forming sentences, sentences as forming paragraphs, and so on (Gough 1972); others argue that the process is a "top-

---

1 For a good introduction to communicative language teaching, see Krashen (1982), Savignon (1983), Yalden (1983, which provides a useful survey of major European developments), and (for practical discussion of methodology) Oller and Richard-Amato (1983).

down" one: the reader starts with a general idea, or scheme, of what should be in the text – this being derived from previously acquired knowledge – and uses this scheme in perceiving and in interpreting graphic cues (Goodman 1967; Smith 1982).

A major issue we would like to raise in this chapter is whether there might be a better characterization of the reading process that would maintain the strengths of a top-down model and, at the same time, provide a way to address such questions as: how and to what degree literate second language readers employ lower-level processing skills and how these interact with higher-level strategies; and whether the second language reading of such students can be accurately described as "sampling, predicting, testing and confirming" (Goodman, cited in Coady 1979:5). While the research of the past ten years represents a major breakthrough, we feel that newer research by a number of lesser-known (at least to language teachers) reading theorists has gone beyond the current set of assumptions of most ESL practitioners. Research on interactive models of reading may allow us to incorporate the insights gained thus far and, at the same time, address possible weaknesses in earlier models.

Weber, for example, has recently noted that the top-down perspective

fails to accommodate important empirical evidence adequately. The interactive models, attempting to be more comprehensive, rigorous and coherent, give emphasis to the interrelations between the graphic display in the text, various levels of linguistic knowledge and processes, and various cognitive activities. (1984: 113)

Support for such a view can also be found in Rumelhart (1977), Stanovich (1980), Ulijn (1980), Perfetti (1985), Singer and Ruddell (1985), and Waltz and Pollack (1985).

Briefly, an interactive model of reading (and note that this is not the "interactive process" mentioned earlier) assumes that skills at all levels are interactively available to process and interpret the text. In its simplest form, such a model subsumes both top-down and bottom-up strategies. This model incorporates the implications of reading as an interactive process – that is, the use of background knowledge, expectations, context, and so on. At the same time it also incorporates notions of rapid and accurate feature recognition for letters and words, spreading activation of lexical forms, and the concept of automaticity in processing such forms – that is, a processing that does not depend on context for primary recognition of linguistic units.[2] Once again Parry (1987) provides a useful summary:

2 This is somewhat oversimplified. The notion "context" itself is a complex issue. Automatic recognition and spreading activation do, in fact, involve subconscious con-

I would suggest, following Rumelhart (1977), Ulijn (1980), and Hill and Larson (1983), that there is in fact an interaction among the levels. The reader starts with the perception of graphic cues, but as soon as these are recognized as familiar, schemata derived from both linguistic knowledge and knowledge of the world in general are brought into play. The proportion of graphic cues that must be perceived varies with individual texts and with individual readers — according to the difficulty of the former, and the knowledge, and confidence in that knowledge, of the latter.

The implications of this model for ESL are numerous, and a few are in direct contrast to currently accepted views. For example, contextual interpretation of lexical items is only a part of the vocabulary skills needed for fluent reading, and may actually interfere if a student over-relies on this strategy (Stanovich 1980). Similarly, certain kinds of "phonics" exercises may be helpful to students (Beck 1981). Basic recognition exercises to improve speed and accuracy of perception may constitute an important component of an effective second language reading program (Stoller 1984b).

For purposes of discussion, such specific issues as these, and many more like them, can perhaps be reduced to three major questions:

1. How does the second language reading of fluent L1 readers differ from that of fluent L2 native speakers? That is, how does the reading of literate learners acquiring *second* language reading skills differ from that of fluent first language readers? More specifically:
2. How do differences in control of grammatical structure affect second language reading processes?
3. How do differences in control of vocabulary affect such processes?

With respect to question 1, many scholars have asserted that a top-down model of reading is essentially a model of the fluent reader (Weber 1984). Such a model, while useful to ESL professionals, will not account for all the needs of students who are acquiring reading skills. ESL students, including students literate in their own languages, may not be fluent readers in relation to the expectations at U.S. academic institutions. And even those who can fulfill such expectations when reading in their native languages may not be able to transfer fluent reading strategies to their second language reading (Clarke 1979; McLaughlin 1985). An interactive model of reading is better able to account for the role of certain bottom-up skills that are important to successful reading acquisition. In a model that accounts for both fluency and acquisition, issues of different scripts and other L1 interference factors can be better understood (or

textual processing of some sort. This is not, however, the sort of context that most reading researchers discuss when they refer to the importance of context. For discussion, see Balota, Pollatsek, and Rayner (1985), Perfetti (1985), and Stanovich and West (1983).

at least the complexity of the problems involved can be better understood). An interactive model would predict, for example, that at earlier stages of development the differences in reading in different languages would be greater than at more advanced stages of development. Conversely, top-down models seem to predict that transfer of reading skills will automatically occur. Superior perceptual (bottom-up) skills are seen as a result, rather than as one of the causes of, superior top-down strategies.

With respect to question 2, an interactive model would suggest that reading requires a relatively high degree of grammatical control over structures that appear in whatever readings are given to ESL students. In research by Cohen et al. (1979, reprinted as Chapter 11 in this volume), for example, so-called heavy noun phrases (that is, noun phrases like "holding cells in buffer after irradiation before placing them on nutrient agar plates") were identified as major impediments to comprehension for second language readers. This aspect of reading is often passed over too lightly in discussions of reading based on top-down models (see Berman 1984).

With respect to question 3, all models of reading recognize the importance of vocabulary. However, the interactive model goes further. Not only is a large vocabulary important, it is a prerequisite to fluent reading skills. Since automatic word *recognition* is more important to fluent processing of text than context clues as a first strategy, large-scale development of recognition vocabulary is crucial (van Dijk and Kintsch 1983; Perfetti 1985). Moreover, the importance of vocabulary is related not only to the number of words, but also to the number of times that these words are encountered and retrieved in texts. This is partly a matter of pure perceptual development, and interactive models grant far more importance to perceptual processing – that is, the rapid, accurate identification of features at various formal levels – than do strictly top-down models. Top-down models assume that poor readers are word-bound, that they do not know how to use context, or are afraid to try to use context even though transfer of reading skills would suggest that they should be able to do so. Much evidence that supports an interactive model suggests, in contrast, that poor readers simply have not acquired automatic decoding skills (Stanovich 1980; Mitchell 1982). They therefore spend much more processing time in guessing from the context, which is just the sort of skill a top-down model suggests is lacking. One reason fluent readers have time to guess from context without slowing down is that they do not often have to do so. For fluent readers, contextual interpretation skills do not overload processing capacities. Poor readers, in contrast (assuming no physiological problems), spend too much processing time on "thinking about" the words rather than automatically recognizing them.

Some general implications for the teaching of second language reading

All of these issues should be important concerns of reading researchers, especially in an ESL context. We should not, however, lose sight of the fact that these issues have a direct impact as well on ESL classroom methods and materials (or at least they should have such an impact.)[3] To the extent that an interactive model is a more convincing model of the reading process, we must ask ourselves what all this means for the classroom. For the teaching of any kind of second language reading, there seem to be two general implications:

1. Some time must be devoted in reading classes to such relatively bottom-up concerns as the rapid and accurate identification of lexical and grammatical forms. Even students who have developed strong top-down skills in their native languages may not be able to transfer these higher-level skills to a second language context until they have developed a stronger bottom-up foundation of basic identification skills.
2. On the other hand, some time must also be devoted to such top-down concerns as reading for global meaning (as opposed to mere decoding), developing a willingness to take chances (that is, to make educated guesses at meaning in the absence of absolute certainty), and developing appropriate and adequate schemata for the proper interpretation of texts. From the very beginning, successful readers do employ such strategies, even while developing their bottom-up skills. Reading of any kind of text must be treated as real reading, that is, reading for meaning. No student should ever be forced or encouraged to limit him- or herself to mere decoding skills.

In short, for second language readers, especially, *both* top-down and bottom-up skills and strategies must be developed, and developed conjointly, since both contribute directly to the successful comprehension of text.

Some limitations of models in relation to teaching

For second-language reading programs as a whole, however, it must be kept in mind that abstract models of the reading process have a limited contribution to make. For one thing, such models are, in general, models of the "ideal," completely fluent reader with completely developed knowledge systems and skills; whereas the second language reader is, almost by definition, a developing reader with gaps and limitations in both of these categories. For another, we have no clear idea at this time of how

---

3 For a comprehensive, and practical, introduction to the teaching of second language reading, see Nuttall (1982). For a survey of methods appropriate to academic reading programs, see Dubin, Eskey, and Grabe (1986).

readers in general combine bottom-up and top-down processes, much less how particular readers do so. In practice, we are therefore still very dependent on each student's natural ability to learn, and our working goal must be to facilitate, not to mechanically control, that learning.

Even more to the point, a number of major issues surrounding the design and implementation of such programs have very little to do with models. We must, for example, make a clear distinction between the building up of particular skills and strategies, or of relevant knowledge, and reading itself. Both top-down and bottom-up skills can, in the long run, only be developed by extensive reading over time. Classroom work can point the way but cannot substitute for the act itself: people learn to read by reading, not by doing exercises.

This last raises the major pedagogical question of exactly how, and to what degree, the teacher of second language reading should intervene in his or her students' learning. Current recommendations range from, at one extreme, total nonintervention (Krashen and Terrell 1983) – just mix students and books and get out of the way (one observer has called this the "garden of literacy" approach) – to, at the other extreme, the kinds of highly structured approach represented by most textbooks (Troyka 1978, for example) which present themselves as reading courses (in which everything read and every skill dealt with is carefully selected, sequenced, and controlled).

In the real world, the answer to this general question will of course vary from program to program, depending on such factors as the age and proficiency of the students, their educational needs, time available, and so forth. But there do appear to be at least three program constants, specific program differences aside. One is quantity of reading: the program must result in students doing enough reading to increase their skills and knowledge significantly. A reading program that does not involve much reading is clearly a contradiction in terms – and a waste of the teacher's and the students' time. A second and related constant is appropriate materials. What the students read must be relevant to their real needs and interests, and they must be ready, willing, and able to read it.

A final, and arguably the most important, constant is the judgment of the teacher, for it is often the teacher who really determines how much and what his or her students read. Although the reading teacher may do very little of what we normally think of as teaching, he or she may play a crucial role in the students' developing (or failing to develop) second language reading skills. The students must of course do the learning for themselves, but the teacher can often have a major effect on whether any given student chooses to go on reading in a language. A good teacher – or a bad one – can make a critical difference in performing a number of significant functions.

It is first of all the teacher who must *create* the world of reading in a particular class. It is the teacher who must stimulate interest in reading, who must project his or her enthusiasm for books, and who must help students to see that reading can be of real value to them. It is also the teacher who must choose, or edit, or modify, or even, in some circumstances, create appropriate materials for students with varied needs and purposes to read in challenging but not overwhelming amounts and in a sequence of increasing difficulty which will lead to improvement, but not to frustration. Bringing students and appropriate materials together is a very large part of the reading teacher's job.

With respect to instruction, it is once again the teacher who must introduce, and provide practice in, useful reading *strategies* for coping with texts in an unfamiliar language. For the second language reader, who is often, as noted, an insecure reader, pre-reading strategies – like the ancient and venerable SQ3R[4] – are even more important than they are for the native reader, and the teacher must therefore coach the students in their use. The teacher must also induce students to abandon the word-by-word approach to reading by introducing exercises, like timed readings, which force the students to read faster, and exercises that, for similar reasons, force students to read in meaningful "chunks." And the teacher must help students learn to read different texts at different rates, and with greater or lesser attention to detail, for different purposes. Students must learn to skim for the main idea and to scan for specific kinds of information, and they may also have to learn to read critically, to make informed evaluations of an author's arguments.

It is, finally, the teacher who must provide students, in classes and individually, with feedback as needed. Every second language reader runs into brick walls that even the most useful of strategies cannot breach, and that no reading teacher can predict in advance. At these times, however, the teacher can serve as a marvelous all-purpose reference tool to resolve uncertainties. Even more important, by providing help when needed, the teacher can keep his or her students reading as they work toward the ultimate goal of acquiring a new reading habit which can go on providing knowledge and pleasure long after the teacher has passed from the scene.

Some specific applications

Top-down applications

Carrell (1987, reprinted as Chapter 16 in this volume) provides an excellent discussion of teaching to develop top-down reading skills. To

4 SQ3R = Survey, Question, Read, Recite, Review. For discussion in a second language context, see Yorkey (1982:154–155).

that discussion we would make just one major addition, which is that the *content* and *quantity* of texts that second language students are asked to read may be the most important determinants of whether, and to what degree, such students do in fact develop these skills. Krashen (1982) has argued that the subject matter of second language classes should be both interesting and relevant, a claim that is especially appropriate to reading. Even in our first language we find it difficult and boring to read material that is not especially interesting or relevant. Thus the chances we will make the special effort required to read such material in a second language – and to read it in the kind of quantity required for developing strong comprehension skills – seem very slim indeed. Anyone designing second language reading programs in which he or she expects the students to acquire significant top-down reading skills in the language must therefore find materials that the students will be genuinely interested in reading, and develop a workable format for assigning this material in substantial amounts over considerable periods of time.

In general there are only two ways to do this. Given the fact that students differ in their interests, as well as in their skills and potential rates of progress, one way is to develop a program that allows for a very high degree of individualization. In such a program the students may be required to do as much reading as possible, but they make their own choices of reading material from among a wide selection of appropriate texts. This is the *reading lab approach* (for discussion, see Stoller 1986), one format that meets the basic criteria of interesting materials and sufficient quantity. It has the additional advantages of allowing each student to progress at his or her own rate, to develop schemata in some area of interest, and to compile a personal record of reading.

It has, however, some disadvantages. It presupposes a substantial library of materials, and, since there are no texts that every student reads, it limits the kinds of group work that can be done and tends to isolate reading from other parts of the curriculum – or any other shared experiences. For students who are not strong self-motivators – who, for example, have not developed the habit of reading in depth in their own languages – this may be a major problem. One possible solution to that problem is a second way of organizing second language reading programs. This is the *content-centered approach*, another – but very different – format which provides for interesting reading in sufficient quantity. There are many variations of this basic theme – English for specific purposes (ESP) courses for particular academic or occupational groups (e.g., courses for science majors, or nurses), "adjunct" courses attached to other academic courses (e.g., courses designed to aid nonnative speakers enrolled in a psychology or a computer science course), and so-called sheltered courses, which are limited to, and tailored to the special needs of, nonnative speakers in academic programs (e.g., an introduction to English literature for international students only). A feature common to all is that they attempt to provide what Grabe (1986) has called a "critical mass" of information on a subject for the class as a whole to explore at some depth, and this in turn provides a natural occasion for reading in that subject extensively.

Appropriate pre- and postreading work also emerges naturally in the form of introductory lectures or films, ongoing discussions of the subject matter, and, following the reading, the production of oral or written presentations, which provide real motivation for reading about the subject. Student interest is stimulated by classroom give and take. There is a natural blending of skills – listening, speaking, reading, and writing – as the students collectively pursue a common intellectual goal. Reading is no longer isolated: It simply becomes an integral part of the normal educational process. It is no longer taught as an end in itself but as a means (which in "real" life it always is) to a more familiar end – like earning a passing grade in a course or simply learning more about an interesting subject. The major drawback, of course, is the loss of individual choice. Finding subjects that everyone is interested in is a near hopeless task, but it can be argued that learning to take an interest in *new* subjects is something that every student must do in any case. It can also be argued that a fundamental part of any teacher's job is *making* subject matter interesting.

It should finally be noted that these two approaches – individualized and content-centered – may be combined within a single program. Some time can be given to content-centered group activities and some to individualized reading in a lab or extensive outside-reading program format. At very low student ability levels, this is also typically the result of employing a Language Experience approach, if it is implemented properly (see Carrell 1987).

Bottom-up applications

In the chapter that follows, Carrell (1987) also discusses the teaching of bottom-up reading skills, stressing especially the teaching of key vocabulary items and, in the area of grammar, the teaching of various cohesive devices. To this discussion we would add a number of suggestions for addressing two additional areas of concern.

One is the early development of automatic identification skills in relation to the language in its written form. Simply knowing the meanings of some set number of (for example) words does not ensure that a reader will be able while reading to process those words both rapidly and accurately. Whatever a reader may know in the abstract, a failure to identify immediately, or the *mis*identification of, some form can disrupt

Key Word

see	I sea	see	sew	saw
fin	I fan	fine	fin	fun
cry	I cry	fry	try	dry
on	I un	in	an	on
two	I tow	toe	too	two
won	I own	win	won	now
games	I gain	games	game	gains
dish	I fish	disk	dash	dish

Figure 1   A word recognition exercise (from Stoller 1984b)

the reading process. Too many such disruptions can undermine comprehension of the text as a whole, even for the reader with good top-down strategies. Good readers in their native languages may find their attempts to read English texts in a similar way "short-circuited" (Clarke 1979) by repeated failure to identify linguistic forms on the page.

The problem has two dimensions, one cognitive – for successful decoding, the reader must of course know the meanings of the forms – and one perceptual – the reader must also recognize, instantaneously, the forms in their visual representations. Just as we learn to recognize old friends, but sometimes stumble when confronted with mere acquaintances (whom, in some sense, we "know"), so we must make old friends of written forms if we are to decode texts fluently, and thereby give ourselves time to make sense of the new information they contain.

To develop identification skills, second language teachers might do well to employ what are sometimes called "rapid recognition" exercises – that is, exercises in which the students are required to identify, quickly and accurately, linguistic forms at various levels. For beginners, the teacher might even provide some practice in identifying forms as simple as numbers, or clusters of numbers, in left-to-right sequences, before moving on to letters and such clusters of letters as the rules of the spelling system allow (*sch* but not *shc*). But these exercises should merely serve as warm-ups for the far more important task of learning to identify English words in print. Words seem to have a status in language akin to that of molecules in physical structures, and good readers become remarkably adept at recognizing thousands of them at a glance. Good readers can, in fact, be distinguished from those who read less well by means of nothing more than their skill in recognizing individual words in context-free settings both more rapidly and more accurately (Stanovich 1980; van Dijk and Kintsch 1983; Perfetti 1985).

Word-recognition exercises come in many forms (for example, see Figure 1; for further discussion, see Stoller 1986). For more advanced students there are variants that can be extremely challenging – exercises, for example, in which students must match not just forms with forms but meanings with meanings, key words with synonyms or antonyms.

It should of course be obvious that doing exercises is not the primary means of developing identification skills. The primary means is reading itself – extensive reading over time. But such exercises, taken in small doses – perhaps the first few minutes of a class – do serve some important purposes. One is consciousness raising: they draw the reader's attention to the central importance of developing identification skills in English. This is important for those who have learned to read in a language that employs a radically different writing system (like Arabic or Chinese), and may be even more important for those who have learned to read in a language that employs the same alphabet with different letter-sound values (like Spanish j, pronounced /h/). They may also serve to pinpoint specific problem areas and, since they are always timed, may establish a foundation for future reading-rate development work.

A final step at the simple recognition level is phrase identification – a first step toward the crucial skill of "chunking," or reading in meaningful groups of words (Nuttall 1982 calls them "sense groups"). This is an especially crucial skill for reading English, a language in which sequences of words frequently function as single lexical items (*in spite of, put up with*) and syntactic constructions carry much of the meaning (*eating chicken* as opposed to *chickens eating*). Like rapid word-recognition exercises, these exercises should be taken in small doses (for an example, see Figure 2; for further discussion, see Stoller 1986) and for much the same reasons – with one important addition. It is in doing exercises like these that second language readers are first exposed to the notion that they can process English in meaningful phrases, that is, in units larger than the word. Learning that they can in fact do this constitutes a crucial breakthrough for many second language readers, one on which the reading teacher must build when students read texts for meaning, as described below.

The second major area of concern is rate building. Rapid word and phrase recognition are merely means to the real-world end of reading real texts successfully – that is, reading real texts at a reasonable rate with comprehension appropriate to the reader's purposes. Good readers, by definition, read fast, which means that with each fixation of their eyes they very quickly process good-sized chunks of text and thereby good-sized chunks of meaningful discourse in building up a meaning for the text as a whole. By contrast, many readers of a second language (even some of those who read well in their first language) try to read word by word, a strategy that effectively destroys their chances of comprehending very much of the text. Taking in, at each fixation, so little information, and fragmenting sense units, such readers place an intolerable strain on their memory systems (for discussion, see Smith 1982),

A. Key phrase: *lazy day*
  crazy day
  hazy day
  cloudy day
  lazy day
  windy day
  nasty day
  lazy day

B. Key phrase: *on the floor*

on the book	in the flood
on the bay	in the blood
on the door	on the floor
in the door	on the door
on the floor	on the flower
in the lore	in the flour
in the flood	on the floor

C. Key phrase: *drive a car*

drive a truck	rent a car	drive cars
drive a bus	drive a car	car driver
dry a car	wash a car	drive a tractor
park a car	drive a truck	drive two cars
buy a car	buy a truck	drive a car
drive a car	buy a bar	drive a bus

Figure 2   Phrase recognition exercises (from Adams 1969)

so that by the time they have made their painful way to the bottom of the page they have long since forgotten what the top was about.

Thus the major bottom-up skill that readers of a second language must acquire is the skill of reading as fast in that language as their knowledge of it will allow them to, in relation to their reading purposes. Specific rates must of course be adjusted to the reader's purpose in reading a particular text (along a spectrum that runs from skimming for the main idea – something less, perhaps, than we would normally call reading – to close reading for, say, an upcoming exam), but the principle holds, and doing any kind of reading at much less than 200 words a minute is certain to affect comprehension adversely.

For rate building, many systems of paced and timed readings are available, and many means of incorporating such work into second language reading programs as a whole have been suggested (for discussion, see Mahon 1986), but here as in the case of recognition exercises it should be obvious that formal rate-building work should be limited to a few minutes per class and should serve very similar purposes – consciousness raising, the identification of problem areas, and, most of all, the breaking down of any psychological barriers to reading faster in English. Major increases in reading rate can only follow, once again, from extensive reading in the language over time.

One interesting footnote to the rate-building issue concerns the role of words in the normal reading process, specifically words which the reader does not know. Most specialists agree that if a text contains too many of these for particular readers, no strategy – bottom-up *or* top-down – can make such a text accessible to them,[5] but second language readers do of course encounter *some* unknown words in most texts they undertake. In most cases, this is in fact the best means of increasing their control of English vocabulary. But second language readers are frequently panicked by the occurrence of unknown words, and they stop reading to look them up in dictionaries, thereby interrupting the normal reading process. In response to this problem, many second language texts recommend various strategies for guessing the meaning of unknown words from context, by using semantic and syntatic clues or even morphological analysis. Similarly, the working out of cloze passages has been presented as the prototype of reading for the second language learner, since these passages, by definition, contain a certain number of unknown words (those omitted). Such exercises may in fact be effective in weaning students away from their dictionaries, but, with respect to the normal reading process, the problem with guessing-from-context strategies is that, like running to the dictionary, they tend to encourage readers to stop reading. In the interest of developing good reading habits, the best "strategy" for dealing with an unknown word may well be to keep reading until the meaning of that word begins to make itself plain in relation to the larger context provided by the developing discourse as a whole. Perhaps we must learn to make a clearer distinction between reading itself and the complementary skill of building a larger sight vocabulary.

Central to all of these bottom-up concerns (including those raised by Carrell 1987) and the ultimate goal of whatever reading teachers decide to do about them is the concept of *automaticity* (for discussion, see La Berge and Samuels 1974; McLaughlin, Rossman, and McLeod 1983; Samuels and Kamil 1984, reprinted as Chapter 2 in this volume). To put that concept into the simplest possible terms, good readers process

---

5 Edward Fry, for example, has argued (1963) for three levels of readability. Texts in which students encounter no more than 1 new word in 100 he assigns to the "independent reading level" (students should be able to read unaided). Texts in which they encounter no more than 5 new words in 100 he assigns to the "instructional reading level" (students should be able to read with some classroom support). Texts in which they encounter more than 5 new words in 100 he assigns to the "frustration reading level" (students should not attempt to read). Cf. Perfetti (1985:86): "When about 9% of the words were unfamiliar, recall of the semantic content units of the text...was only about 19%."

language in the form of written text without thinking consciously about it, and good second language readers must learn to do so too. It is only this kind of automatic processing which allows the good reader to think instead about the larger meaning of the discourse – to recover, on the one hand, the message that the author intended to convey and, on the other hand, to relate that new information to what the reader knows and feels about the subject, and to his or her reasons for reading about it. In short, it is only this kind of *local* processing that allows for *global* reading with true comprehension.[6]

References

Adams, W. R. 1969. *Increasing reading speed*. London: Macmillan.

Balota, D., A. Pollatsek, and K. Rayner. 1985. The interaction of contextual constraints and parafoveal visual information in reading. *Cognitive Psychology* 17: 364–390.

Beck, I. 1981. Reading problems and instructional practice. In *Reading Research*, Vol. 2, G. Mackinnon and T. Walker (Eds.), 53–95. New York: Academic Press.

Berman, R. 1984. Syntactic components of the foreign language reading process. In *Reading in a foreign language*, J. C. Alderson and A. H. Urquhart (Eds.), 139–156. New York: Longman.

Carrell, P. 1983. Some issues in studying the role of schemata, or background knowledge, in second language comprehension. *Reading in a Foreign Language* 1(2): 81–92.

1987. Fostering interactive second-language reading. In *Initiatives in communicative language teaching*, Vol. 2, S. Savignon and M. Berns (Eds.), 145–169. Reading, Mass.: Addison-Wesley. [A revised version appears as Chapter 16 in this volume.]

Carrell, P. L., and J. C. Eisterhold. 1983. Schema theory and ESL reading pedagogy. *TESOL Quarterly* 17(4): 553–573. [Reprinted as Chapter 5 in this volume.]

Clarke, M. A. 1979. Reading in Spanish and English: evidence from adult ESL students. *Language Learning* 29: 121–150.

Clarke, M. A., and S. Silberstein. 1977. Towards a realization of psycholinguistic principles in the ESL reading classroom. *Language Learning* 27(1): 135–154.

Coady, J. 1979. A psycholinguistic model of the ESL reader. In *Reading in a second language*, R. Mackay, B. Barkman, and R. R. Jordan (Eds.), 5–12. Rowley, Mass.: Newbury House.

Cohen, A., H. Glasman, P. R. Rosenbaum-Cohen, J. Ferrara, and J. Fine. 1979. Reading English for specialized purposes: discourse analysis and the use of student informants. *TESOL Quarterly* 13: 551–564. [Reprinted as Chapter 11 in this volume.]

6 Perfetti (1985) presents a more complex review of local processing as the key to reading comprehension abilities. He does agree that without adequate word recognition skills, comprehension will be lost accordingly.

Dijk, T. A. van, and W. Kintsch. 1983. *Strategies of discourse comprehension.* New York: Academic Press.

Dubin, F., D. E. Eskey, and W. Grabe (Eds.). 1986. *Teaching second language reading for academic purposes.* Reading, Mass.: Addison-Wesley.

Eskey, D. E. 1973. A model program for teaching advanced reading to students of English as a foreign language. *Language Learning* 23(2): 169–184.

Fry, E. 1963. *Teaching faster reading.* Cambridge: Cambridge University Press.

Goodman, K. S. 1967. Reading: a psycholinguistic guessing game. *Journal of the Reading Specialist* 4: 126–135.

Gough, P. B. 1972. One second of reading. In *Language by ear and by eye*, J. F. Kavanagh and I. G. Mattingly (Eds.). Cambridge, Mass.: MIT Press.

Grabe, W. 1986. The transition from theory to practice in teaching reading. In Dubin and Eskey (Eds.), 25–48.

Hill, C., and E. Larson. 1983. *What reading tests call for and what children do.* Washington, D.C.: National Institute of Education.

Krashen, S. D. 1982. *Principles and practice in second language acquisition.* New York: Pergamon.

Krashen, S. D., and T. D. Terrell. 1983. *The natural approach.* Hayward, Cal.: Alemany.

LaBerge, D., and S. Samuels. 1984. Toward a theory of automatic information processing in reading. *Cognitive Psychology* 6: 293–323.

Mahon, D. 1986. Intermediate skills: focusing on reading rate development. In Dubin, Eskey, and Grabe (Eds.), 77–102.

McLaughlin, B. 1985. *Second language acquisition in childhood.* 2nd ed. Hillsdale, N.J.: Erlbaum.

McLaughlin, B., T. Rossman, and B. McLeod. 1983. Second language learning: an information-processing perspective. *Language Learning* 33: 135–158.

Mitchell, D. C. 1982. *The process of reading.* New York: Wiley.

Nuttall, C. 1982. *Teaching reading skills in a foreign language.* London: Heinemann.

Oller, J. W. Jr., and P. A. Richard-Amato (Eds). 1983. *Methods that work.* Rowley, Mass.: Newbury House.

Parry, K. J. 1987. Reading in a second culture. In *Research in reading in English as a second language*, J. Devine, P. L. Carrell, and D. E. Eskey (Eds.). Washington, D.C.: TESOL.

Perfetti, C. A. 1985. *Reading ability.* New York: Oxford.

Rumelhart, D. E. 1977. Toward an interactive model of reading. In *Attention and performance*, Vol. 6, S. Dornic (Ed.), 573–603. New York: Academic Press.

Samuels, S. J., and M. Kamil. 1984. Models of the reading process. In *Handbook of reading research*, P. D. Pearson (Ed.), 185–224. New York: Longman. [An abridged version appears as Chapter 2 in this volume.]

Savignon, S. J. 1983. *Communicative competence: theory and classroom practice.* Reading, Mass.: Addison-Wesley.

Singer, H., and R. Ruddell (Eds.). 1985. *Theoretical models and processes of reading.* 3rd ed. Newark, Del.: International Reading Association.

Smith, F. 1983. *Understanding reading: a psycholinguistic analysis of reading and learning to read.* 3rd ed. New York: Holt, Rinehart and Winston.

Stanovich, K. E. 1980. Toward an interactive-compensatory model of individual differences in the development of reading fluency. *Reading Research Quarterly* 17: 157–159.

Stanovich, K. E., and R. West. 1983. On priming by sentence context. *Journal of Experimental Psychology: General* 112: 1–36.

Stoller, F. 1984a. Designing an effective reading lab. *Team* 49: 1–13.

    1984b. Implications of the interactive model of reading for recognition skills instruction. Paper presented at the 18th TESOL Conference, Houston, March.

    1986. Reading lab: developing low level reading skills. In Dubin, Eskey, and Grabe (Eds.), 51–76.

Troyka, L. Q. 1978. *Structured reading*. Englewood Cliffs, N.J.: Prentice-Hall.

Ulijn, J. 1980. Foreign-language reading research: recent trends and future prospects. *Journal of Research in Reading* 3: 17–37.

Waltz, D., and J. Pollack. 1985. Massively parallel parsing: a strong interactive model of natural language interpretation. *Cognitive Science* 9: 51–74.

Weber, R.-M. 1984. Reading: United States. *Annual Review of Applied Linguistics* 4: 111–123.

Yalden, J. 1983. *The communicative syllabus: evolution, design, and implementation.* New York: Pergamon.

Yorkey, R. C. 1982. *Study skills for students of English.* 2nd ed. New York: McGraw-Hill.

16 Interactive text processing: implications for ESL/second language reading classrooms

Patricia L. Carrell

The models and theory chapters in this volume, specifically Chapter 3 (Anderson and Pearson) and 5 (Carrell and Eisterhold), provide the theoretical underpinnings of this pedagogical chapter.

In recent research on second language reading (Carrell 1983; Carrell and Wallace 1983), it has been found that second language readers may not effectively utilize knowledge-based processes or top-down processing (i.e., specific contextual information they were supplied with) to facilitate comprehension. They may engage almost exclusively in text-based processing to the detriment of comprehension. By contrast, in other studies (Steffensen, Joag-dev, and Anderson 1979; Johnson 1981; Carrell 1981), some evidence has been found of overreliance on top-down processes. Thus, overreliance on either mode of processing to the neglect of the other mode has been found to cause reading difficulties for second language readers. Some second language readers are not efficient interactive text processors, either because they attempt to process in a totally bottom-up fashion, and may be effortful decoders at that, or because they attempt to process in a totally top-down fashion and are hence subject to schema failures or schema interference – see Carrell, Chapter 7 of this volume, for a discussion of the causes of text-boundedness and schema interference. For such inefficient second language readers, what can the second language reading teacher do?

This chapter proposes teaching a number of comprehension strategies designed to help nonnative readers to become interactive readers. In discussing these classroom suggestions, I shall classify them into two groups: (1) those designed to teach students to make effective use of the bottom-up processing mode, and (2) those designed to teach students to make effective use of the top-down processing mode. This distinction is primarily for ease of presenting and discussing these strategies, for to some extent the strategies discussed from the perspective of one pro-

This chapter is a revised version of Patricia L. Carrell, 1987, Fostering interactive second-language reading, in *Initiatives in communicative language teaching*, Vol. 2, S. Savignon and M. Berns (Eds.), 145–169. Reading, Mass.: Addison-Wesley. Reprinted with permission of Addison-Wesley.

cessing mode also have an effect on the other processing mode, and on the general metacognitive awareness by second language readers that effective reading calls for an efficient *interaction* of both processing modes.

Implications for second language reading classrooms

Given the role of schemata in reading comprehension, the following are suggestions of some classroom implications and applications of this view of second language reading. Suggesting applications of theory to pedagogy is always dangerous and must be prefaced with several caveats: (1) although these suggestions are based on both theoretical and experimental, empirical research, for the most part they have not been subjected to classroom-based, pedagogical research, and where they have been tested in classrooms, they have not been tested in wide varieties of pedagogical settings; (2) a class of adults literate in their native language is generally assumed, although most suggestions would also be applicable or adaptable to classes for children or for adults illiterate in their native language; (3) there are potential differences in how these suggestions might apply at different levels of proficiency in the second language (some of these are mentioned); (4) although these suggestions are offered from the perspective of a schema-theoretic view of reading, insofar as schema theory is compatible with a general psycholinguistic model of reading, some may also be implied by other aspects of the psycholinguistic approach; (5) since some suggestions are compatible with any reader-centered, communicative approach to reading, they may already be happening in second language reading classrooms; (6) this list is by no means exhaustive.

Bottom-up processing

As mentioned in the introduction to this volume, the introduction of a top-down processing perspective has had a dramatic effect on models of second language reading. From earlier views of second language reading as a rather passive linguistic decoding process, to more contemporary views of second language reading as an active, predictive process, the field today is strongly influenced by top-down processing perspectives. However, lest the top-down view of second language reading be seen as a *substitute* for the bottom-up, decoding view, rather than its complement, several researchers have recently felt the need to emphasize that efficient and effective second language reading requires *both* top-down and bottom-up strategies operating interactively (Rumelhart 1977, 1980; Sanford and Garrod 1981; van Dijk and Kintsch 1983; and, in this volume, Eskey, Chapter 6; Eskey and Grabe, Chapter 15; and Carrell, Chapter 7). Eskey (Chapter 6) terms this recognition of the importance of bottom-up processing, of the help second language readers need in simple decoding tasks, "holding in the bottom." In this part of the chapter I shall discuss two areas of pedagogy that can assist second language readers to improve their bottom-up, language-decoding skills, that is, to "hold in the bottom": grammatical skills and vocabulary development.

GRAMMATICAL SKILLS

Several studies have shown the important role played by grammatical knowledge in native and nonnative reading. Among native English-speaking children (in Britain), Chapman (1979) found a relationship between reading ability and ability to complete anaphoric relations in a cloze test, and he concluded that mastery of such textual features – including cohesive ties (Halliday and Hasan 1976) – is a central factor in fluent reading and reading comprehension. Cohen and his colleagues (1979, reprinted as Chapter 11 in this volume) found that foreign readers of English texts in the sciences and economics often did not pick up on conjunctive words in their specialized texts. Cohen et al. argued that nonnative readers read more locally than do native speakers and, because they do not attend to conjunctive ties, they have trouble synthesizing information across sentences and paragraphs. Mackay (1979) and Cowan (1976) have similarly argued that recognition of conjunctions and other intersentential linguistic devices is crucial to the information-gathering skills of second language readers. Thus, "holding in the bottom," enhancing second language readers' bottom-up decoding skills, should include classroom instruction on the cohesive devices of English (substitution, ellipsis, conjunction, lexical cohesion), and their function across sentences and paragraphs. Such instruction can make students aware of how ideas in a text are unified by these cohesive elements. Williams (1983) has not only discussed the importance of recognizing cohesive ties in reading in a foreign language, but has suggested teaching materials and methods to bring this about. Specifically, he proposes a system of symbols and textual markings that teach foreign readers how to use cohesive signals in order to increase their reading comprehension. Chapman (1983) has published an entire book on the teaching of cohesion and its relationship to reading development; see also Carrell (1986) for a review of this book and Carrell (1982) and subsequent replies in the Forum section of the *TESOL Quarterly* for discussion of the limitations of cohesion.

Connor (1984) has studied both cohesion and coherence in advanced ESL learners' writing and discovered that although advanced ESL writers use about the same proportion of cohesive devices as native writers, they lack the variety of native writers. This is especially true in the category of lexical cohesion, where ESL writers tend to overuse repetition and underuse synonyms and collocation. For example, in compositions written on the topic of tests and testing situations, a native speaker used the following lexical collocations: "methods of measuring," "a set of questions," "a satisfactory means of measuring a student's achievement," "means of testing," "gauge a student's mastery," and "administering examinations." Writing on the same topic, a nonnative speaker exhibited limited use of synonyms and relied almost exclusively on repetitions: "tests," "the tests," "put scores," "good scores," "bad scores," "scores of tests," "tests." Connor attributes this to general deficiencies in ESL learners' vocabularies, and comments that this appears to be related to similar results with good and poor native English writers (Witte and Faigley 1981). This brings us to the second major area of classroom instruction designed to enhance second language readers' bottom-up decoding skills – vocabulary development.

VOCABULARY DEVELOPMENT

Vocabulary development and word recognition have long been recognized as crucial to successful bottom-up decoding skills. However, schema theory has shed new light on the complex nature of the interrelationship of schemata, context, and vocabulary knowledge. Unlike traditional views of vocabulary, current thinking converges on the notion that a given word does not have a fixed meaning, but rather has a variety of meanings around a "prototypical" core, and that these meanings interact with context and background knowledge. Consider the following examples of the verb "kick" in English:

The punter kicked the ball.
The baby kicked the ball.
The golfer kicked the ball.

(Anderson et al. 1977: 368)

Readers will construct different images for the words *ball* and *kick* because of the influence of the different subject noun phrases. Different kinds of balls are visualized, and the act of kicking is different in each of the sentences. If readers do not have the background experiences associated with types of kicking and things that can be kicked, then the comprehension of the lexical items and the sentences as a whole will be affected. Thus, knowledge of individual word meanings is strongly associated with conceptual knowledge – that is, learning vocabulary is also learning the conceptual knowledge associated with the word. On the one hand, an important part of teaching background knowledge is teaching the vocabulary related to it, and, conversely, teaching vocabulary may mean teaching new concepts, new knowledge. Knowledge of vocabulary entails knowledge of the schemata in which a concept participates, knowledge of the networks in which that word participates, as well as any associated words and concepts.

Teachers must become aware of the cross-cultural differences in vocabulary and how meaning may be represented differently in the lexicons of various languages. For example, the words *cut* and *carve* have distinct meanings in English; but the meanings are represented by one word in French, *couper* (Macnamara 1972). Thus, a French speaker learning the English words will have to learn semantic distinctions in the concepts of *cut* and *carve*, in addition to learning the words. For some suggestions on semantically based vocabulary teaching methods, see D. Johnson and Pearson (1978).

Correlations between knowledge of word meanings and ability to comprehend passages containing those words are all high and well established in first language reading studies (Anderson and Freebody 1981). Such evidence, of course, fails to establish knowledge of word meanings as a *cause* of comprehension. Direct support for a causal relationship must be sought in the several instructional studies that have investigated the effect of preteaching vocabulary on passage comprehension.

Comprehension studies in both first and second language reading that employ prereading instruction in word meanings have been both successful and unsuccessful in accomplishing a significant effect. While any conclusions drawn from an analysis of only a few studies should be seen as tentative, several characteristics seem to distinguish effective from ineffective teaching programs. (See Stahl and Fairbanks 1986 for a meta-analysis of studies concerned with effects of vocabulary instruction on comprehension and on learning of word meanings). Preteaching vocabulary in order to increase learning from text will be more successful if the words to be taught are key words in the target passages, if the words are taught in semantically and topically related sets so that word meanings and background knowledge improve concurrently, if the words are taught and learned thoroughly, if both definitional and contextual information are involved, if students engage in deeper processing of word meanings, and if only a few words are taught per lesson and per week. Attempts to teach word meanings without determining that they are key to the target passages, without teaching word meanings and background knowledge concurrently, without teaching words thoroughly, or teaching more than a few words per lesson or per week, are probably doomed to failure.

Research specific to second language reading has shown that merely presenting a list of new or unfamiliar vocabulary items to be encountered in a text, even with definitions appropriate to their use in that text, does not guarantee the learning of the word or the concept behind the word, or of improved reading comprehension on the text passage (e.g., Hudson 1982, reprinted as Chapter 13 in this volume). In one study, three different types of vocabulary instruction before or concurrent with reading the target passages failed to produce any significant facilitating effects on the reading when compared to the absence of any vocabulary instruction (P. Johnson 1982).

Rather, to be effective, an extensive and long-term vocabulary development program accompanying a parallel schemata or background-knowledge-development program is probably called for. Instead of pre-teaching vocabulary for single reading passages, teachers should probably be preteaching vocabulary and background knowledge concurrently for sets of passages to be read at some later time. In effect, this recommendation would result in a type of "spiral curriculum" (Bruner 1960), wherein knowledge and vocabulary taught about a topic would assume knowledge and vocabulary learned previously about that topic and would provide a new foundation of knowledge and vocabulary on which later knowledge and vocabulary about that topic could be built. Every second language curriculum should have a general program of parallel concept/background knowledge development and vocabulary development. After all, the problem of vocabulary development in a second language is not simply a matter of teaching new labels for familiar concepts; it may also involve teaching new concepts.

Finally, on the topic of linguistic, bottom-up decoding skills in second language reading, I am reminded of the results of empirical research by Clarke (1979; 1980, reprinted as Chapter 8 in this volume) and Cziko (1978), which suggest that competence in the second language (grammar and vocabulary) may place a ceiling on second language reading ability. The implications are that "good reader" top-down reading skills may be hampered as a result of limited language proficiency, and that reading in a second language may be parasitic on language to a larger degree than first language reading.

However, be that as it may, Hudson (1982) has found that schema production, top-down processing, is very much implicated in the so-called short circuit of second language reading, and that schemata can override language proficiency as a factor in comprehension. Therefore, with such effects in mind, let us now consider teaching techniques/strategies which can help students make more effective use of the top-down processing mode.

Top-down processing

BUILDING BACKGROUND KNOWLEDGE

Schema theory research shows that the greater the background knowledge a reader has of a text's content area, the better the reader will comprehend that text (Pearson, Hansen, and Gordon 1979; Taylor 1979; Stevens 1980). The implication of this is that some students' apparent "reading problems" may be problems of insufficient background knowledge.

One of the most obvious reasons that a particular schema may fail to exist for a second language reader is that the schema is specific to a given culture and is not part of a particular reader's background. Studies by Steffensen et al. (1979), Johnson (1981), and Carrell (1981) have shown that the implicit cultural knowledge presupposed by a text and the reader's own cultural knowledge interact to make texts based on one's own culture easier to read and understand than syntactically and rhetorically equivalent texts based on a less familiar culture.

The same may be said of texts demanding specific background knowledge which is discipline-specific (e.g., economics texts, science texts) (Alderson and Urquhart 1985, reprinted as Chapter 12 in this volume).

The related pedagogical question is: "Can we improve students' reading by helping them build background knowledge on the topic prior to reading, through appropriate prereading activities?" The available research suggests an affirmative answer to this question. A number of first language studies with children support the existence of a causal relationship between background knowledge and comprehension (McWhorter 1935, cited in Smith 1963; McDowell 1939, cited in Smith 1963; Graves and Cooke 1980; Graves and Palmer 1981; Graves, Cooke, and LaBerge 1983). For example, Stevens (1982) increased learning from text compared with a control group for tenth-grade students reading a history passage by teaching them relevant background information for that passage. In another study, Hayes and Tierney (1982) found that presenting background information related to the topic to be learned helped readers learn from text regardless of how that background information was presented or how specific or general it was.

Unfortunately, while these studies support the notion that improving background knowledge can improve comprehension and learning from text, they do not give us clear guidance on the best ways of accomplishing this teaching. Failing definitive pedagogical research on which teaching methods work best in building background knowledge — for example, direct versus symbolic experiences, direct versus incidental instruction, explicit versus deductive instruction — the best the classroom reading teacher can do is to experiment with a number of prereading activities. Direct teaching of appropriate background knowledge can be accomplished through lectures, such as that used by Stevens, or various other types of prereading activities; viewing movies, slides, pictures; field trips; demonstrations; real-life experiences; class discussions or debates; plays, skits, and other role-play activities; text previewing; introduction and discussion of the key vocabulary to be encountered in the text (see previous discussion of vocabulary development); key-word/key-concept association activities; and even prior reading of related texts. Until research tells us otherwise, it is probably wise to assume that these prereading activities work best when used in varying combinations.

Carrell and Eisterhold (1983, reprinted as Chapter 5 in this volume) discuss the importance of text-previewing activities for second language readers because of the potential of cultural specificity of text content. Also useful are text previewing activities such as those suggested by Swaffar (1981), which include the previewing of text genre as well as of text content.

Of particular relevance for second language readers at lower levels of proficiency and with limited vocabularies in the second language, for whom meaning tends to break down at the word level, are prereading activities involving key-word or key-concept association tasks. Pearson and Johnson (1978) propose the use of word association tasks in instruction settings to yield a diagnosis of what students already know and what they need to know about a key concept. Initial associations made by students may be of different types (superordinates, subordinates, attributes, definitions, synonyms, antonyms, contradictories, contraries, reverses, personal experiences, or even similar-sounding words). As the students volunteer these associations, the teacher writes them on the blackboard; the teacher may go even further to organize the associations into the form of a "semantic map" for the students (D. Johnson and Pearson 1978). Figure 1 illustrates such a semantic map. Reflection on these associations may then form the basis for further class discussion. Langer (1981) has found that through such class discussion students may significantly enrich their networks of associations. In attempting to get students to "stretch" their concepts, Pearson and Johnson (1978) and Pearson and Spiro (1982) encourage the teacher to use analogies, comparisons, even metaphors to build bridges between what the students already know about a concept and what they may need to know in order to read and understand a particular text. Obviously, it is also helpful for the teacher to offer several examples of the new concept, as well as several examples of what it is not, so students have a sense of the parameters of the concept.

Different prereading activities may be more or less effective with different proficiency levels. In one study, Hudson (1982) compared one type of explicit prereading activity (which consisted of having students briefly view a set of cue pictures, discuss the pictures, and then individually generate a set of predictions about what they expected to find in the passage) to another type of prereading activity (a type of vocabulary activity). In general, he found that the former type of prereading activity had a significantly greater facilitating effect on reading comprehension compared to the latter. However, close examination of the data showed

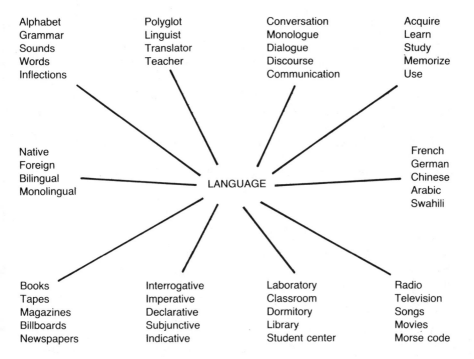

Alphabet	Polyglot	Conversation	Acquire
Grammar	Linguist	Monologue	Learn
Sounds	Translator	Dialogue	Study
Words	Teacher	Discourse	Memorize
Inflections		Communication	Use

Native			French
Foreign			German
Bilingual	LANGUAGE		Chinese
Monolingual			Arabic
			Swahili

Books	Interrogative	Laboratory	Radio
Tapes	Imperative	Classroom	Television
Magazines	Declarative	Dormitory	Songs
Billboards	Subjunctive	Library	Movies
Newspapers	Indicative	Student center	Morse code

Figure 1   Semantic map for "language"

that the effect was significant only for beginning and intermediate level ESL readers; at the advanced levels neither one of these two prereading activities was any better than the other. In fact, at the advanced level there were no significant differences among those two types of prereading activities and a third type – a read and reread activity.

Some existing second language reading materials include token amounts of prereading exercises, usually in the form of prefacing passages with prereading, information-seeking, or prediction questions for the reader to keep in mind while reading (e.g., Grellet 1981). Further, some texts that have comprehension questions following the passages suggest that these may be used as prereading questions (e.g., Baudoin et al. 1977). Others intersperse questions throughout a reading passage (e.g., Allen and Widdowson 1974). These question-posing, prediction, prereading exercises supposedly function to motivate students to read what follows for a purpose – that is, to gain the requisite information to answer the questions. They also supposedly function to get the student to predict, within a general content area, what the text will be about. However, even if they do perform these two functions, in many reading situations they are too limited to be the only type of prereading activity.

At best, these kinds of prereading questions function to help readers predict which prior, existing knowledge to access; they will not do much toward actually building that knowledge in the reader. Various other types of prereading activities of the kinds previously listed may be needed in order to help second language readers both to build the background knowledge they need for their reading and to show them how to activate or access such knowledge in the process of reading, once it exists. Pre-reading activities must accomplish both goals: building new background knowledge as well as activating existing background knowledge. As Stevens says: "A teacher of reading might thus be viewed as a teacher of relevant information as well as a teacher of reading skills" (1982:328).

ACTIVATING BACKGROUND KNOWLEDGE

Organized methods.   Several organized approaches and methods for facilitating reading through activation of background knowledge have been proposed in the literature. By "organized" I mean methods that have been given a label or name, have been at least somewhat codified, and are already published and accessible in the pedagogical literature. I shall mention only a few of these: The Language Experience Approach (LEA; Hall 1981; Rigg 1981; Stauffer 1980); Extending Concepts Through Language Activities (ECOLA: Smith-Burke 1980); Directed Reading-Thinking Activity (DRTA; Stauffer 1980); the Experience-Text-Relationship method (ETR; Au 1979); the PreReading Plan (PReP; Langer 1980, 1981); and, finally, the Survey-Question-Read-Recite-Review method (SQ3R; Robinson 1941). I will attempt to summarize what these methods seem to have in common; for further information and the details of each method, interested readers should refer directly to the cited references or to Barnitz (1985), which has an extended discussion of each method.

All of these methods train the reader to *do* something *before* reading in order to activate appropriate background knowledge – either creating the text themselves (LEA), setting a communication purpose for reading (ECOLA), predicting what a text will be about (DRTA), sharing prior experiences on the topic (ETR), free associating on the topic (PReP), or surveying the text (SQ3R). This prior activation of background knowl-edge also gives the reader a purpose for reading.

In addition, all of these methods have the reader read the text against the background of the activated knowledge. Finally, they all have the reader *do* something *after* reading to synthesize the new information gained from the text with their prior knowledge – for example, discussing the text (LEA, SQ3R), writing their interpretations (ECOLA, SQ3R), reviewing the text to confirm hypotheses or prove conclusions (DRTA), relating text content to prior knowledge (ETR), or reformulating knowledge (PReP).

Text-mapping strategies.   A number of instructional strategies have evolved recently to help make readers aware of the rhetorical structure of texts. These strategies are also intended to help readers use knowledge about the rhetorical organization of a text to guide and organize their interaction with the text. These strategies have arisen from research on text analysis of both expository and narrative texts, but this discussion will be limited to expository, or informational, texts.

Generally speaking, text mapping involves selecting key content from an expository passage and representing it in some sort of visual display (boxes, circles, connecting lines, tree diagrams, etc.) in which the relationships among the key ideas are made explicit. Four such thrusts – "networking" (Dansereau et al. 1979), "mapping" (Anderson 1978), "flowcharting" (Geva 1980, 1983), and "top-level rhetorical structures" (Meyer 1975; Bartlett 1978) have all been used successfully as instructional tools. Students use text cues to define the fundamental relationships as they manifest themselves in expository texts. Networking, mapping, and flowcharting require students to diagram how the ideas and their relationships are represented within the text; Meyer's top-level rhetorical structure approach requires students not only to identify the hierarchy of ideas but to label these patterns as well (e.g., as time order, comparison, collection of descriptions, or cause/effect). Figure 2 describes these four of Meyer's top-level organization patterns and illustrates words that are typical clues to each organizational pattern. Figure 3 illustrates a classroom exercise that can be used to train students in identifying each of these top-level organizations (Mikulecky 1985:275–276). Figures 4 and 5 are an example of flowcharting a text, from Geva (1983:386–387). Geva (1980, 1983), Taylor and Beach (1984), and Bartlett (1978) have all shown significant effects of teaching text structure in instructional settings with native speakers of English. Carrell (1985) shows similar significant facilitating effects of explicit instruction on Meyer's top-level organization patterns with readers of English as a second language. If students are not familiar with these rhetorical structures before teaching, such teaching may build the schemata as well as teach students to activate the schemata.

Teaching predicting.   In addition to teaching students techniques of previewing texts (see, e.g., Mikulecky 1985), other techniques can be used to teach second-language readers to predict text content. These include: (1) exposing a text bit by bit (either sentence by sentence, or clause by clause) and asking readers to predict the contents of the next

TIME ORDER

Time Order – information organized in a chronology, time sequence

Words that are clues or signal words often used when writing in chronological or time order:

first, next, last, in the end, days, dates, soon, later, finally, eventually, times, later on, in the meantime, afterwards, not long after, at the end, at last, right away, in the beginning.

COMPARISON/CONTRAST

Comparison/Contrast – information organized to show similarities, differences, advantages, disadvantages. Speaker's perspective may be neutral or may take a position.

Words that are clues or signal words of a comparison or contrast:

but, different, however, like, contrary to, comparative forms (e.g., faster, slower), rather, on the contrary, as, in the same way, instead, yet, similarly, on the other hand.

COLLECTION OF DESCRIPTIONS

Collection of descriptions – information organized by a simple listing of facts or ideas relating to the same topic.

Words that are clues or signal words of a collection of descriptions:

some, others, many, a few, other, also, first, second, third, finally, in addition, lastly, all.

CAUSE AND EFFECT

Cause and Effect – information organized by showing the cause or causes of an event or situation, of the effects of some event or situation, or both.

Words that are clues or signal words of a cause/effect pattern:

result, cause, effect, lead to, due to, consequently, because of, create, become, come about.

Figure 2   Meyer's patterns of top-level organization

part. Fillmore (1981), Connor (1985), and Steffensen (1985) have successfully used this technique as a research tool, but it can also be used
as an instructional device; (2) giving only the first and last sentences of
a paragraph of a text, and asking students to reconstruct what has been
omitted; (3) asking students to determine the original order of a number
of detached paragraphs, or (4) asking students to unscramble two in-
termingled texts (Crane 1984; Westhoff 1981). Cloze texts, another
technique used mainly in testing, can also be used in teaching students
to develop strategies for contextual guessing, to not depend on word-
by-word processing (Greenewald 1981; Hosenfeld et al. 1981; Westhoff
1981; Schulz 1983). In all of these exercises, learners have to read the
text with a handicap – something is missing and they need to fill the
gap, reduce the uncertainty, solve a problem. To enable them to do so,
and to thus learn a strategy for so doing, the information they need in
order to solve the problem must be completely available. Therefore, the
texts used for these exercises should be relatively easy.

Directions: Here are four paragraphs about Sir Isaac Newton. Read each paragraph, and then choose one sentence from the extra sentences below and write the letter for that sentence next to the paragraph in which it would fit best. One of the sentences will not be used.

Paragraph 1

Sir Isaac Newton worked on many important scientific problems. First, there was his development of the laws of motion. He also made important discoveries about optics and the nature of color. His other work included ideas about astronomy, chemistry, and logic. And finally, he produced the *Principia*, a book which explained his law of universal gravitation.

Paragraph 2

Isaac Newton was born in England in 1642. He went to Trinity College, Cambridge University, in 1661 at the age of 18. In 1665, the plague swept through England, and Newton left school and returned to his family home in Woolsthorpe. It was there that he began most of his best work. He published his famous book, the *Principia*, in 1682. And in 1699 he was made the director of the English Mint. Sir Isaac Newton died in 1727 and he is buried in Westminster Abbey.

Paragraph 3

Although the two men were both geniuses, Isaac Newton and Albert Einstein have very little else in common. True, they both did their most important and famous work before the age of 26. But there are great differences between them. "Proper behavior" was most important to Newton, while Einstein liked to be different. Newton spent his later years working for the government, while Einstein spent his entire life doing science.

Paragraph 4

Newton did most of his best work during his stay in Woolsthorpe from 1665 to 1668. Many writers have tried to find out what caused him to produce all of those great ideas in such a short time. Was it the peace and quiet of the small town that caused his creative powers to increase? The causes may never be known, but the effects of Newton's genius are still felt today.

Extra Sentences:

a. Some people think that a falling apple caused Newton to think of the law of universal gravitation.
b. Present-day physicists have discovered limits to the mechanical universe which Newton described.
c. In addition, he invented differential and integral calculus.
d. They say Isaac Newton never smiled, but Albert Einstein had a great sense of humor.
e. In fact, by age 26, he had already completed most of his best work.

Figure 3   Exercise in identifying patterns (From B. S. Mikulecky, Reading skills instruction in ESL, in "On TESOL '84," P. Larson et al. (Eds.), pp. 275–6. © 1985 by Teachers of English to Speakers of Other Languages. Reprinted by permission of the publisher and B. S. Mikulecky.)

WAVES

Waves are caused, as nearly everyone knows, by the wind. Two classes of waves may be distinguished: the long rollers at the coast, and the far more irregular forms of the open sea, where waves of all sizes and types are present. The size and speed of waves depends not only on the wind's speed but on the length of time the wind has been blowing, and the unbroken stretch of water over which it blows as well. Very strong winds tend to beat down the waves' height and to reduce wave speed. On the other hand, less violent but steady winds often produce wave speed greater than that of the wind itself. The average maximum wave length is about 36 feet, although occasional higher waves have been measured.

Figure 4   Text of "Waves" (From E. Geva, 1983, Facilitating reading comprehension through flowcharting, Reading Research Quarterly 18(4): 387. Reprinted with permission of E. Geva and the International Reading Association.)

Reporting *how* the prediction was made is one of the most important parts of this learning process. In order to give as many learners as possible the proper instructional setting to enable a maximal number of learners to report at the same time, group work or pair work should be used.

Anomaly/nonsense.   Pearson and Spiro (1982) have suggested yet another technique to show learners that exclusive reliance on bottom-up processing, word-by-word decoding, is not the way to process texts. They recommend using texts on familiar topics which have embedded in them anomalous words, phrases, and sentences. Students should be asked to stop reading when they encounter something that does not make sense. Discussing the anomalies and why they do not make sense helps to sensitize students to the importance of involving background knowledge and checking textual details against background knowledge. Figure 6 illustrates one way to construct such a text simply by replacing words in an existing text.

A similar exercise may involve the use of nonsense texts, such as Lewis Carroll's poem "Jabberwocky" or Anthony Burgess's *A Clockwork Orange* (see, for example, Figures 7 and 8). Students can be "walked" through these texts and shown that although the content words are nonsense and cannot, therefore, be looked up in a dictionary, one can nonetheless arrive at an understanding of the text. With "Jabberwocky," students learn to predict from their background knowledge of morphological and syntactic facts of English; with *A Clockwork Orange*, they learn to predict from their background knowledge of a content domain (the criminal world).

Other top-down techniques.   The communicative prereading activities described previously, in addition to building appropriate background

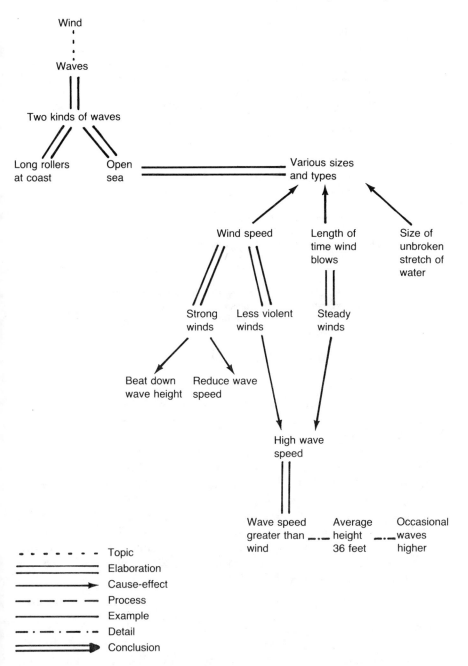

Figure 5 Flowchart of "Waves" text (from Geva 1983: 387, by permission)

FLORIDA

Practically synonymous with the word "vacation," Florida has played the gracious host since Ponce de Leon arrived in 1513. The state is more than just a land of surf, beaches with sand as soft as *concrete*, and recreational opportunities such as Disney World. It also offers great potential for industrial *decline*. The visitor is often tempted to become a resident, and *seldom* does.

Figure 6   (Anomaly)

'Twas brillig, and the slithy toves
  Did gyre and gimble in the wabe:
All mimsy were the borogoves,
  And the mome raths outgrabe.

Figure 7   (From Lewis Carroll's "Jabberwocky," p. 153)

Then we *slooshied* the sirens and knew the *millicents* were coming with *pooshkas* pushing out of the police auto-windows at the ready. That little weepy *devotchka* had told them, there being a box for calling the *rozzes* not too far behind the Muni Power Plant.

Figure 8   (From Anthony Burgess, "A Clockwork Orange," p. 17)

knowledge, would also be part of an instructional program designed to teach students the importance of activating appropriate background knowledge during reading.

For students who overrely on top-down processing, Pearson and Spiro (1982) suggest several techniques that can be used to teach the importance of paying attention to text details. These techniques include use of explicit textual clues in one part of a text to distinguish appropriate from inappropriate multiple-choice possibilities in another part of the text. In addition, students can be encouraged to read carefully for details by making sure they have opportunities to read such texts as directions – for example, for making things, for getting from place to place, for playing games, or for accomplishing a task.

Conclusion

This chapter suggests some activities that can and should go on in second language reading classes to give nonnative readers the skills they need in order to make effective use of both bottom-up and top-down processing modes. Moreover, these classroom activities should also function to make second language readers metacognitively aware that effective reading calls for an efficient *interaction* of both processing modes.

References

Alderson, J. C., and A. Urquhart. 1985. This test is unfair: I'm not an economist. In *Second language performance testing*. P. Hauttman, R. LeBlanc, and M. Bingham Wesche (Eds.), 25–43. Ottawa: University of Ottawa Press. [Reprinted as Chapter 12 in this volume.]

Allen, J. P. B., and H. G. Widdowson. 1974. *English in physical science*. London: Oxford University Press.

Anderson, R. C., and P. Freebody. 1979. *Vocabulary knowledge*. Technical Report No. 136. Urbana: University of Illinois, Center for the Study of Reading.

Anderson, R. C., R. E. Reynolds, D. L. Schallert, and E. T. Goetz. 1977. Frameworks for comprehending discourse. *American Educational Research Journal* 14(4): 367–381.

Anderson, R. C., and P. D. Pearson. 1984. A schema-theoretic view of basic processes in reading comprehension. In *Handbook of reading research*, P. David Pearson (Ed.), 255–287. New York: Longman. [Reprinted as Chapter 3 in this volume.]

Anderson, T. H. 1978. *Study skills and learning strategies*. Technical Report No. 104. Urbana: University of Illinois, Center for the Study of Reading.

Au, K. Hu-Pei. 1979. Using the experience-text-relationship method with minority children. *The Reading Teacher* 32(6): 677–679.

Barnitz, J. 1985. *Reading development of nonnative speakers of English: Research and instruction*. Language in Education series, ERIC Clearinghouse on Language and Linguistics. Center for Applied Linguistics/Harcourt, Brace, Jovanovich.

Bartlett, B. J. 1978. Top-level structure as an organizational strategy for recall of classroom text. Unpublished doctoral diss., Arizona State University.

Baudoin, E. M., E. S. Bober, M. A. Clarke, B. K. Dobson, and S. Silberstein. 1977. *Reader's choice: a reading skills textbook for students of English as a Second Language*. Ann Arbor: University of Michigan Press.

Bruner, J. S. 1960. *The process of education*. New York: Vintage Books.

Carrell, P. L. 1981. Culture-specific schemata in L2 comprehension. In *Selected papers from the ninth Illinois TESOL/BE annual convention, the first midwest TESOL conference*, R. Orem and J. Haskell (Eds.), 123–132. Chicago: Illinois TESOL/BE.

1982. Cohesion is not coherence. *TESOL Quarterly* 16(4): 479–488.

1983. Three components of background knowledge in reading comprehension. *Language Learning* 33(2): 183–207.

1984a. Schema theory and ESL reading: classroom implications and applications. *Modern Language Journal* 68(4): 332–343.

1984b. Evidence of a formal schema in second language comprehension. *Language Learning* 34(2): 87–112.

1984c. The effects of rhetorical organization on ESL readers. *TESOL Quarterly* 18(3): 441–469.

1985. Facilitating ESL reading by teaching text structure. *TESOL Quarterly* 19(4): 727–752.

1986. Review of *Reading development and cohesion*, L. J. Chapman. *Language Learning* 36(3): 377–385.

Carrell, P. L., and J. C. Eisterhold. 1983. Schema theory and ESL reading pedagogy. *TESOL Quarterly* 17(4): 553–573. [Reprinted as Chapter 5 in this volume.]

Carrell, P. L., and B. Wallace. 1983. Background knowledge: context and familiarity in reading comprehension. In *On TESOL '82*, M. Clarke and J. Handscombe (Eds.), 295–308. Washington, D.C.: TESOL.

Chapman, L. J. 1979. Confirming children's use of cohesive ties in text: pronouns. *The Reading Teacher* 33(3): 317–322.

1983. *Reading development and cohesion*. London: Heinemann.

Clarke, M. A. 1979. Reading in Spanish and English: evidence from adult ESL students. *Language Learning* 29(1): 121–150.

1980. The short/circuit hypothesis of ESL reading – or when language competence interferes with reading performance. *Modern Language Journal* 64(2): 203–209. [Reprinted as Chapter 8 in this volume.]

Cohen, A., H. Glasman, P. R. Rosenbaum-Cohen, J. Ferrara, and J. Fine. 1979. Reading English for specialized purposes: discourse analysis and the use of student informants. *TESOL Quarterly* 13(4): 551–564. [Reprinted as Chapter 11 in this volume.]

Connor, U. 1984. A study of cohesion and coherence in English as a second language students' writing. *Papers in Linguistics* 17(3): 301–316.

1985. In search of the ideal bilingual reader using a new interview research method. Manuscript. Indianapolis: Indiana University.

Cowan, J. R. 1976. Reading, perceptual strategies and contrastive analysis. *Language Learning* 26(1): 95–109.

Crane, F. J. 1984. Reading strategies for before, during and after. Workshop presented at the 1984 Illinois TESOL/BE State Convention, Chicago, Illinois.

Cziko, G. A. 1978. Differences in first- and second-language reading: the use of syntactic, semantic and discourse constraints. *Canadian Modern Language Review* 34(3): 473–489.

Dansereau, D. F., K. W. Collins, B. A. McDonald, C. D. Holley, J. Garland, G. Dickhoff, and S. H. Evans. 1979. Development and evaluation of a learning strategy program. *Journal of Educational Psychology* 71(1): 64–73.

Dijk, T. A. van, and W. Kintsch. 1983. *Strategies of discourse comprehension*. New York: Academic Press.

Fillmore, C. J. 1981. Ideal readers and real readers. In *Georgetown University Roundtable on Languages and Linguistics 1981*, Deborah Tannen (Ed.), 248–270. Washington, D.C.: Georgetown University Press.

Geva, E. 1980. *Metatextual notions and reading comprehension*. Unpublished doctoral diss., University of Toronto.

1983. Facilitating reading comprehension through flowcharting. *Reading Research Quarterly* 18(4): 384–405.

Graves, M. F., and C. L. Cooke. 1980. Effects of previewing difficult short stories for high school students. *Research on Reading in Secondary Schools* 6(1): 38–54.

Graves, M. F., C. L. Cooke, and M. J. LaBerge. 1983. Effects of previewing difficult short stories on low ability junior high school students' comprehension, recall, and attitudes. *Reading Research Quarterly* 18(3): 262–276.

Graves, M. F., and R. J. Palmer. 1981. Validating previewing as a method of improving fifth and sixth grade students' comprehension of short stories. *Michigan Reading Journal* 15(1): 1–3.

Greenewald, M. J. 1981. Developing and using cloze materials to teach reading. *Foreign Language Annals* 14(3): 185–188.

Grellet, F. 1981. *Developing reading skills: a practical guide to reading comprehension exercises.* Cambridge: Cambridge University Press.

Hall, M. A. 1981. *Teaching reading as a language experience.* Columbus, Oh.: Merrill.

Halliday, M. A. K., and R. Hasan. 1976. *Cohesion in English.* London: Longman.

Hayes, D. A., and R. J. Tierney. 1982. Developing readers' knowledge through analogy. *Reading Research Quarterly* 17(2): 256–280.

Hosenfeld, C., V. Arnold, J. Kirchofer, J. Laciura, and L. Wilson. 1981. Second language reading: a curricular sequence for teaching reading strategies. *Foreign Language Annals* 14(5): 415–422.

Hudson, T. 1982. The effects of induced schemata on the "short circuit" in L2 reading: non-decoding factors in L2 reading performance. *Language Learning* 32(1): 1–31. [Reprinted as Chapter 13 in this volume.]

Johnson, D. D., and P. D. Pearson. 1978. *Teaching reading vocabulary.* New York: Holt, Rinehart and Winston.

Johnson, P. 1981. Effects on reading comprehension of language complexity and cultural background of a text. *TESOL Quarterly* 15(2): 169–181.

1982. Effects on reading comprehension of building background knowledge. *TESOL Quarterly* 16(4): 503–516.

Langer, J. A. 1980. Facilitating text processing: the elaboration of prior knowledge. In *Reader meets author/bridging the gap*, J. A. Langer and M. T. Smith-Burke (Eds.), 149–162. Newark, Del.: International Reading Association.

1981. From theory to practice: a prereading plan. *Journal of Reading* 25(2): 152–156.

Mackay, R. 1979. Teaching the information-gathering skills. In *Reading in a second language*, R. Mackay, B. Barkman, and R. R. Jordan (Eds.), 79–90. Rowley, Mass.: Newbury House.

Macnamara, J. 1972. Bilingualism and thought. In *The language education of minority children*, B. Spolsky (Ed.), 60–76. Rowley, Mass.: Newbury House.

McDowell, H. R. 1939. A comparative study of reading readiness. Unpublished master's thesis, University of Iowa.

McWhorter, O. A. 1935. Building reading interests and skills by utilizing children's first-hand experiences. Unpublished master's thesis, Ohio University.

Meyer, B. J. F. 1975. *The organization of prose and its effects on memory.* Amsterdam: North-Holland.

Mikulecky, B. S. 1985. Reading skills instruction in ESL. In *On TESOL '84,*

P. Larson, E. L. Judd, and D. S. Messerschmitt (Eds.), 261–277. Washington, D.C.: TESOL.

Pearson, P. D., J. Hansen, and C. Gordon. 1979. The effect of background knowledge on young children's comprehension of explicit and implicit information. *Journal of Reading Behavior* 11(3): 201–209.

Pearson, P. D., and D. D. Johnson. 1978. *Teaching reading comprehension.* New York: Holt, Rinehart and Winston.

Pearson, P. D., and R. J. Spiro. 1982. The new buzz word in reading is "schema." *Instructor* May 1982: 46–48.

Rigg, P. 1981. Beginning to read in English the LEA way. In *Reading English as a second language: moving from theory,* C. W. Twyford, W. Diehl, and K. Feathers (Eds.), 81–90. Monographs in Language and Reading Studies, No. 4. Bloomington: Indiana University Press.

Robinson, R. P. 1941. *Effective study.* New York: Harper and Row.

Rumelhart, D. E. 1977. Toward an interactive model of reading. In *Attention and performance,* Vol. 6, S. Dornic (Ed.), 573–603. New York: Academic Press.

    1980. Schemata: the building blocks of cognition. In *Theoretical issues in reading comprehension,* R. J. Spiro, B. C. Bruce, and W. F. Brewer (Eds.), 35–58. Hillsdale, N.J.: Erlbaum.

Sanford, A. J., and S. C. Garrod. 1981. *Understanding written language.* New York: Wiley.

Schulz, R. A. 1983. From word to meaning: foreign language reading instruction after the elementary course. *Modern Language Journal* 67(2): 127–134.

Smith, N. B. 1963. *Reading instruction for today's children.* Englewood Cliffs, N.J.: Prentice-Hall.

Smith-Burke, M. T. 1980. Extending concepts through language activities. In *Reader meets author/bridging the gap,* J. A. Langer and M. T. Smith-Burke (Eds.), 163–179. Newark, Del.: International Reading Association.

Stahl, S. A., and M. M. Fairbanks. 1986. The effects of vocabulary instruction: a model-based meta-analysis. *Review of Educational Research* 56(1): 72–110.

Stauffer, R. G. 1980. *The language experience approach to the teaching of reading.* New York: Harper and Row.

Steffensen, M. S. 1985. Children's reading and cultural interference. Paper presented at 1985 TESOL Convention, New York.

Steffensen, M. S., C. Joag-dev, and R. C. Anderson. 1979. A cross-cultural perspective on reading comprehension. *Reading Research Quarterly* 15(1): 10–29.

Stevens, K. 1980. The effect of background knowledge on the reading comprehension of ninth graders. *Journal of Reading Behavior* 12(2): 151–154.

    1982. Can we improve reading by teaching background information? *Journal of Reading* 25(4): 326–329.

Swaffar, J. K. 1981. Reading in a foreign language classroom: focus on process. *Unterrichtspraxis* 14(2): 176–194.

Taylor, B. M. 1979. Good and poor readers' recall of familiar and unfamiliar text. *Journal of Reading Behavior* 11(4): 375–380.

Taylor, B. M., and R. W. Beach. 1984. The effects of text structure instruction on middle grade students' comprehension and production of expository text. *Reading Research Quarterly* 19(2): 134–146.

Westhoff, G. J. 1981. *Voorspellend lezen.* [Predictive reading]. Doctoral diss., Utrecht University.

Williams, R. 1983. Teaching the recognition of cohesive ties in reading in a foreign language. *Reading in a Foreign Language* 1(1): 35–53.

Witte, S. P., and L. Faigley. 1981. Coherence, cohesion, and writing quality. *College Composition and Communication* 22(2): 189–204.

17 The relationship between general language competence and second language reading proficiency: implications for teaching

Joanne Devine

Rosenblatt (1978), Widdowson (1979), and others have argued persuasively that successful reading is an act of creation: the reader *creates* meaning through the interaction with a text. In this view, the meaning of a text does not reside in a fixed, static form frozen within the words on the page. Rather, it emerges anew in each encounter of a reader with a text. A text, then, does not contain meaning as such but, as Widdowson suggests, potential for meaning, which readers, both native and non-native, will realize in varying degrees. This ability to create meaning (what is usually referred to as comprehension) depends critically on, and in fact may be said to presuppose, another kind of interaction – that of various types of information the reader brings to the reading task and information available in the text itself. (See Grabe, Chapter 4 of this volume, for a full treatment of the various senses of the term *interactive*.) Eskey (1986) identifies two categories of knowledge that must interact if there is to be "full, or at least native-like, comprehension of written texts" (p. 17): knowledge of form and knowledge of substance. Formal knowledge includes recognition of graphophonic, lexical, syntactic/semantic, and rhetorical patterns of a language; knowledge of substance encompasses cultural, pragmatic and subject-specific information. My purpose is not to rehearse the relative contribution of each of these types of knowledge to successful reading in a second language (for such a discussion, see Chapters 6 by Eskey, 7 by Carrell, and 15 by Eskey and Grabe in this volume; as well as Carrell 1987, reprinted as Chapter 16 in this volume), but to consider in some detail the role of general language proficiency as it contributes to second language readers' ability to create meaning through interaction with a text and the implications of this role for the teaching of reading in a second language.

Before turning to a discussion of the role of general language competence in second language reading, it is important to note that not all classroom teachers and reading researchers regard second language readers' level of proficiency in the new language as a critical factor in the success or failure of those readers as they attempt to interact with a text in the second language. For example, Jolly (1978, reported in Alderson 1984) and others (Groebel 1980; Mott 1981) suggest that it is first language reading ability rather than the degree of control of the new language that determines a reader's capacity to read in a second language. Successful reading, according to Jolly, requires "the transference of old skills, not the learning of new ones" (1978; quoted in Alderson 1984:2). This view underlies a large body of second language reading research conducted in what is frequently referred to as the "psycholinguistic model of reading" (see Rigg 1977a, and 1977b, reprinted as Chapter 14 in this volume; Clarke 1979; Romantowski 1981; Connor 1981; Devine 1981). In this research, the consistent patterns of reading performance for readers from a wide variety of language backgrounds lent credence to Kenneth Goodman's oft-quoted assertion that "the reading process will be much the same for all languages" (1973:27). Because of the "universality" of the reading process, success in second language reading was seen as the result of the transfer of good reading strategies from the first language. Likewise, reading failure in a foreign language was viewed as directly attributable to poor reading in the native language. Classroom instruction aimed at improving second language reading typically focused on teaching "good" reading strategies which were thought to be lacking in the first language.

By the 1970s it was widely acknowledged that psycholinguistic research, with its emphasis on universal features of the reading process and transfer of first language reading strategies, had made a significant contribution to the understanding of reading in a second language. However, growing criticism of the use of oral reading samples (especially miscue analysis, which lies at the heart of the psycholinguistic model of reading) in research and evaluation (Wixson 1979; Leu 1982), coupled with a growing body of research which failed to demonstrate a strong relationship between reading ability in the first language and reading ability in a second language (see Alderson 1984 for an excellent critical summary of this research), has led to renewed interest in the role of language proficiency in second language reading. Despite the emphasis on similarities in the reading process in all languages, even during the heyday of the psycholinguistic period of second language reading, most researchers remained sensitive to the role of language competence in second language reading success, as evidenced by Clarke and Silberstein's observation: "Our students' efficiency in using reading skills is directly dependent upon their overall language proficiency – their general language skills" (1977:145).

The critical interaction of language proficiency and reading ability is now generally well accepted. Most researchers and classroom teachers, in fact, take as a given that second language readers must reach a certain level of second language competence before they can effectively read in the second language. As Eskey and Grabe (Chapter 15, this volume) assert: "Reading requires a relatively high degree of grammatical control over structures that appear in whatever readings are given to [L2] students" (p. 226). Given the wide acceptance of this assumption, it seems appropriate to begin with a review of the relevant research on the relationship of general language competence and second language reading proficiency.

Second language reading as a language problem

Psycholinguistic research aside, until relatively recently, much second language reading pedagogy was based not on insights provided by research but on the assumption that instructional attention focused on improving language proficiency would result in increased reading achievement. This notion derived in part from the audiolingual method (Bloomfield 1942), popular in foreign language teaching from the late 1940s into the 1970s. Adhering strictly to the belief in the primacy of spoken language, audiolingual advocates usually banned all second language reading during the early stages of language instruction. Typically, students were not even exposed to written language until some command of spoken language was evident. (This was certainly the case in my own ESL teaching experience in the early 1970s; reading activities at all levels emphasized language instruction rather than reading instruction.) In this view, second language reading problems were regarded as symptomatic of the larger failure to gain control of the spoken forms of the target language.

While not endorsing the audiolingual method, Yorio (1971) agreed that the problems of second language readers are due to a lack of familiarity with the new language. In his view, this inadequate knowledge of the target language inhibits the use of essential textual cues in reading: "The reader's knowledge is not like that of the native speaker; the guessing or predicting ability necessary to pick up cues is hindered by the imperfect knowledge of the language" (1971:108). Interference from the native language compounds the problem of imperfect command of the second language, making the task of the second language reader even more complex. This analysis of the role of language competence (and L1 language interference) in second language reading achievement seemed to support the then frequent practice of delaying reading instruction until a critical level of language proficiency had been reached. But, as Alderson (1984) points out, Yorio's formulations were not based on empirical evidence. Subsequent research has, however, provided tentative support for Yorio's contention that L2 reading problems, particularly at beginning levels, might well be regarded more generally as language problems.

The evidence supporting the hypothesis that L2 reading problems are due to inadequate knowledge of the target language comes from research on three closely related questions:

1. Does limited proficiency in a foreign language restrict general reading ability in that language?
2. Does limited proficiency in a foreign language restrict readers from using very specific types of textual information, such as discourse constraints, when reading in that language?
3. Is there a "threshold of linguistic competence" (Cummins 1979) which readers must reach before they can read successfully in a second language? How can that threshold, if it exists, be defined?

Question 1

Research into the first of these questions has broadly examined the role of language proficiency in L2 reading, with an eye to determining if a significant relationship exists between the level of language competence and the level of reading ability in the second language. Alderson, Bastein, and Madrazo (1977), in a study of Mexican subjects reading in both their native Spanish and in English, found a significant correlation between proficiency in English and reading comprehension of a text in English, leading them to conclude that language competence was the best predictor of reading success in a second language. Results of a study by Aron (1980) provide support for this conclusion. (For a full critical discussion of research by Alderson et al. 1977, Chihara et al. 1977, and Cummins 1979, see Alderson 1984.)

Devine (1987) studied the question of the relationship between L2 language proficiency and oral reading performance longitudinally. The progress of twenty beginning-level ESL students was followed for an academic year; during that period, both reading samples and language proficiency data were collected at three-month intervals. It was hypothesized that as general language proficiency increased, reading behavior would become more efficient, especially in regard to the use of effective strategies involving semantic cues in the text. Analyses showed significant correlations between gains in language competence and the use of effective reading strategies (as defined by both the type of oral reading strategies used and by successful comprehension). Perhaps more interestingly, the positive correlations with increased reading achievement emerged only for those measures of language proficiency that were holistic; gains on discrete point grammar and vocabulary tests showed no or negative correlation with gains in L2 reading ability. Devine concludes that the study affirms, at least for oral reading, the relationship between language proficiency and reading proficiency. She suggests, moreover, that if language instruction is to have a positive impact on second language reading, that instruction should be holistic or integrative, since the relationship between proficiency in the language and reading performance obtains only when language competence is considered as a set of interacting abilities rather than as individual, isolated skills.

In a series of related studies involving classroom observations of and interviews with Hebrew EFL students, Berman (1984) investigated the hypothesis that knowledge of syntactic features of a language (certainly a central component of language proficiency) is essential for "unraveling of parts of sentences and correct perception of their grammatical and rhetorical interrelations," activities important for "reading fluency in general" (p. 139). In this view, readers must be able to manipulate the structural aspects of a second language in order to understand the propositional content of a second language text – successful readers are able to get at the "kernel" or core of sentences by unraveling the syntax. Subjects in one of the studies were asked to read either syntactically adapted or unaltered English texts and respond to both text-specific and general idea questions. It was hypothesized that readers encountering more "transparent" syntax would have a considerably easier time comprehending the text than would those readers confronted with unaltered (and hence more complex) syntax. While all readers made more mistakes on text-specific questions, those who read the syntactically adapted text scored consistently higher on both types of questions. Berman interprets these results as support for her hypothesis. Further study of Hebrew EFL readers, based on classroom observation and analysis of recall protocols, confirmed the earlier findings: knowledge of syntax (and by extension, achievement of a level of language proficiency) enhances L2 reading ability.

Other recent studies have generally affirmed a relationship between poor reading ability in a second language and inability to manipulate the syntactic features of that language (see for example Cooper 1984 and Field 1985). Other research suggests that low language competence may hinder the L2 reader in yet another significant way – by restricting reading speed. Cohen et al. (1979, reprinted as Chapter 11 in this volume) found that ESL readers often took up to six times as long as native readers to complete a text. Presumably, at least some of that time was spent trying to process difficult syntax; indeed, the readers in this study evidenced inability to process syntactic cues critical to text comprehension. As Eskey and Grabe (Chapter 15 in this volume) remind us, reading time spent on close decoding is, more often than not, reading time misspent.

Question 2

Researchers investigating the second question concerning the relationship between language proficiency and L2 reading have, in a sense, asked a more specific version of the first question. Chihara et al. (1977), Cziko (1978, 1980), and Cooper (1984), among others, have focused on the extent to which a second language reader's ability to use very particular types of textual information when reading in a second language depends upon that reader's level of language proficiency. In a study comparing the ability of native speakers of English and Japanese to comprehend "sequential" (normal) prose and scrambled prose in English, Chihara et al. found that increasing language proficiency was related to increasing ability to understand both types of prose. The authors conclude that greater language competence allows readers to utilize context constraints more efficiently.

Cziko (1978, 1980) compared the reading strategies of limited and advanced English language proficiency French students with those of native English speakers as both groups read in English. Advanced English proficiency French readers behaved very much like native English speakers, demonstrating a sensitivity to syntactic, semantic, and discourse constraints operating in the text; low language proficiency readers, on the other hand, usually employed such "poor" reading strategies as attempting to reproduce exactly the orthographic features of text words. Lower proficiency readers appeared to rely on bottom-up strategies for processing information in a text, whereas native and advanced proficiency readers relied on both graphic and contextual cues as well as more general nontextual information, or higher-order schemata. Cziko suggests that reader strategies – the ability to use the various types of textual constraints – are related to competence level in the language.

A study by Cooper (1984), while highlighting the role of attitudinal factors in second language reading, adds support to Cziko's findings. Cooper examined the performance of "practiced" and "unpracticed" nonnative readers of English enrolled at the University of Malaya. "Practiced" readers had pursued much of their earlier education in English, and had demonstrated the ability to cope with university-level texts in English; "unpracticed" readers, on the other hand, although they had studied English, had been educated in their native language. They exhibited great difficulty in dealing with English language texts, and as a result, upon entering the university, they required special courses concentrating on developing reading skills in English. After establishing that the two groups of readers were equally capable of reading academic texts in their native language, Cooper examined features of English that might be possible sources of reading difficulty for the unpracticed readers: the meaning of affixes, word meaning in context, syntactic meaning (tense, aspect, modality, etc.), grammatical and lexical cohesion, and intersentential relationships. Scores from tests on these aspects of written English in each case correlated highly with scores of general reading comprehension for the two groups of readers. Cooper concludes:

Unpractised readers differed primarily from practised readers in their ability to use the linguistic clues in the larger context to determine meaning. They found it especially difficult to deduce word meaning from context, to understand lexical cohesion, and to understand the meaning relationships between sentences. (1984:133)

Cooper also notes that unpracticed readers were severely handicapped by their inadequate English vocabulary. Significantly, the vocabulary deficits of the unpracticed readers were primarily of two types: "sub-technical" words common across a number of disciplines ("contrast," "similarity," etc.) and sentence connectors such as "despite" and "nevertheless." Especially in the case of connectors, it can be argued that unpractised readers' vocabulary deficits are a cause of their inability to build coherent (and perhaps cohesive) texts. Other researchers (Cowan 1976; Cohen et al. 1979; and Mackay 1979) have also observed that second language readers typically experience difficulty with conjunctive vocabulary and hence often fail to successfully comprehend L2 texts.

Question 3

The general findings of research on questions 1 and 2 – that low reading achievement in a second language is significantly related to low general proficiency in that language and that readers with low L2 language proficiency are especially handicapped in their ability to utilize contextual constraints and cohesive devices when reading in the target language – have led some researchers to suggest that there is a threshold of linguistic competence necessary for successful L2 reading. Clarke (1980, reprinted as Chapter 8 in this volume) refers to this threshold in his discussion of a "linguistic ceiling," suggesting that low proficiency restricts a reader's ability to interact with a second language text. Hudson (1982, reprinted as Chapter 13 in this volume) does not argue against the ceiling effect of low language proficiency; rather, he suggests that this effect can be mitigated by a reader's ability to activate appropriate schemata.

Cummins (1979), studying the reading behavior of bilingual English/French subjects, maintains that the purported positive effects of balanced bilingualism, such as cognitive and academic progress, appear only after a "threshold of linguistic competence" has been reached. This notion is consonant with the findings of research (discussed above) which suggests that L2 readers will not be able to read effectively until they develop some proficiency in the target language. If a threshold of linguistic competence does in fact exist for second language readers, it is quite natural, especially for classroom teachers, to attempt to define that threshold. But Cummins and others (e.g., Alderson 1984) point out that "threshold" cannot be understood as an absolute term; it must be seen as varying from reader to reader (perhaps related to the cognitive and conceptual development of the individual reader) and from task to task (an idea consistent with the research findings of Berman 1984 and others). The usefulness of the concept of a linguistic threshold for successful L2 reading, then, depends on the answers to a number of related questions, summarized by Alderson:

... to what extent is it [the linguistic threshold] syntactic, semantic, conceptual, discoursal? Does the level of the threshold vary for different learners, and for different tasks? Is it conceivable that good first-language readers will require a lower threshold before being in a position to utilize their good reading strategies? Will the attainment of a higher level of competence compensate for a poor first-language reader? (1984: 21)

These, of course, are precisely the questions that research into the relationship between language proficiency and reading performance must begin to address.

Grabe (1986) contends that successful second language reading depends upon the possession of a "critical mass of knowledge," of which only one part is strictly linguistic knowledge. This type of knowledge is, of course, important to L2 reading; indeed, in Grabe's view readers must reach a stage of automatic processing of the syntactic patterns encountered in a text (as well as in the processing of the vocabulary; see Eskey and Grabe, Chapter 15). But linguistic knowledge must interact with two other "strands" of knowledge to form the "critical mass" needed for successful L2 reading: background knowledge assumptions and relevant formal and content schemata. Background knowledge assumptions consist of the information base that permits readers to make often nonobvious connections between seemingly independent realms of knowledge that they possess. These assumptions arise in large part from prior reading experience; they allow for speculative thinking. In short, background knowledge assumptions permit discovery and creative thinking, activities necessary for proficient reading. The role of schemata in reading has, of course, been explored at some length in this volume (see Chapter 3 by Anderson and Pearson, Chapter 5 by Carrell and Eisterhold, and Chapter 7 by Carrell). Second language readers with sufficient knowledge in each of these three "strands" are in possession of the "critical mass of knowledge" required for L2 reading; they can then begin to "read in ways similar to successful students in their own language." Grabe suggests that achievement of "critical mass" might be said to make the point at which "a reader stops learning to read and only reads to learn" (1986:36).

Linguistic knowledge of the type that forms the "threshold" then can be regarded as part of a larger interacting network of information needed by the second language reader. It is necessary but not, by itself, sufficient for successful L2 reading. Grabe's insights into the role of language proficiency in second language reading are the first steps in answering the important questions that Alderson poses concerning the nature of the "linguistic threshold." However, empirical research as such into the precise nature and measurement of this "threshold of linguistic competence" and its contribution to successful L2 reading remains to be done.

The research into the relationship between language competence and L2 reading reviewed earlier perhaps raises more questions than it answers; nonetheless, it is possible to offer a number of general pedagogical suggestions based on the findings. In offering these suggestions, I encourage the reader to recall Carrell's (1987) list of caveats, which must preface all attempts to apply theory and empirical research directly to classroom teaching.

General language competence and L2 reading proficiency: implications for teaching

Discussion of the pedagogical implications of research into the relationship between general language competence and L2 reading is divided into three sections, corresponding to the general research questions posed earlier. In the first section I offer suggestions based on the findings of studies investigating impact of limited proficiency in a foreign language on general reading ability in that language (question 1). The next section focuses on pedagogical implications of research into the potential restrictions of low L2 language proficiency on second language readers' ability to use specific types of textual information (question 2). Finally, in the third section, I suggest ways in which the classroom teacher might begin to define "linguistic threshold" as it applies to proficient L2 reading and to assist readers in achieving the necessary "threshold" for successful second language reading (question 3).

Question 1

Research investigating the relationship between general language proficiency and L2 reading ability suggests a number of conclusions. First, success in reading in a second language is related to the level of proficiency in the language; the higher the level (to a point), the better the chances that a reader will successfully comprehend a text. Second, knowledge of syntax enhances L2 reading ability. The research suggests that poor second language reading is in part the result of the failure to manipulate the syntactic features of the target language. A final suggestion is that the slow reading rate of L2 readers, with the problems that rate creates for comprehension (see Eskey and Grabe, Chapter 15), can be traced to low general competence in the second language.

The idea that second language readers must reach a level of general language competence in order to read successfully in the target language is no longer seriously challenged. More controversial are suggestions of how to ensure that L2 readers attain the minimal level of needed competence. While there are currently few advocates of the audiolingual practice of withholding written material until oral language proficiency has been demonstrated, the research finding that limited L2 proficiency inhibits reading in the second language does suggest that readers must first become at least marginally proficient in the target language before they can hope to read in that language. Some preliminary program of L2 language instruction thus seems in order. Elley (1984), however, offers a different perspective on the relationship between language proficiency and reading success. In a study of the reading difficulties of second language learners in Fiji, Elley suggests that reading may function to increase language proficiency; rather than viewing reading problems as resulting from low language proficiency, he attributes his Fijian subjects' weaknesses in the second language (English) to their lack of exposure to written material at an early stage in L2 development. In this view, written material serves as a source of linguistic data which promotes the growth of general language competence; increased language competence in turn enhances reading ability.

To ensure that this symbiotic relationship develops – that is, reading promotes language competence and increased language competence enhances reading ability – Elley (1984) and others (Cooper 1984; Devine 1987) recommend that even low-proficiency students be exposed to an ample amount of linguistic data, including a large supply of reading materials. Devine (1987) summarizes:

The teacher should provide a rich linguistic environment in which readers will be exposed to topically interesting and situationally appropriate language samples. This might be accomplished through the use of tapes, dialogues, and even carefully screened reading materials which even low-language proficiency readers could follow. The language would be learned, as much as possible, through reading, not as a prerequisite for reading.

The idea that reading can serve as a vehicle for learning a second language and as a result enhance reading ability in that language – that is, L2 learners can learn to read by reading – is consistent with the "reading lab" approach outlined by Stoller (1986). Among other things, readers at all levels are exposed to a variety of high-interest reading materials in the reading lab; furthermore, class time is devoted to actual reading of these materials without the active intervention of the instructor. This activity is valuable in a number of important ways, not the least of which is that it presents readers with rich linguistic data.

Related to the general finding that reading ability in a second language is closely related to the level of competence in the language is the observation that it is specifically the lack of syntactic knowledge that prohibits readers from successfully comprehending L2 texts (Berman 1984; Cooper 1984). It follows from this that there may be pedagogical techniques, such as the use of grammatically simplified texts, that would allow second language readers to overcome their syntactic deficiencies.

While evidence does suggest that young children learning to read in their native language may indeed profit from the use of texts containing shorter, syntactically simplified sentences (Kintsch and Vipond 1979), some researchers have questioned the adequacy of these types of reading materials for beginning second language readers. Shook (1977), Blau (1981), and others have criticized the "oversimplified syntax" that results from the application of a readability formula to L2 reading texts. In a study titled "The Effects of Syntax on Readability for ESL Students in Puerto Rico," Blau found that lower readability material, which was characterized by short, grammatically simple sentences, actually tended to impede the comprehension of beginning ESL readers. She concludes that "choppy, unnatural sentences are difficult to read... Readers do indeed seem to benefit from the information regarding relationships that is revealed by complex sentences" (p. 525).

The apparent contradiction between findings such as Berman's, which suggest that second language readers more readily understand texts containing "transparent syntax," and those such as Blau's, which appear to demonstrate that simplified syntax may actually interfere with L2 readers' ability to comprehend texts, can perhaps be resolved by reference to Davies's (1984) observations about the process of "simplification" as it applies to second language reading texts:

... simplification can be seen as a process in which the teacher ... consciously adjusts the language presented to the learner.... Simplification ... of reading materials refers to the selection of a restricted set of features from the full range of language resources for the sake of pedagogic efficiency. (pp. 182–3)

Davies notes further that, in linguistic terms, there is no absolute measure of simplicity; texts are simple only with respect to the needs of a specific audience. Those altered texts that enhance the comprehension of the reader are thus "simplified" texts, regardless of the particular syntactic changes that have been effected. The "oversimplified syntax" that Blau cautions against clearly does not result in simplification (in Davies's sense) but rather in a fundamental disruption of original texts.

There are obvious pedagogical implications concerning the use of simplified or altered texts in the L2 reading classroom that follow from these observations. Since almost all beginning-level second language readers are simply incapable of handling the syntactic complexities of unaltered L2 reading materials, the common practice of simplifying those materials makes good pedagogical sense. However, as Alderson and Urquhart warn, "simplification must be seen to refer to a wide range of procedures…the resulting text should be more appropriate for the audience" (1984a: 197–8). Reading teachers might then want to apply criteria of "appropriateness" rather than of "simplicity" when choosing or creating L2 reading materials. "Appropriateness" would undoubtedly result in part from syntactic simplification, but might also be related to such features as the amount of redundancy in a text (see Haynes 1984 for discussion) and textual "density" or "heaviness" (Berman 1984).

A third observation arising from studies of the relationship between general language proficiency and L2 reading ability is that second language learners read far more slowly than their native counterparts; thus they tax the short-term memory and thereby reduce the likelihood of successful comprehension (see Eskey and Grabe, Chapter 15). Since syntactic processing no doubt accounts in large measure for the slow reading rate of L2 readers, classroom techniques that encourage readers to make syntactic guesses as a strategy for increasing reading speed are recommended. Cloze procedures would be particularly useful in this regard. (See Alderson 1979 and Brown 1984 for a complete treatment of cloze procedure.) Exercises designed especially to increase reading speed would also help discourage the tedious word-by-word decoding that often characterizes second language reading. See Stoller (1986), Mahon (1986), and Anderson (1986) for useful suggestions concerning building L2 reading rate.

Question 2

Research into the effects of limited language proficiency on a reader's ability to use specific type of textual information has focused primarily on identifying the specific cues that are typically problematical for the second language reader. Among those frequently cited as sources of L2 reading difficulties are the following: textual constraints (syntactic, semantic, and discoursal), grammatical affixes, tense, aspect, modality, grammatical and lexical cohesion, intersentential connectors, and a range of technical and subtechnical vocabulary. The importance of control over these features for successful second language reading is not at issue. Rather, the question that the classroom teacher must answer is how best to help readers learn to use these types of textual information. One of the most obvious suggestions is to simply teach these features to second language readers. My purpose here is not to offer a "how to" guide for teachers on the ways to teach L2 readers everything they need to know about tense, modality and so forth; see Carrell (1987); Eskey and Grabe (Chapter 15); Dubin, Eskey, and Grabe (1986); Williams (1983); Mackay, Barkman, and Jordan (1979), and others for specific pedagogical suggestions.

What I offer here instead is a very general observation about instruction in any language feature, syntactic or lexical, in the L2 classroom: that instruction should be holistic or integrative rather than discrete point. My own research (1987) indicates that no or negative correlation exists between scores on various discrete point tests and advances in second language reading ability. This finding suggests that if language instruction is to have a positive impact on reading performance, that instruction should not isolate the components of language. Teachers are discouraged from constructing language exercises and drills focused on the target features that remove those features from the type of full language context in which they normally occur. L2 students, especially at beginning levels, should be exposed to texts that allow them to encounter complete, self-contained samples of actual written language. Real written language, after all, provides numerous examples of the very structures and vocabulary items that readers need to know and can thus serve as the focus of instruction. These ideas are, of course, consistent with the central pedagogical observation offered in the preceding section; reading of real, if simplified, texts should be at the heart of any second language reading program.

Question 3

Most L2 reading instructors and researchers would agree that second language readers must attain a level of proficiency in the target language before there can be genuine interaction with texts in that language. Although studies focusing on "the threshold of linguistic competence" necessary for successful L2 reading have, to date, provided little hard evidence on the nature and measurement of this threshold, researchers have posed critical questions about this threshold and have begun to speculate on its interaction with other types of knowledge required for proficient second language reading. Two ideas that emerge from these speculations are of special pedagogical interest. The first is that the linguistic threshold almost assuredly varies from task to task and from reader to reader. The second is that linguistic knowledge must critically interact with nonlinguistic knowledge in L2 reading.

Alderson (1984) notes that the more difficult the reading task, the higher the linguistic threshold is likely to be, an observation readily confirmed by readers confronting different types of reading material in their native languages. These native readers quite naturally adjust their reading behavior according to the type of text, employing one strategy for reading a novel, for example, and quite a different one for reading highly technical material (Devine 1984). Reading instructors should encourage second language readers to develop this same flexibility in their reading of different types of text in the target language. Dubin (1986) offers very valuable suggestions for enhancing the development of text-appropriate strategies; she also demonstrates the ways in which a variety of brief, real-language source materials (newspapers, magazines, etc.) can be adapted for class use.

Although complex syntactic patterns and highly specialized vocabulary undoubtedly pose special problems for the second language reader (and may thus raise threshold), not all second language reading difficulties can be traced to specific language features of a text. As many of the contributors to this volume have convincingly demonstrated, the reader's conceptual background will in part determine how accessible reading material will be. Linguistic threshold then will vary, not only from text to text, but also as a function of the background information a reader brings to a text. Although it can be expected to vary greatly from reader to reader, usually, the more a reader knows about the general subject of a text, the lower the linguistic threshold is likely to be. (See Hudson 1982 for experimental evidence on the impact of teaching background information.) Reading teachers must be attentive to these differences in background knowledge and should help readers prepare for a text by providing relevant background information. Carrell's suggestions (1987) are especially useful in this regard.

Relative to the second idea mentioned above, Grabe (1986) reminds us once again that proficient L2 reading depends on the interaction of various types of knowledge – linguistic, background, and schematic – which must come together to form a "critical mass." While asserting that these types of knowledge must function simultaneously in successful reading, he also suggests, at least indirectly, that for pedagogical purposes an important distinction can be made in the L2 classroom "between language processing difficulties and information processing difficulties" (p. 37). The classroom teacher may want to choose materials that reflect this useful distinction. These texts would contain carefully controlled language patterns when unfamiliar and conceptually demanding material is introduced; perhaps a simplified (in Davies's 1984 sense) text could be produced. At other times, when conceptual content is more familiar either because of a reader's background or as a result of explicit instruction, the text would contain more complex language patterns. Increasingly, readers would be expected to become more independent, that is, fully capable of dealing with both conceptually and linguistically complex material in the second language.

Conclusion

In this chapter, I have attempted to discuss recent research investigating the relationship of general competence and L2 reading proficiency and to draw very general pedagogical implications from that research. It should be evident from this discussion that much important research remains to be done in this area, especially concerning the notion of "linguistic threshold" and the particular ways it applies to second language reading. The pedagogical suggestions offered here, while they await empirical testing, are consistent with, indeed complement, those offered by Carrell (1987) and Eskey and Grabe (Chapter 15), and fully support an interactive approach to second language reading.

References

Alderson, J. C. 1979. The cloze procedure and proficiency in English as a foreign language. *TESOL Quarterly* 13(2): 219–228.

———. 1984. Reading in a foreign language: a reading problem or a language problem? In Alderson and Urquhart (Eds.) 1984b, 1–24.

Alderson, J. C., S. Bastien, and A.-M. Madrazo. 1977. A comparison of reading comprehension in English and Spanish. Research and Development Unit Report No. 9, mimeo. UNAM, Mexico City.

Alderson, J. C., and A. H. Urquhart. 1984a. Postscript on Davies. In Alderson and Urquhart (Eds.), 1984b, 196–198.

Alderson, J. C., and A. H. Urquhart. 1984b. *Reading in a foreign language.* New York: Longman.

Anderson, N. J. 1986. Increasing the reading rate of ESL students. *TESOL Newsletter 5.*

Aron, H. 1980. Comparing reading comprehension in Spanish and English by adult Hispanics entering a two-year college. In *Proceedings of the Third International Conference on Frontiers in Language Proficiency and Dominance Testing*, R. O. Silverstein (Ed.), 165–173. Occasional Papers on Linguistics, No. 6. Carbondale, Ill.: Southern Illinois University, Department of Linguistics.

Berman, R. 1984. Syntactic components of the foreign language reading process. In Alderson and Urquhart (Eds.) 1984b, 139–156.

Blau, E. K. 1981. The effect of syntax on readability for ESL students in Puerto Rico. *TESOL Quarterly* 16(4): 517–528.

Bloomfield, L. 1942. *Outline guide for the practical study of foreign language.* Baltimore, Md.: Linguistic Society of America.

Brown, J. D. 1984. A cloze is a cloze is a cloze? In *On TESOL '83*, J. Handscombe, R. A. Orem, and B. P. Taylor (Eds.), 109–119. Washington, D.C.: TESOL.

Carrell, P. L. 1987. Fostering interactive language reading. In *Initiatives in communicative language teaching*, Vol. 2, S. Savignon and M. Berns (Eds.), 145–169. Reading, Mass.: Addison-Wesley. [Reprinted as Chapter 16 in this volume.]

Carrell, P. L., and J. C. Eisterhold. 1983. Schema theory and ESL reading pedagogy. *TESOL Quarterly* 17(4): 553–573. [Reprinted as Chapter 5 in this volume.]

Chihara, T., J. Oller, K. Weaver, and M. A. Chavez-Oller. 1977. Are cloze items sensitive to constraints across sentences? *Language Learning* 27(1): 63–73.

Clarke, M. A. 1979. Reading in Spanish and English: evidence from adult ESL students. *Language Learning* 29(1): 121–150.

1980. The short circuit hypothesis of ESL reading – or when language competence interferes with reading performance. *Modern Language Journal* 64(2): 203–209. [Reprinted as Chapter 8 in this volume.]

Clarke, M. A., and S. Silberstein. 1977. Towards a realization of psycholinguistic principles in the ESL classroom. *Language Learning* 27(1): 135–154.

Cohen, A., H. Glasman, P. Rosenbaum-Cohen, J. Ferrara, and J. Fine. 1979. Reading English for specialized purposes: discourse analysis and the use of student informants. *TESOL Quarterly* 13(4): 551–564. [Reprinted as Chapter 11 in this volume.]

Connor U. 1981. The application of Reading Miscue Analysis to diagnosis of English as a second language learner's reading skills. In *Reading English as a second language: moving from theory*, C. W. Twyford, W. Diehl, and K. Feathers (Eds.), 47–55. Bloomington: Indiana University School of Education.

Cooper, M. 1984. Linguistic competence of practised and unpractised non-mature readers of English. In Alderson and Urquhart (Eds.), 1984b, 122–135.

Cowan, J. R. 1976. Reading, perceptual strategies and contrastive analysis. *Language Learning* 26(1): 95–109.

Cummins, J. 1979. Cognitive/academic language proficiency, linguistic interdependence, the optimum age question and some other matters. *Working Papers on Bilingualism* 19: 197–205.

Cziko, G. A. 1978. Differences in first and second language reading: the use of syntactic, semantic and discourse constraints. *Canadian Modern Language Review* 34: 473–489.

1980. Language competence and reading strategies: a comparison of first- and second-language oral reading errors. *Language Learning* 30(1): 101–116.

Davies, A. 1984. Simple, simplified, and simplification: what is authentic? In Alderson and Urquhart (Eds.), 1984b, 181–196.

Devine, J. 1981. Developmental patterns in native and nonnative reading acquisition. In *Learning to read in different languages*, S. Hudelson (Ed.), 103–114. Washington, D.C.: Center for Applied Linguistics.

1984. ESL readers' internalized models of the reading process. In *On TESOL '83*, J. Handscombe, R. A. Orem, and B. P. Taylor (Eds.), 95–108. Washington, D.C.: TESOL.

1987. General language competence and adult second language reading. In *Research on reading English as a Second Language*, J. Devine, P. L. Carrell and D. E. Eskey (Eds.). Washington, D.C.: TESOL.

Dubin, F. 1986. Dealing with texts. In Dubin, Eskey, and Grabe (Eds.), 127–160. Reading, Mass.: Addison-Wesley.

Dubin, F., D. E. Eskey, and W. Grabe (Eds.). 1986. *Teaching second language reading for academic purposes.* Reading, Mass.: Addison-Wesley.

Elley, W. B. 1984. Exploring the reading of second-language learners in Fiji. In Alderson and Urquhart (Eds.), 1984b, 281–297.

Eskey, D. E. 1986. Theoretical foundations. In Dubin, Eskey, and Grabe (Eds.), 2–23.

Field, M. L. 1985. A psycholinguistic model of the Chinese ESL reader. In *On TESOL '84*, P. Larson, E. L. Judd, and D. S. Messerschmitt (Eds.), 171–183. Washington, D.C.: TESOL.

Goodman, K. S. 1973. Psycholinguistic universals of the reading process. In *Psycholinguistics and reading*, F. Smith (Ed.), 21–29. New York: Holt, Rinehart and Winston.

Grabe, W. 1986. The transition from theory to practice in teaching reading. In Dubin, Eskey, and Grabe (Eds.), 25–48.

Groebel, L. 1980. A comparison of students' reading comprehension in the native language with their reading comprehension in the target language. *English Language Teaching Journal* 35(1): 54–59.

Haynes, M. 1984. Patterns and perils in second language reading. In *On TESOL '83*, J. Handscombe, R. A. Orem, and B. P. Taylor (Eds.), 163–176. Washington, D.C.: TESOL.

Hudson, T. 1982. The effects of induced schemata on the "short circuit" in L2 reading: non-decoding factors in L2 reading performance. *Language Learning* 32(1): 1–31. [Reprinted as Chapter 13 in this volume.]

Jolly, D. 1978. The establishment of a self-access scheme for intensive reading. Paper presented at the Goethe Institute, British Council Colloquium on Reading, Paris, October.

Kintsch, W., and D. Vipond. 1979. Reading comprehension and readability in educational practice and psychological theory. In *Perspectives on memory research: essays in honor of Uppsala University's 500th Anniversary*, L-G. Nilsson (Ed.), 329–365. Hillsdale, N.J.: Erlbaum.

Leu, D. 1982. Oral reading error analysis: a critical appraisal of research and application. *Reading Research Quarterly* 17(3): 420–437.

Mackay, R. 1979. Teaching the information-gathering skills. In Mackay, Barkman, and Jordan (Eds.), 79–90.

Mackay, R., B. Barkman, and R. R. Jordan (Eds.). 1979. *Reading in a second language.* Rowley, Mass.: Newbury House.

Mahon, D. 1986. Intermediate skills: focusing on reading rate development. In Dubin, Eskey, and Grabe (Eds.), 77–102.

Mott, B. W. 1981. A miscue analysis of German speakers reading in German and English. In *Learning to read in different languages*, S. Hudelson (Ed.), 54–68. Washington, D.C.: Center for Applied Linguistics.

Rigg, P. 1977a. Reading in ESL. In *On TESOL '76*, J. Fanselow and R. H. Crymes (Eds.), 203–210. Washington, D.C.: TESOL.

1977b. The Miscue-ESL Project. In *On TESOL '77*, H. D. Brown, C. A. Yorio, and R. H. Crymes (Eds.), 106–118. Washington, D.C.: TESOL. [Reprinted as Chapter 14 in this volume.]

Romantowski, J. 1981. A psycholinguistic description of miscues generated by selected bilingual subjects during the oral reading of instructional material as presented in Polish readers and in English basal readers. In *Learning to read in different languages*, S. Hudelson (Ed.), 21–26. Washington, D.C.: Center for Applied Linguistics.

Rosenblatt, L. 1978. *The reader, the text and the poem: the transactional theory of the literary work.* Carbondale, Ill.: Southern Illinois University Press.
Shook, R. 1977. Discourse structure in reading. *TESOL Reporter* 10, Nos. 2, 3, 4.
Stoller, F. 1986. Reading lab: developing low-level reading skills. In Dubin, Eskey, and Grabe (Eds.), 51–76.
Widdowson, 1979. The process and purpose of reading. In *Explorations in applied linguistics*, H. Widdowson (Ed.), 171–183. New York: Oxford University Press.
Williams, R. 1983. Teaching the recognition of cohesive ties in reading in a foreign language. *Reading in a Foreign Language* 1(1): 35–53.
Wixson, K. L. 1979. Miscue analysis: a critical review. *Journal of Reading Behavior* 11(2): 107–115.
Yorio, C. A. 1971. Some sources of reading problems in foreign language learners. *Language Learning* 21(1): 107–115.

Index

The following abbreviations are used in the index: *ch*, chapter; *f*, figure on page; *t*, table on page.